Redrawing Local Government Boundaries

Edited by John Meligrana

Redrawing Local
Government Boundaries:
An International Study of Politics,
Procedures, and Decisions

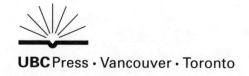

UBC Press · Vancouver · Toronto

© UBC Press 2004

All rights reserved. No part of this publication may be reproduced, stored in a retrieval system, or transmitted, in any form or by any means, without prior written permission of the publisher, or, in Canada, in the case of photocopying or other reprographic copying, a licence from Access Copyright (Canadian Copyright Licensing Agency), www.accesscopyright.ca.

15 14 13 12 11 10 09 08 07 06 05 04   5 4 3 2 1

Printed in Canada on acid-free paper

National Library of Canada Cataloguing in Publication

Redrawing local government boundaries : an international study of politics, procedures and decisions / edited by John Meligrana.

Includes bibliographical references and index.
ISBN 0-7748-0933-7

1. Local government – Cross-cultural studies. 2. City planning – Cross-cultural studies. 3. Boundaries. I. Meligrana, John, 1966-

JS78.R42 2004   320.8   C2004-900362-3

Canadä

UBC Press gratefully acknowledges the financial support for our publishing program of the Government of Canada through the Book Publishing Industry Development Program (BPIDP), and of the Canada Council for the Arts, and the British Columbia Arts Council.

Printed and bound in Canada by Friesens
Set in Stone by Brenda and Neil West, BN Typographics West
Copy editor: Dallas Harrison
Proofreader: Carina Blåfield

UBC Press
The University of British Columbia
2029 West Mall
Vancouver, BC V6T 1Z2
604-822-5959 / Fax: 604-822-6083
www.ubcpress.ca

Contents

Figures and Tables / vii

Acknowledgments / ix

1 Introduction / 1
John Meligrana

2 Redrawing Local Boundaries: Deriving the Principles for Politically Just Procedures / 19
Ronan Paddison

3 Goals for Municipal Restructuring Plans / 38
Andrejs Skaburskis

4 Annexation Activity and Policy in the United States / 56
Greg Lindsey

5 Canadian Experiences of Local Government Boundary Reform: A Comparison of Quebec and Ontario / 75
Raphaël Fischler, John Meligrana, and Jeanne M. Wolfe

6 The Two Waves of Territorial Reform of Local Government in Germany / 106
Hellmut Wollmann

7 Changeless Boundaries Do Not Fix a Changing History: The Map of the Spanish Local Government / 130
Abel Albet i Mas

8 Changing Local Government Boundaries in Israel:
The Paradox of Extreme Centralism versus Inability to Reform / 154
Eran Razin

9 Confusing Responses to Regional Conflicts: Restructuring
Local Administrative Boundaries in Korea / 172
Dong-Ho Shin

10 Reorganizing Urban Space in Postreform China / 189
Jianfa Shen

11 Local Government Reorganization in South Africa / 206
Robert Cameron

12 Conclusion: Changing Local Government Boundaries in
Different Political-Ideological Environments / 227
John Meligrana and Eran Razin

Contributors / 240

Index / 243

Figures and Tables

Figures

4.1 Primary annexation method and average annual number of annexations, USA, 1990-98 / 59
5.1 Municipalities in the Montreal metropolitan area / 82
5.2 Amalgamated municipalities and regional county municipalities, Montreal metropolitan area / 98
6.1 German *Länder* and municipal governments / 108
7.1 Municipal map of Catalonia, Spain, 2002 / 146
7.2 County *(comarca)* map of Catalonia, Spain, 2002 / 147
7.3 Provincial boundaries of Catalonia, Spain, 2002 / 148
7.4 Barcelona's metropolitan area and its twenty-seven internal municipal boundaries, 2002 / 149
8.1 Local government boundaries, Israel, 2001 / 157
8.2 Local government boundaries in the Tel Aviv metropolitan area, 2001 / 158
8.3 Urban and rural local authorities in the Lachish region, 2001 / 159
9.1 Regional context of Korea and Korean provincial boundaries / 173
9.2 Administrative hierarchy of Korean local government system / 174
10.1 Chinese provincial and municipal governments / 193
10.2 Schematic diagram of various boundary changes in China / 194
11.1 Provinces and metropolitan areas, South Africa / 207
11.2 Provincial and municipal government boundaries, South Africa / 220

Tables

3.1 Summary of goals for boundary restructuring plans / 50
4.1 Annexation methods used in the United States / 58
4.2 Frequency and characteristics of annexation in the United States / 63
4.3 Annexation schedule and characteristics of four northeast annexations / 70
6.1 Demographic changes between 1968 and 1978 (German Federal Republic) / 115

6.2 Changes to counties between 1968 and 1978 (German Federal Republic) / 117
6.3 Changes to the number of municipalities between 1990 and 1998 (East Germany) / 123
6.4 Changes to counties between 1990 and 1998 (East Germany) / 125
7.1 Total number of municipalities in Spain, 1900-2000 / 135
7.2 Number of municipalities according to population, Spain, 1999 / 136
7.3 Number of municipalities according to surface area, Spain, 2000 / 137
7.4 Number of local bodies, Spain, 2000 / 138
8.1 Number of local authorities in Israel, 1951-2001 / 155
10.1 Number of cities and the share of city population and city nonagricultural population in total population in China, 1949-2000 / 198
11.1 Summary of South African local governments by population, area, and density / 215
11.2 Tribal authorities by province, South Africa / 217
11.3 Number of local governments by category in South Africa, 2000 / 219

Acknowledgments

This book's publication was supported by funds made available from research grants awarded by the Office of Research Services and the School of Graduate Studies, Queen's University.

The book project received advice and encouragement from many colleagues, including Hok-Lin Leung, Andrejs Skaburskis, and Len Evenden. It was further supported by technical and editorial support from Kevin Muir. Vital direct and indirect assistance was received from Angie L'Abbé and Jo-Anne Rudachuk.

Many thanks to my parents and family for their love and support. Thanks also to my partner, Maria Natividad.

The authors are also grateful for the support received from Randy Schmidt and Ann Macklem at UBC Press.

Jianfa Shen acknowledges a direct research grant from the Chinese University of Hong Kong, project code 2020659.

Andrejs Skaburskis would like to thank Gary Paget, Brian Walisser, and Kenneth MacLeod of the British Columbia Ministry of Municipal Affairs for their valuable comments on an early version of his chapter. That work was supported by a grant from the Social Sciences and Humanities Research Council of Canada.

All errors remain the responsibility of the editor.

1
Introduction
John Meligrana

Local government boundaries are under extreme pressure for reform. Changing the areal jurisdiction of the most basic level of government appears to be a ubiquitous and ongoing problem confronting many nations. It seems that no nation is immune from local government boundary problems; they afflict African, Asian, European, and North American nations alike. Simply stated, local governments around the world must govern territories that are increasingly out of sync with the economic, environmental, social, and regional demands of an ever-urbanizing world. Given the global dimension of this phenomenon, an international comparative study of various legal and regulatory procedures used to reform the territorial jurisdictions of local governments is both warranted and overdue. This book's international perspective is extensive through its inclusion of case studies of eight nations located in four continents: USA, Canada, Spain, Germany, Israel, Korea, China, and South Africa.

To date, the procedures used to redraw local political jurisdictions have been given little serious attention by either scholars, policy makers, or lawmakers. Theory is weak in explaining and understanding the various procedures used to redraw local government boundaries. As a result, the redrawing of municipal boundaries in many nations has been ad hoc. Officials in various governments have few theories, guidelines, or sets of "best practices" to help them in their boundary decisions. This also means that no intellectual framework exists to record any benefits that might occur serendipitously through ad hoc practice. This book's selection of a common policy tool (i.e., local government boundary reform) and comparison of procedures for its use and implementation among several nations provide the empirical information needed to begin to construct generalizations and inform best practices with respect to municipal boundary reform.

The book's focus on the procedures for redrawing local government boundaries provides a vehicle through which to examine several key points regarding this type of local government reform. First, annexation procedures act as filters through which territorial options are debated and considered. Examining them exposes the spatial ideas and models driving the debate regarding the areal arrangement of local units of government. Furthermore, doing so provides an international understanding of an important urban growth management technique – that is, adjusting political boundaries to meet the real dimensions of urban spaces. As mentioned below, the spatial mismatch between urban areas and political areas emerges in each case study as an important driver of boundary reform. Previous research tended to discuss ideal spatial forms of local government territories without acknowledging the procedures needed to achieve such ultimate spatial forms. This book fills that gap by examining not only the spatial forms discussed in each nation but also the forums and manners in which they were decided upon.

Second, tracking annexation procedures exposes the key actors and institutions and their interest in changing or maintaining local government boundaries. As a result, the local government system is described, examined, and discussed as a necessary precursor to understanding the nature of boundary disputes and/or reforms in each nation. Each case study represents a unique mix of institutions and actors in the process of deciding upon local government boundary changes. Furthermore, annexation procedures, and any changes to them over time, provide clues to changes in government approaches as the result of changing ideologies and economic and political circumstances in each nation.

Third, and flowing from the previous point, municipal annexations inform the relationship among various levels and types of government institutions. Tracing changes to local government boundaries involves unpacking the state structure of each nation. The case studies provide a diverse range of states along the continuum of strong unitary systems to loose federal systems. The examination of annexation procedures, collectively demonstrated by the case studies, unveils the manner by which intergovernmental agencies interact to provide policy responses to important public problems.

The introductory chapter is organized into three sections. The first reviews the book's organization and research questions. The next section provides a summary of each national case study. The final section explains the book's comparative approach to the international study of the reform of local government boundaries.

Organization of the Book

Although the book does not adopt a specific theoretical focus that guides each national case study, the theoretical undertones of the case studies are the subject of this introduction as well as two separate chapters (Chapters

2 and 3). To begin with, this introductory chapter outlines four specific frameworks – (1) geography of the local boundary problem, (2) boundary procedures, (3) institutions and actors, and (4) broader regional and urban contexts – that assist in setting the case studies within a comparative framework.

Chapters 2 and 3 provide discussions of contemporary ideas and theories regarding study of the reform of local government territories. First, Ronan Paddison (Chapter 2) provides an overview of the nature of local boundaries and the issues involved in their redrawing. He then offers three propositions that could lead to a more just system of local government boundary restructuring: (1) that it meet local preferences and needs, (2) that it be a fair, transparent, and relatively accessible process, and (3) that neither central nor local political elites wholly determine it. Second, Andrejs Skaburskis (Chapter 3) fleshes out some of the theories and concepts regarding local government boundary reform introduced by Paddison. Skaburskis identifies some pragmatic goals for municipal restructuring plans.

The concluding chapter, by John Meligrana and Eran Razin, revisits the ideas and theories regarding local government boundary reform introduced by Paddison and Skaburskis in light of the evidence presented by the case studies. The concluding chapter provides a summary and analysis of the convergence and divergence in international trends in the procedures to reform local government boundaries.

Chapters 4-11 explore how the legislative, economic, political, and institutional contexts of each nation shaped the debates on and changes to local government boundaries. Each chapter, in varying degrees, examines four key areas: (1) the formal procedures, in theory and practice, and whether they were reformed; (2) the political game – attributes of the conflicts, the actors, their interests and relative power, court intervention, and so on; (3) local government boundary change as reflecting broader social and political changes; and (4) the implications for the spatial development of the urban system and for equality, efficiency, and participation issues. Specific questions are addressed. What are the goals and objectives of local government boundary reform? What are the procedures for extending the territory of a local government? What are the various roles and perspectives of different actors (stakeholders) in the redrawing of local government boundaries? And have the procedures changed over time?

To answer these questions, this book brings together an international group of scholars, from both developing and developed nations and from a variety of academic backgrounds (geography, public administration, political science, and urban planning), to provide a comprehensive and multidisciplinary perspective on the study of local government boundary reform. Not only are the authors internationally recognized scholars, but also many are (or were) active members of boards, commissions, and other government agencies responsible for dealing with local government boundary reform. Thus, each chapter provides an interesting mix of both scholarly and professional (pragmatic) perspectives on this topic. Each author provides a detailed investigation of government documents, reports, and legislation not readily accessible to the English reader.

Case Studies: An Overview of Local Boundary Changes in Eight Countries

United States

In Chapter 4, Greg Lindsey compares the different policies and procedures, and ultimately the different approaches, of annexation throughout the United States arising from its federalist system. Individual states reserve the authority to make changes to municipal government boundaries in that system. To a degree, Lindsey also introduces generic types of annexation procedures referred to either explicitly (see Chapters 5 and 8) or implicitly by the authors of the other national cases.

Lindsey begins by comparing the five types of annexation procedures, from determination by the local population to determination by the courts. He finds that the majority of states use popular determination and municipal determination as the primary methods of annexation (closer to the local level), while significantly fewer use legislative, quasi-legislative, or judicial determination (more removed from the local level). Annexation procedures, Lindsey notes, have featured a trend of increasing opportunities for municipalities and local residents to participate and an associated rise in the complexity of policies and procedures. The level of annexation appears to have been consistent in the past thirty years, but the character has changed: between 1970 and 1998, the number of total annexations and the number of states involved with annexation remained fairly consistent; however, the populations and population densities involved in these annexations decreased significantly.

In this context, Lindsey notes that investigating annexation policies and procedures is particularly important. He suggests four themes of issues concerning annexation. First, political issues arise primarily from the right of self-determination versus the municipality's ability to expand and annex easily. Second, economic and fiscal issues emerge mainly from decisions concerning tax increases and service needs (and service wants) for newly annexed areas. Third, annexation criteria, service delivery equity, and rights to remonstration are the most notable administrative issues associated with annexation. Fourth, there is a range of other issues, such as environmental issues associated with stormwater management, that emerges with annexation.

Illustrating how these issues play out in a practical example, Lindsey uses Fort Wayne, Indiana, as a case study of annexation strategies and policies. Fort Wayne developed its annexation strategy based on comprehensive studies recommending the absorption of contiguous areas. Recognizing many of the above-mentioned issues, the city adopted a phased annexation strategy for its contiguous areas by taking advantage of delaying provisions in the state legislation. Concurrently, municipal officials encouraged active public participation in the annexation activities; however, the city failed to address the protests of the people and therefore incurred the involvement of the courts. Ultimately, the Fort Wayne case study reveals the results of a comprehensive strategy for a city that led the state in the amount of land annexed in the 1980s and 1990s.

Concluding, Lindsey notes a range of possible priorities for further research. For instance, while he maintains that states are main actors in the process, either by directly annexing or by establishing procedures for local governments, the implications of public participation must be further researched. This research is especially important, Lindsey points out, as popular determination states tend to have fewer annexations than municipal determination states.

Canada

Jeanne M. Wolfe, Raphaël Fischler, and John Meligrana present information in Chapter 5 on local government boundary restructuring undertaken within Ontario and Quebec, Canada's two most populous and urban provinces. Both Ontario's and Quebec's reforms to their annexation and amalgamation procedures for deciding boundary disputes reveal much regarding provincial interests versus those of local governments and citizens. Overall, the boundary reforms in both provinces disclose Canada's constitutional condition that municipalities are merely "creatures of the province." Both Ontario's and Quebec's Ministries of Municipal Affairs played central roles in shaping the debates and conditions under which municipal boundary restructuring could take place. Both provincial ministries showed a capacity to bring tremendous changes to the territorial maps of their local government systems. However, the manner in which and the degree to which each province used this power show the diversity of approaches that can be taken within the same constitutional setting.

Even though both provinces had absolute power to redraw municipalities, neither used it exclusively. Both provinces sought to establish procedures whereby local municipalities could decide, or have input into, any revisions to the territorial status quo. Quebec's method was perhaps gentler than Ontario's since its emphasis was on voluntary boundary restructuring and the use of more carrots than sticks to encourage boundary reform. Ontario, however, sought to establish boundary reforms that would insulate it from being drawn into what were usually fierce political contests over territory waged by neighbouring municipalities. When Ontario did act, it was usually swiftly and resulted in dramatic changes to its local government map.

The authors identify three distinct periods of boundary reform in each province. In Quebec, they were (1) the 1960s and early 1970s, a time of starts and stops, (2) the period of great municipal reforms at the end of the 1970s and implemented in the 1980s, and (3) another time of transformation in the late 1990s, with major amalgamations. Each period was characterized by both major interventions by the provincial government and ongoing programs to encourage municipal amalgamations. In Ontario, institutions and legislation governing annexation divide the province's procedures for redrawing municipal boundaries into three phases. The first and longest phase covers the period from the 1950s to 1982, when a quasi-judicial agency, the Ontario Municipal Board (OMB), had virtually complete jurisdiction over annexations as granted to it by the province. The second phase, 1982 to 1995, began with new legislation to enlarge the role of locally elected officials and the provincial Ministry of Municipal Affairs to resolve boundary disputes without recourse to the OMB. The third phase, 1995 to the present, has been characterized by more streamlined annexation and amalgamation procedures to restructure the territories of local governments.

Ontario and Quebec have both divergent and convergent histories with respect to their treatment of the "boundary problem." The most obvious divergence was in the types of municipal boundary changes. Quebec firmly avoided annexations in favour of municipal amalgamations and consolidations. The province's strategy of municipal boundary reform was to group existing municipal governments into a more "logical" territorial configuration. In Ontario, annexation was preferred, amalgamations being a method of last resort or a consequence of frequent and sustained annexations. In fact, the amalgamations undertaken to form regional municipalities during the late 1960s and early 1970s may have fanned the flames of annexation by municipalities untouched by this regional reform. Only toward the mid-1990s did amalgamation become more central to the Ontario government's campaign to reduce the number of municipalities.

Furthermore, both provinces also diverged with respect to the reform of county boundaries. Ontario's municipal boundary reform did not disturb the historic county boundaries but grafted regional municipalities out of the existing territorial dimensions of its historic county system. Quebec, however, abandoned the county boundary in its creation of regional county municipalities (RCMs). The divergence is also evident in the fact that Ontario's regional municipalities were restricted to the urban areas of the province, while Quebec's institution of RCMs was more geographically extensive.

The authors note that Ontario's boundary disputes were long settled by quasi-judicial determination by the Ontario Municipal Board, while in Quebec there was no formal commission or board. The OMB set standards regarding the size of annexation and specified that the annexing municipality had the burden of proof in establishing a need for more land. Although the OMB established a standard and, to a degree, a predictable method for deciding boundary disputes, the process was usually slow, expensive, and adversarial. The OMB did not solve the chronic boundary problem of many Ontario municipalities, as the authors reveal through an analysis of a few case studies. Moreover, the complexities of boundary issues became too much for the OMB.

The creation of regional municipalities in Ontario and regional county municipalities in Quebec represents an important convergence in the comparative experiences of boundary reform in these provinces. These reforms, which established a two-tier system of local government, created the template for the municipal amalgamations and the dramatic decline in the number of local governments. By the 1990s, the provincial governments in Quebec and Ontario sought to restructure the areas covered by regional municipalities.

Unfortunately, it appears that neither Ontario nor Quebec has been able to solve the chronic boundary problems of its municipal governments. Both provinces are currently studying or actively pursuing further boundary reform. In this regard, the provinces converge on a crucial point: the inherent policy of the provincial governments has always been to reduce the number and enlarge the area or territory of local governments. It appears that no other strategy has been considered.

Germany

In Chapter 6, Hellmut Wollmann examines Germany's experience with altering the territorial jurisdiction of its local governments. He examines Germany's two distinct periods of local government territorial reform. The first occurred in the "old" Federal Republic during the late 1960s and early 1970s, and the second, after reunification, occurred in East Germany starting in the early 1990s.

Wollmann argues that, like other European countries (particularly Sweden and the United Kingdom), Germany experienced, during the "planning-oriented" late 1960s and early 1970s, a wave of territorial local government reforms. He states that the factors and discourses shaping the reform agenda were massive shifts in the settlement structure, rising debate on regional planning, an expansive ("social democratic") welfare state, and functional reform. To improve the administrative efficiency and planning capacity of the municipalities and counties, the federal states *(Länder)* proceeded to drastically redraw the boundaries of the local governments through large-scale (and often conflict-ridden) territorial reforms and amalgamations. In doing so, most *Länder* followed what has been termed the "North European" pattern (with large-scale amalgamation) rather than the "South European" model (with small-scale or no territorial changes). Thus, with significant differences between the *Länder*, the number of municipalities was cut, in total, from 24,000 to some 8,400 and that of counties from 425 to 237.

West Germany adopted two strategies, along a continuum, in the reorganization of municipal government territories. At one end of the continuum was the variant ("Strategy I") to redraw the boundaries of all existing municipalities by way of merging (amalgamating) them and forming (territorially and demographically enlarged) "unitary municipalities" *(Einheitsgemeinden)*. At the other end of the continuum was the variant ("Strategy II") in which all existing municipalities, even the small ones, were retained as *political* local government units, while a set of *joint authorities* was created of which the municipalities were members and that served them as their *administrative* support unit.

After German reunification, from 1990 onward, the East German *Länder* followed suit in carrying out territorial reforms, at first mainly at the county level and more recently also at the municipal level. Hence, Germany's institutional and local government history provides ample examples, in conspicuous interregional and intertemporal variance, of the legal preconditions, strategies, and consequences of local government territorial reforms.

Spain

Abel Albet i Mas focuses in Chapter 7 on Spain's historical development and current status of municipal government legislation and the primary dysfunctions of its current municipal structure. Spain's contemporary structure of local government was established in the Decree of 1812, which recognized the legal status of municipalities, compared to the diverse structure previously remaining from the ancien régime. Until 1931, legislation concerning municipal organization changed over twenty times, and another twenty bills were not passed. Albet i Mas highlights seven pieces of legislation until 1955 that shaped Spain's contemporary municipal structure, noting the alternating absolutist, liberal, and conservative philosophies inherent in each.

Albet i Mas notes that local government reform was scarcely mentioned in much of the legislation prior to 1955. Although many pieces of legislation distinguished different forms and procedures of municipal restructuring, by the end of the 1960s there never appeared to be a unitary, systematic approach by any piece of legislation detailing municipal restructuring. Legislation in 1966 encouraged and provided financial incentives for amalgamation and annexation and accounted for the reduction of about 1,000 municipalities by 1977, at which time the financial incentives were abandoned. This legislation was the only piece concerning municipal restructuring in the "legislative desert" of the 1960s and much of the 1970s in Spain.

Since that time, a ministry directive has sought to reduce the number of municipalities where there is adequate local support or, conversely, where there is a sufficient lack of opposition. Many changes occurred during this period: for instance, one *diputación* ("provincial council") eliminated about 25 percent of its municipalities. However, despite the issue of excessive fragmentation, annexation, not amalgamation, has been the primary means of local change, but this change has not occurred without serious effects on local community history and identity. Albet i Mas notes that, in this period for some areas, there were insensitivities in renaming municipalities and faulty functional criteria used in decision making.

In 1979, significant political changes again began to take effect. The Spanish Constitution established the local level as a formal level of government under the administration of both the central and the regional governments. Further legislation was also enacted and established the basis for local regulations, recognized different local entities, and detailed the rights, responsibilities, and functions of local governments and residents. The Catalan Municipal Act particularly was more specific than the central government's legislation.

Current municipal legislation in Spain offers a range of restructuring options, including amalgamation, annexation, segregation, boundary changes, and name changes, but these suggested changes have been limited by the legislation's and, for that matter, the public's acceptance of the current municipal system. Spanish municipal legislation also permits a range of other local entities, such as municipal associations that provide a range of services to several municipalities. Presumably, these additional local entities have added to Spain's problems of local government fragmentation.

The lack of action on behalf of the Spanish central government in establishing a systematic reform has resulted in the maintenance of the fragmented local government system. This is most noticeable in a number of dysfunctions, including enclaves within other jurisdictions, arbitrary boundaries, or municipalities split by international boundaries.

Albet i Mas concludes that local government reform in Spain has been difficult because of public attitudes toward such change: people associate their municipality with their civic and political identity. He further concludes that, although the excessive fragmentation of Spain's local government system has been recognized for much of the past 200 years, there have never been policies or legislative efforts targeted at resolving the problem. Ultimately, the first step toward such a reform is clarifying and realigning the functions and responsibilities of each government level.

Israel

In Chapter 8, Eran Razin compares Israel's procedures in municipal boundary changes with those of other democracies, evaluates Israel's changing context for these procedures, and discusses the causes of reform failures in Israel. The basis of its boundary change procedures, Razin notes, is a remnant of the British colonial legislation that granted authority to the Ministry of the Interior for commission appointments and final decision making for establishing, abolishing, or changing the boundaries of municipalities.

Israel's procedures for local boundary changes are identified as being highly centralized (more so than other countries), simple, and lacking relevant criteria. The three modifications that have occurred have been modest, concerning local industrial councils, minimum thresholds for new local authorities, and the transfer of local revenues between local authorities. Razin suggests that these modifications to the procedures may represent an attempt to limit the minister's absolute power in decision making but, better yet, represent the intervention of other ministries in the process.

Razin does note that, although the legal framework for changes has remained relatively intact, the centralized decision-making authority of the Ministry of the Interior has diminished significantly since the 1980s. This diminishment can be attributed to several factors, including the increase in pluralist ethnoreligious politics; the competition within the central government between ministries with stakes in the decisions, particularly the Ministry of Finance's financial interventions and constraints; and the constant scrutiny by Israel's High Court of Justice of the government's procedures and policies.

Changes to these procedures at the end of the twentieth century progressed in three directions: (1) a change toward the "American" model of self-determination; (2) a change toward a more streamlined set of procedures for growth and development; and (3) a change to formalize the requirements and time frames of the procedures in writing. Procedures were established in writing in 2001 by the minister of the interior, but an indication of their effectiveness is not yet available.

Concluding, Razin notes that, by the end of the 1990s, the highly centralized powers granted to the minister of the interior remained, but significant new pressures were now exerted by other parties. Ultimately, only minor, modest steps have been achieved toward a comprehensive reform of Israel's local government system. Four main factors contributed to this failure: the lateness of local government reform on the public agenda, the existence of national parties at the local level, the heterogeneous ethnoreligious landscape, and the political fragmentation complicating national reform.

Korea

Dong-Ho Shin in Chapter 9 details Korea's recent local governance reform, primarily focusing on the main actors, principles, legal foundations, and political processes. This reform has progressed on Korea's rapid industrialization and subsequent urbanization, which have created various spillover effects and regional conflicts. Korea's current administrative hierarchy consists of the central, provincial, and municipal levels. The provincial level consists of Seoul metropolitan city, other metropolitan cities, and provinces. Metropolitan cities are urban areas separated from provinces, often former provincial capitals, and report directly to the central government. The special Metropolitan City of Seoul differs from its counterparts in that its governor is equivalent to central government ministers, unlike provincial governors, who are one tier lower.

The current government structure is a result of the changes made since 1945, after the end of Japanese colonial rule. Provincial boundaries were remnants of the Chosun Dynasty of the later nineteenth century, and, given geographical barriers preventing adequate communication between regions, strong regional identities exist in Korea. Metropolitan cities were separated from the provinces after 1945 based on the rationale that the interests of urban areas are better served by their own governments, despite strong provincial disapproval. Municipal boundaries changed little before 1960, but since that time many areas were classified as cities, and many townships were incorporated. Ultimately, the numerous provincial and municipal boundary adjustments have resulted in complexities for urban and regional governance in Korea, as a result of a highly fragmented government system and individualistic behaviours.

Shin highlights the complexities associated with the local government fragmentation resulting from local government reforms in case studies of Kyungki Province and Kyungnam Province. Kyungki Province, Korea's most economically active province, has experienced considerable industrialization and urbanization. Its main cities, Seoul and Inchun, separated to form metropolitan cities in 1946 and 1980, respectively. Seoul's growth control policies encouraged population and economic growth in the surrounding province, which saw town centres grow and separate from their hosting counties as new cities. As a result of this fragmentation, Shin argues, interjurisdictional decision making and coordination have suffered. Korea's triangular region, located southwest of Seoul, exemplifies these problems. Shin highlights the differences between the rural setting of the city of Uiwang and the heavily urbanized cities of Ahnyang and Kunpo, the three of which were separated from Silheung County in the 1970s and 1980s. Shin notes the problems of service management associated with insufficient coordination and cooperation among the three cities, and he points out that attempts at unification have failed because of resistance from Uiwang and Kunpo.

Shin's second case study details the separation of Kyungnam's provincial capital of Pusan and the complex relationship that now exists. The conflicts and poor relationships between Pusan and Kyungnam Province are highlighted when he considers the three successful annexation attempts by rapidly developing Pusan, despite protests from Kyungnam Province. Although both parties have sought to promote Pusan to balance Seoul's economic superiority, Pusan and Kyungnam Province have disagreed concerning priorities, whether urban transit line extensions or the locations of landfills.

Reforms until the 1990s in Korea had created a fragmented system of local government enhanced by the country's transition to a more democratic and liberal society. In 1994, the Ministry of Home Affairs announced a plan to correct this fragmentation that pursued widespread municipal amalgamation. While the central government established the reform process and criteria, local governments were involved in the process through municipal referendums on the amalgamation issue. The goal was to amalgamate as many municipalities as possible. Shin finds that these reforms were successful in meeting this goal, but the central government failed in its desire for a totally democratic process, since it often intervened directly in approvals or interpreting referendum results.

Overall, while the amalgamation thrust appears to have been successful in reducing local government fragmentation, Shin argues that it is too early to gauge the achievement of the central government's goals for the reform. He argues that the most important aspect of the reform was the establishment of a platform from which to completely correct a fragmented local government map.

China
In Chapter 10, Jianfa Shen details the city designation and boundary adjustment procedures in postreform China since 1978, a topic that has been virtually neglected in the literature. These reforms, Shen argues, have been necessitated by the rapidly changing economic and social needs in China through rapid urbanization resulting from the country's progress toward a market economy in addition to the state government's trend of government decentralization and the need for stronger urban and regional governance. In this progression, Chinese cities slowly emerged throughout the twentieth century from strong central government control and

provincial monitoring toward political autonomy. Chinese cities currently exist within a six-tier administrative structure, ranging in power from the State Council and provincial-level units to town-/township-/street-level units and villages'/residents' committees. Cities may be designated at the provincial, prefecture, or county level of government, thus creating a confusing array of cities with different designations.

Shen highlights the two main forms of city designation and the three main forms of boundary adjustment that have prevailed in China. The first form of city designation involves the creation of a new city from the separation of urban areas from hosting counties. This form was emphasized prior to 1978 on the rationale of differentiating between different urban and rural interests. The second form of city designation, which has dominated city designation since 1978, involves the redesignation of entire counties as cities. Shen maintains that China's central government has encouraged and facilitated city designation, seeking the creation of cities that are conducive to economic development and growth. The first form of boundary change involved the city administration of counties in a previous prefecture; the second featured the annexation of a city or county as a new urban district; and the third involved amalgamation between two cities, generally a prefecture-level city and a county-level city.

While the process of city designation and boundary reform in China has been dominated by the central government, other local units have had significant input. China's central government develops the guidelines for qualifying candidates and is the final authority for approval of city designation and boundary changes. The provincial, prefecture, and county levels of government are often the initiators of and experimenters with city designation and boundary change reforms, acting as a grassroots feedback mechanism for the central government. Although in 1961 the state government encouraged public participation in the reform process, most issues and decisions are separate from the public realm.

While Shen argues that the local government reforms since 1978 have corrected some of the problems in the previous system, numerous problems have been generated as a result. Separation often resulted in a county's losing its urban centre, often its economic heart. This problem was corrected somewhat by the county designation as a city form, which in turn generated problems of excessive urbanization and industrialization, loss of agricultural land, and complex service coordination. With the city-governing-county form, urban interests often dominated the political arena, while counties increasingly found their needs unmet, and anticipated equal allocations of resources did not materialize. Furthermore, new layers of government added under this form, such as prefecture-level cities, have further complicated China's administrative hierarchy.

In concluding, Shen notes the challenges faced by a developing country in coping with rapid urbanization. The state government's efforts toward local government reform in China are perceived to have been partially successful; however, acute conflicts between city and county interests still remain. Shen maintains that a more transparent and open public participation mechanism is required to solve such conflicts in order to accommodate more successful urban space expansion, reorganization, and reform in China.

South Africa
The last case study is presented in Chapter 11 by Robert Cameron, who presents an analysis of the procedures used in South Africa to restructure the boundaries of local units of government. He identifies several phases of South Africa's local government reorganization that have occurred over nearly a decade. In the mid-1990s, South Africa moved from a racially based system of local governance toward a nonracial system. His analysis focuses on the final phase of this reform, which involves a move toward majoritarian democracy with limited safeguards for minorities.

Cameron begins his chapter with an overview of contemporary problems with the local government system, which include boundaries influenced by gerrymandering, odd sizes, and unclear national goals and standards. He then takes an exclusive look at the Municipal Demarcation Board. This board is the nation's final decision-making body when it comes to the demarcation of local government boundaries. In his analysis, Cameron deconstructs the operations of this board as well as reviews the pros and cons of its governing legislation.

Comparative Approach to Local Government Boundary Reform
Finding a common language and a common topic for nations as diverse as the ones in this book is difficult. However, two key parameters provided direction for each author. Although various types of boundary reform were examined in the case studies, one parameter was a dual focus on annexation, the enlargement of a municipal territory, and amalgamation, the merger of two or more local governments. Furthermore, to simplify terminology regarding the diversity of boundary changes made to local government areas, the following discussion uses the word *annexation* as a generic term to identify all possible types of boundary change. The second parameter was a focus on local units of government, commonly referred to as city or municipal government, and changes to their boundaries. Other levels and types of government as well as other kinds of local government reform are considered only in their connections to the territorial changes to local governments.

Within these two parameters, each nation was selected not only to provide wide global coverage but also because each case informs four key frameworks in the study of local government boundary reform: (1) geography of the local government boundary problem, (2) boundary reform procedures, (3) institutions and actors, and (4) boundary reform in the context of urban and regional governance. To be sure, the emphasis on each framework varies according to the approach of each author and the unique issues of each case study. However, these four key areas provide a continuity among the chapters in their treatment of municipal boundary restructuring within each nation. The following section introduces each framework in relation to the case studies. Although this introduction treats each framework as a distinct factor, they are not mutually exclusive.

Geography of the Local Government Boundary Problem

Boundary reform procedures are established because there are real or perceived problems with the existing territorial forms of local government. In geographical terms, this problem can be conceptualized by the terms "overbound municipality" and "underbound municipality." Application of these concepts provides the rationale for first identifying the mismatch between the legal city (or an urban municipality) and the area of fringe developments and urban spaces. An overbound city has municipal control over the settled urban area in addition to the rural land reserved for future urban uses. The underbound city's municipal control extends only to a proportion of the settled area, leaving portions of urbanized land beyond the city limits without any municipal controls. The concepts of overbound and underbound municipalities imply that there is, or should be, a strict legal division of urban and rural spaces, with cities and towns governing urban areas and rural governments governing rural areas. What emerges from these concepts is the question of where to draw the political and legal divisions between urban and rural.

Municipal boundary changes bring to the fore the relationship between local government reorganization and the transformation of land from rural to urban uses. Rusk (1995), writing from an American perspective, argues that the use of annexation is important in dissolving the notion of the rural-urban fringe area by creating elastic cities that can expand to include the entire sphere of influence of a city-region – that is, rural, urban, and fringe landscapes – under one political jurisdiction. Doing so creates what he terms "cities without suburbs," thereby solving problems of growth management and fiscal and political equality within a city-region. Or, put another way, all urban municipalities should be overbounded. Local government boundary reform, therefore, is an attempt to cope with fringe development, to establish a political space that is overbound.

Overbound cities, or "elastic cities," to use Rusk's (1995) terminology, are more prosperous and enjoy substantially stronger population growth rates than inelastic cities – that is, cities that have not extended their municipal limits. From this perspective, annexation is not just a process of problem solving in which boundaries are adjusted to gain better planning and control over fringe developments but can also be a proactive policy of modernizing local governments. Thus, annexation can be a "solution" to this archaic local political geography and one way to deal with the "boundary problem." The boundary problem arose as local governments were (and still are) slow to change their boundaries to properly overlap the real dimensions of urban land use.

The boundary problem can also be seen in functional terms in which broad principles of boundary configuration provide a litmus test for the effectiveness of the delivery of certain urban services. Lindsey's case study of the United States (Chapter 4) enumerates several substantive issues involved in municipal boundary restructuring, including administrative efficiency, local government finance, public health, the environment, and quality of life. Functional concerns include size (the area needed to provide adequate services or protection), shape (for the appropriate delivery of public services such as sewer lines or emergency services), and containment of economic activities. Therefore, as functions of local government change, so must boundary configurations.

The nations analyzed in this book both confirm and challenge the above conventional thinking regarding the political geography of local governments. In some cases, boundary reform attempted to maintain urban areas within urban municipal governments, while in other cases more elaborate boundary changes resulted in urban and rural areas under one local jurisdiction. Shin's discussion of Korea (Chapter 9) neatly summarizes this point: boundary reform was previously enacted to maintain an "urban-rural separation" (conventional approach) but is now enacted to create an "urban-rural integration" (new approach). Thus, the Korean experience of local boundary changes is in contrast to the American and Israeli experiences (Chapters 4 and 8). Lindsey's study of the United States and Razin's study of Israel show annexation procedures and regulations premised on maintaining a strict political division between rural and urban governments: annexation as a battle between city and countryside. The Canadian (Chapter 5) and Chinese (Chapter 10) experiences fall between the Korean-American-Israeli model; these countries attempted to reform local boundaries to achieve objectives of both urban-rural separation and urban-rural integration. More complex spatial models of boundary reform are found in Cameron's review of South Africa's annexation procedures (Chapter 11).

Boundary Reform Procedures
The case studies reveal that diverse procedures have been developed to address local government boundary problems. The studies show that some procedures have been used to engineer major and dramatic changes to

local boundaries (Canada, Korea, and China), while in other cases the procedures have brought minor or no changes (Spain and Israel). Such a diversity in results can be traced back, to a degree, to the procedures and methods for redrawing local government territories (United States).

The procedures for redrawing local government boundaries, therefore, influence how the "boundary problem" is interpreted. In some cases, specific geographic criteria are built into the procedures for deciding municipal annexations (United States and South Africa), while in other cases the procedures are silent about the geographic variables that are to guide the reform of municipal boundaries (Canada and Spain).

Furthermore, the type of annexation procedure conditions the methods and information used to decide on the appropriate reform of local boundaries. For example, in some cases, annexation is a matter of extensive public debate and approval (Korea), while in other cases quasi-judicial tribunals are the dominant forum for deciding boundary questions (Canada and South Africa). In many cases, annexation procedures are becoming more complex and involving many forums for local boundary changes to be debated and decided.

Annexation procedures may change over time, thereby enhancing or diminishing the power of various public and private actors involved in any boundary dispute. In some cases, public participation has been elevated or enhanced by revisions to annexation procedures (United States, Canada, and Korea), while in other cases the procedures have remained virtually constant over the past several decades (Spain and Israel). Moreover, as mentioned above, interpretations of and solutions to the boundary problem ultimately must be crafted in light of the established procedures for deciding annexations. Case studies of specific annexation decisions and disputes presented here highlight how local institutions and actors have operated within the established annexation procedures to either support or oppose changes to the municipal territorial status quo.

Institutions and Actors

There are various actors and institutions involved in the politics of annexation, each having a different perspective on the boundary problem and whether or not various types of boundary reform represent viable solutions. For example, if annexation is needed, then something is perceived to be "wrong" and needs to be corrected. The logic of this perception is not the issue, but its acceptance as legitimate is a major point. Herein lies the heart of the politics of annexation: it is a political power play to legitimize the existence of a boundary problem and the use of annexation to correct the problem.

Each actor and institution involved in annexation politics has a different take on the study and interpretation of boundary problems. Important for all the case studies is the role of senior levels of government. Most of the authors are critical of senior levels of government for not providing effective leadership and procedures for solving local government boundary problems.

Broader Context of Urban and Regional Governance

The topic of local government boundary reform takes on more importance and meaning when it is looked at in the context of a country's general administrative, developmental, and fiscal structures, in particular with regard to the roles and functions of supramunicipal (e.g., regional) and senior levels of government. Thus, the case studies presented in this book tackle the issue of how local boundary reform is wrapped up in the larger context of governance as it is practised in each nation. Two key points emerge when linking boundary reform to the broader context of governance. First, boundary reform can be an expression of changing approaches and ideologies with respect to governance. For example, both Chapter 5 and Chapter 7 examine how boundary reform procedures have changed, to a degree, as a result of changing government ideologies. Second, boundary reform is examined as part of the environmental and economic challenges associated with globalization. Perhaps Shen's chapter on China best exemplifies how local boundary changes are part of a nation's strategy for economic reform and development. In fact, the underlying theme (treated either explicitly or implicitly by each author) is that, without the reform of local government boundaries, regional and national economic development will be hampered.

Acknowledgment
Portions of the Case Studies section (pp. 7-14) have been contributed by Kevin Muir.

Reference
Rusk, D. 1995. *Cities without Suburbs*. 2nd ed. Washington: Woodrow Wilson Centre Press.

2
Redrawing Local Boundaries: Deriving the Principles for Politically Just Procedures

Ronan Paddison

The ubiquity of local government provides the most obvious testimony to its importance in the processes of governing the state. With few exceptions,[1] all states have a system of local government through which those functions of government that need to be locally delivered can be structured. Such an interpretation perhaps overemphasizes the instrumental role of local government; in liberal democracies, it also functions in a (local) democratic capacity bolstering the legitimacy of the (local) state. Yet what is apparent in the functions ascribed to local government in most states is its central role in the functioning of the state. Nor is this contribution limited to the delivery of local services – local government is commonly used as a vehicle through which the regulatory functions of the state can be mediated while providing the agency through which local economic growth can be fostered.

As part of the state apparatus, local governments are created, and re-created, to serve the objectives of the state. Typically, a local government is subordinate to a central (or more senior) government: its functioning, including its autonomy, the method(s) by which it is financed, and the spatial framework within which it operates are decided within parameters determined, to a considerable degree, by the senior government. This generalization needs to be qualified to take account not only of the different practices evident between states, themselves reflective of political-ideological differences (as the empirical chapters in this volume amply demonstrate), but also of the local political factors that influence how local government is re-created. How local government is structured and restructured needs to take account of local factors, ensuring that boundary reform is a dialogue between actors representing different scales and interests.

It is in urban areas that questions of local government boundary structure and reform assume their greatest salience. Two types of question predominate: whether and how urban areas should be separated from their rural hinterlands and how the governing of the urban area itself should be organized. Given the complexity of the city, and the juxtaposition of vested (territorial) interests, it is small wonder that reconfiguring the political map so readily becomes a contested exercise. Yet, as an essential component of the wider system of local governance, boundary reform is contested because of the nature of cities and their governing.

Cities, it could be argued, are more effective as sites for wealth accumulation than they are as sites for local democratic governance. It is perhaps all too easy to accept uncritically the fact that, particularly with the beginning of industrial capitalism, the development of large cities and the urbanization of society have been primarily intended to serve the needs of capital. Cities harness economies – of agglomeration, transfer, externality, and scale – and have proved to be the vital loci through which economic growth can be achieved. It is no accident that all of the wealthy nations, those within the Organisation for Economic Co-operation and Development (OECD), contain major metropolitan areas and are defined by high levels of urbanization. Previously, cities or, more properly, towns had functioned as economic links in trade and production systems, but it was not until the emergence of industrial capitalism that scale, and its accompanying traits of physical extensiveness and social diversity, marked out cities as human settlements in ways that we recognize today. But if it was with industrial urbanization in the nineteenth century that networks of large cities emerged, then with populations of a million or more problems of governance also quickly became apparent.

Urbanization, the development of towns and cities, has typically raised the question of whether they should be governed separately from the rural areas that surround them. The processes of distinguishing between urban and rural described by Jianfa Shen in postreform China (see Chapter 10) mirror changes in Britain starting in the 1830s and elsewhere in Europe with the development of urban centres. Frequently, local government boundaries were drawn to separate town and countryside. Whatever the justification for the separation, it has rarely proved to be stable: urban growth has ensured that questions of annexation have been enduring, while the debate as to whether urban should be separate from rural has been ongoing. What is striking is how these questions repeat themselves cross-nationally, albeit with variations.

While the scale of the contemporary city distinguishes it in part from earlier types of settlement, there are other defining features, as urban sociologists have sought to show. In his classic statement, Wirth (1938) argued that, alongside size, density and social heterogeneity defined cities and city living (although his analysis, along with some others, tended to conflate urban society with industrial society). Undeniably, urban societies were not just quantitatively different from their pre-urban counterparts but also qualitatively different. Social relations were more instrumental and contractual, less intimate, for citizens; virtually all fellow inhabitants were strangers (Simmel 1908/1950). These relations were defined by the physical proximity of rich and poor and by a level of social diversity (particularly in immigrant societies) unimaginable in pre-urban society. Born of industrial capitalism, the burgeoning cities of nineteenth-century Western Europe and North America, together with colonial urban outposts such as Melbourne, had traumatic impacts on contemporaries living through the transformation.[2] Although the problems of rapid urban growth were expressed largely in social terms, increasingly they were seen to overlap with normative understandings of how cities should be governed.

One of the more obvious outcomes of city living was the complex net of spatial externalities, intentional or accidental, positive or negative, that crisscrossed the urban area, creating cartographies of advantage and disadvantage. Some demanded control: those that were life threatening, notably public health, and those that were a threat to social order (or, more precisely, the dominant social order). Even more fundamentally, controlling such issues was necessary insofar as a failure to address them could undermine the economic prosperity of the city. Control requires some form of government harnessed through institutions whose remit would be the managing of a public service for the public (common) good. (Implementation of the Police Act in 1829 in England is a classic example.) But in the provision, how are questions of its government to be decided? And by whom? Over what territorial area should the service be provided? Should provision be a local responsibility or delivered by the central government? If the former, then should there be a system of monitoring to ensure the effectiveness of local delivery? Who is to pay for the service? Who is to make decisions as to how the service is to be provided, and should this decision making be democratic and open or not? Governing cities, even the provision of a single public good, ineluctably raises a plethora of questions, for many of which – precisely because of the effects of different value positions – resolution is not expressible in terms of right or wrong (though, in the case of service delivery, it may be plausible to talk in terms of its more or less effective provision).

Nearly all the chapters in this volume focus on the practices of local government boundary reform in democratic states. It is a focus that is wholly rational – in command societies, local government units and boundaries are imposed rather than open to negotiation[3] – but nevertheless is based on an assumption fundamental in its implications: namely, that the processes of boundary restructuring are open to local democratic negotiation. In many of the countries examined in this volume, a tradition of local democracy is embedded within the overarching state, perhaps enshrined constitutionally or, where it is not, so much a part of the political culture that it is part of the taken-for-granted world.

The idea(l)s of democracy do not sit unproblematically with the governing of cities. Clearly, the scale and social diversity of the city, as introduced earlier, imply that notions of democratic governance along the lines of the Greek city-state are anachronistic to say the least, yet their example continues to have an influence as to what democratic practice in the modern city might aspire to. Being able to muster citizens to take democratic decisions in the *agora* is replicable in the contemporary world only in institutional practices such as the New England town meeting, clearly not in cities.[4] In the city-state, citizenship was restricted, gendered, and defined by wealth, but in the emergent industrial city the demand for democratic control of the local public sphere could be met only indirectly through elections and local representative forms of democracy. Defined on the basis of a territorial collectivity, local government can negate individual preferences for the collectively expressed preference. This tyranny of the majority has fundamental implications for boundary reform (as we shall see), as it does for democratic practice in general.

In fact, as Crick (1983) has astutely observed, democracy is a promiscuous term, capable of generating multiple interpretations. Furthermore, claims that local democratic institutions function democratically, whatever the reality and however "being democratic" is defined, need to take into account the interplay of political processes. In other words, local democratic processes, decisions on how to structure and restructure local government boundaries, are politicized territorial games in which power relations play a critical role in outcomes. This is to underline the promiscuity of the term "democracy" rather than to deny it. How (to take one example) are we to interpret its meaning where decisions on boundaries are perceived as being imposed locally by some higher (but also democratically elected) level of jurisdiction, a central state, where the outcome is clearly at odds with local preferences? Both levels of government can claim political legitimacy for their actions. Such cases are far from exceptional, demonstrating the "scalar contradictions" of the multilevel, territorially pluralist, democratic state.

These introductory remarks serve as a backdrop to the discussion of the wider philosophical implications of local government boundary restructuring and its theorization. In the discussion that follows, it is assumed that local boundary restructuring takes place within an overarching democratic state. Rather than define the term "democracy," I want to suggest minimal defining criteria for it – that it is an open, accountable, and responsive system of government and decision making, recognizing that collectively expressed preferences may "need" to override those of the individual but be able to be an effective forum for plurivocal demands. (Denying this need would be a denial of a system of local government, an argument that will be revisited in the discussion of public choice theory.)

The premise of (local) democracy is necessary to an understanding of the politics and processes of local boundary reform. I want to outline some propositions relating to a reform process in which the institutional procedures leading to territorial outcomes are just and are seen to be just. In raising the question of justness, the argument lays itself open to accusations of idealism. My intention here is normative, to suggest key propositions defining a just system of local government boundary restructuring as an "ideal type" against which the reality of processes and outcomes can be assessed. (The assessment is conducted more in the empirical chapters and in the editorial conclusion of this volume, though some pointers are suggested in this chapter.) Before I outline the arguments, we need to consider one other assumed feature of the argument: the nature of boundaries. An understanding of their nature will allow us to contemplate the implications of boundary redrawing.

The Nature of Local Boundaries: Inclusion, Exclusion, Territoriality, and Power Mapping

Any understanding of boundaries must accept their duality: they are both inclusionary and exclusionary. The act of drawing boundaries defines a sense of commonality, perhaps some form of political community, and grants explicit recognition to the differences that distinguish those inside from those outside the boundary. Closely linked with the concept of territoriality (Sack 1986; Storey 2001), boundaries define the limits of those spaces deemed important, whether for social, cultural, political, or economic reasons or (as is more often the case) some mix of them. In cities, as in other spaces, boundaries abound. Most are de facto boundaries, marking (say) one urban neighbourhood from another or the turf claimed by a certain gang. Some are *de jure*, given legal status, of which the most common (and important) is the political boundary.

As "natural" as established boundaries may appear, their reality is more convincingly explained through social constructivism. The reasoning here can borrow arguments used to explain territoriality. As Sack (1986, 219) has argued, territoriality "is a device to create and maintain much of the geographic context through which we experience the world and give it meaning." Territory provides the ground space for everyday practice, but critically it is also a vital component of self-identity. In the hierarchy of political organization, the linkages between territory, identity, and political life are strongest at the level of the nation, the nation-state, whose spatial expression is afforded through the national territory. Through what Sack terms the "tendencies of territoriality," it is possible to see exactly how boundaries fit into the overall argument. That is, territoriality becomes a means of claiming exclusive ownership, the spatial limits to which are made explicit through the delimitation of a precise boundary.

Fundamentally, as Storey (2001, 16) points out, "these boundaries indicate territorial control and, hence, power over prescribed space." But, reflecting their social construction, boundaries are not drawn randomly on the map; their delimitation is defined by those spaces that have social meaning and that in turn can be used to define the limits of a territorially defined social collectivity.

A social constructivist explanation of boundaries may be of particular significance in the case of local government boundaries because of the relative frequency with which local boundary change occurs. Historically, national boundaries, the limits of the separate states, have been more stable than local political boundaries. Wars and more consensual modes of political negotiation have been the basis for a significant "volume" of boundary changes between states, but quantitatively this volume palls by comparison with the frequency of local boundary changes. Local boundaries are more malleable than their national counterparts, processes of identity building within new territorial limits being plausible through the agency of political-territorial socialization.[5] This is not to deny that local identities do not provide powerful bases for action and resistance. The practice of local boundary reform has an abundance of historical examples to demonstrate that restructuring frequently engenders vociferous resistance. Yet few would be prepared to give the ultimate sacrifice to forestall a local boundary threat, as is precisely an explicit obligation of the citizen to the state. Nor are the foundations of local boundaries usually buttressed by complex, historically articulated, constructed ideas of territory and nation that harbour the potential for political extremism and have been the basis for all-embracing conflict.

It is largely because of the ways in which the uneven development of the (inter)national economy unfolds and its effects at the regional, metropolitan, or more local scale that the need for (substate) boundary changes recurs. Industrial societies, for example, and even more postindustrial societies, are characterized by their level of geographical mobility. Cities early in the industrial phase were described as pedestrian in their geographical scale; in the cities of North America of the 1870s, it is estimated that as many as 87 percent in the labour force either walked or cycled to their workplaces. By 1990, the car accounted for 95 percent of the journeys to work in extensive urbanized regions in North America (Hart 2001). The extent to which political boundaries have kept pace with rapid metropolitan growth, as John Meligrana has shown in the previous chapter, demonstrates the extent to which cities are under- or overbounded. More fundamentally, the needs of capital, and the institutional capacity to steer its effects locally, provide what are often technocratic reasons for refashioning political boundaries so that they keep pace with the dynamics of metropolitan physical and economic growth.

In spite of the frequency of local boundary restructuring (or calls for it), and in spite of any arguments about their relative malleability, local government boundaries can be of long historical standing. In some systems, their longevity ossifies the political map. There are ticklish questions here of the temporality of change. What periodization defines ossification? Put alternatively, in advanced postindustrial societies, how frequently does local government boundary restructuring resurface on the political agenda? Systems such as the network of French *départements* or local government divisions in some of the Australian states, which have been more or less stable since the nineteenth century, early in that century in the case of France, demonstrate the durability of local boundaries. In many cases, the durability has existed in spite of attempts by a higher level of government to refashion the map.

Reasoning for the resistance to change returns the argument to the essential nature of boundaries: they define the limits of locally apportioned space, creating an inside and an outside, and they define the territorial arenas in which (formal) power bases are constituted and in which local rule and control can be exercised. Boundaries are fundamental to place-based identities, and, as successive *Eurobarometer* surveys show, for example, the locality is second only to the member nation-states of the European Union for the strength of territorial attachments that citizens bestow on the different levels of political institutions affecting everyday lives (Hooghe and Marks 2001). The intensity of local identity is contingent on the specific institutional, political, and social geographies that define the individuality of place, but in many cases it provides powerful resistance to change. Informal power politics, mediated through communities and other local political associations, together with the agency of the individual, combine in this respect with the clout represented by local political elites, whose power base may be threatened by reform proposals. Few politicians are willing participants in territorial suicide, just as informal associative groups are enthusiastic defenders of their territorial interests. It is almost a law of local boundary restructuring that there will be powerful forces intent on maintaining the status quo.

One final aspect defining the nature of (local) political boundaries needs to be highlighted: their territorial precision. Political boundaries are geometrically precise, unlike many de facto territories, whose limits have more or less fuzzy edges. Yet the paradox is that redrawing (local) political boundaries is often expressed in terms of making them coterminous with the geographies created by de facto divisions: the fitting of suburban jurisdictions in a metropolitan area to the cartographies of class (or sometimes ethnic) division,[6] and the attempt to restructure boundaries to accord with labour and/or retail catchment areas, are common methods used to prescribe the boundaries of local governments. But the geographies created by everyday practices are not only dynamic but also fuzzy. The precision of the political boundary creates its own contradictions, not least in the border regions themselves, in which in-betweenness is excluded normally as a possibility.

Three Propositions in Search of a More Just System for Local Government Boundary Restructuring

In this section, I want to develop three propositions that contribute to an understanding of how local government boundary reform could be made a fairer process. Like boundary reform itself, this is a fraught exercise. By emphasizing the problem of fairness, an obvious question is fair to whom? Fair to those actors less powerful within the reform process is one way to respond to the question. Typically, boundary redefinition infringes on powerful territorial interests; how boundaries are redrawn reflects those interests and the unequal power relations through which changes become mediated.

Local autonomy is never an absolute but is constrained by the policies and preferences of higher levels of government and authority (as well as by market forces). Indeed, as a form of political decentralization, local government, however necessary for the effective democratic governance of the national territory, exists because of some higher level of jurisdiction. In Australia, for example, as in Canada, local government is talked of as a "creature" of the separate states/provinces in the federation, a description used to underline that it is the states or provinces and not the federal government that have constitutional responsibilities for local councils.[7] In Britain, usually described as a relatively centralized unitary state, local autonomy is significantly constrained by central fiat. During the 1980s, a period when central-local relations were strained, left-controlled councils tried to maintain local state welfarism that was otherwise being reformed by a right-wing central government, but it was possible for the centre to resolve the issue by abolishing authorities, including the Greater London Council, in spite of local preferences. Such examples demonstrate the inequalities of power relations; fairness needs to counter the inequalities so that the less powerful are at least heard, if not more.

The three propositions are not exhaustive. Nor are they meant to be definitive. Rather, I state them (not in any order of importance) as hypotheses in which, following their descriptions, it is possible to unravel the implications to which they give rise. Such arguments need to accept that local government systems, together with the methods used to revise their territorial structures, differ considerably between countries and, in the case of federal states in particular, often within them. This diversity defies the plausibility of being able to suggest a universal, fair methodology for boundary reform, particularly since superimposed over these methods are the different value positions given to the ends that local governments should serve. These goals – differently emphasized as political education through participation in local democratic practices, efficient and equitable service delivery, strategic area-wide coordination, local control, and accountability – conflict not just in the different geographies emphasized by them but also because of the different emphases given to them by actors in the reform process.

Proposition 1: Local Government Restructuring Should Meaningfully Address Local Preferences and Needs

Stated this baldly, such a proposition might appear redundant. Yet to the functioning of *local* government, it is fundamental. Although an ambiguous term, "addressing local preferences and needs" will require institutions capable of being responsive to the nuances of local diversity. Yet arguing that local preferences and needs should be meaningfully addressed through boundary reconfiguration is not to say that such a principle should be allowed to dominate. As I will argue in the final proposition, boundary determination and restructuring should be a balance between central and local interests and preferences.

A system of local government enables collective provisions to be established on a democratic footing by the representatives who are voted into power but who are capable of being ousted through the electoral process if they fail to meet local preferences and needs. The onus is on local government to be sufficiently small so that it is able to be responsive. But what is meant by small? Furthermore, if local governments are small, and given that the "rights" of local autonomy give political legitimacy to local action, what are the implications for those functions that the local government is otherwise typically responsible for (e.g., planning) that might need to be catered to within wider geographical areas? We will look at these issues through the two contrasting situations, metropolitan fragmentation and a more consolidated structure.

Clearly, a metropolitan area fragmented into a large number of separate local jurisdictions directly answers the question of smallness. The origins of such fragmentation probably lie in the historical development of the urban area; as it expanded, new suburbs and neighbourhoods emerged whose citizens expected to be served with basic public goods. Thus, in Australia, fragmentation of the contemporary metropolitan area was initiated in the nineteenth century. As a city expanded and new suburbs were established, many sought incorporation to give separate local government status, mainly to ensure public provision of roads, street lighting, local policing, and other basic services. Many of these early councils persist and have resisted calls for their amalgamation,[8] although they may have been subject to local boundary revision. It is a pattern of *local* local government repeated elsewhere, in which boundaries conform closely to the territorialities created by the historically cemented de facto socioeconomic geographies into which a city is divided. It is a structure that self-evidently gives expression to local preferences and needs but (in the absence of any overarching body) simultaneously reduces the capacity of local governance to steer the overall growth of the city or to be able to address its problems either strategically or equitably.

Arguments for the political fragmentation of cities so as to match the mapping of local preferences are given theoretical support through public choice theory. At root, the theory contends that local government will be more responsive to local preferences and needs than will some higher level of government. It will tend to provide services uniformly within its jurisdiction. In public choice terms, a balkanized city will be more responsive to individual citizen preferences than will a unified city, particularly once the question of payment for services (through local taxation) is introduced. In his famous statement on metropolitan fragmentation, Tiebout (1956) argued the case for it on the ground that the citizen as local taxpayer-cum-service consumer would be able to choose from among the multiplicity of local jurisdictions the local government offering the service-tax bundle most closely matching her or his preferences. In fact, public choice theories question inherited orthodoxies on the role of local representative democracy. As Bailey (1999, 266) argues, "put simply the idea of one politician representing all individual citizens in his or her own constituency irrespective of political persuasion is questionable." This is not an argument for abandoning local representative democracy so much as it is an argument for ensuring that local government units are small – the greater the proximity between citizen and local council, the more the latter will be responsive. This, it is argued, is all the more necessary as cities become increasingly diverse and multicultural. As rational as such arguments might appear, there is a paucity of empirical evidence to support them. It is by no means evident that "proximity" will become reflected in more responsive service provision. Proximity arguments run the risk of social/spatial determinism, overlooking underlying inequalities in who has access to political processes. Nor in the case of Tiebout's "exit and migration" strategy is there survey evidence to show that choosing the "right" local council is consistently a significant factor in intrametropolitan movement.

Public choice ideas (or derivatives of them) have been influential in the wider project of neoliberal restructuring and in the widespread adoption of privatization, marketization, and deregulation practices in local governments in both advanced and developing economies. Ultimately, such ideas provide the theoretical (and ideological) tools for an assault on the premise on which local service provision rests, and hence on local government, where even in the smallest units it is possible that collectively expressed preferences will be at odds with those of the individual. While this may appear to be a hypothetical position as far as local government boundary reform is concerned, the development of practices emphasizing the citizen as consumer may be a way of circumventing the need for boundary reorganization. Thus, in Britain, public choice ideas have been given expression through functional, as opposed to political, decentralization. Paradoxically, in comparison with many other countries in Europe, in Britain local government units tend to be large (Hellmut Wollmann's "North European type" in Chapter 6 of this volume). However, through the implementation of Parental Choice, for example, in which parents have the right to choose their child's school, decentralization is taken to the individual. Its effect is to "deborder" locally provided services, reducing the need for local boundary reforms.

If public choice theories buttress balkanization of the city, consolidationist arguments point to its flaws, advocating that boundary reform should enable the city's limits to expand in line with its growth or its anticipated development. Annexation and amalgamation are the means by which consolidation can be achieved. Failure to annex adjacent rural areas enables residents of such areas to become free riders (see Chapter 4 in this book). Resistance to consolidation can be tempered through "federalization of the city," the creation of two tiers of local government. Thus, the London Government Act of 1965 created a metropolitan-wide authority responsible for strategic planning, public transport provision, and other city-wide concerns, accompanied by a lower tier of thirty-two boroughs whose responsibilities included local planning and housing.

Consolidationists use different theories to support their case. Belief in local democratic theory is fundamental – the capacity of a locally elected body to provide services efficiently to the populace within its jurisdiction. Furthermore, to the extent that the local government may have difficulty in being responsive, this problem can be reduced through the extension of democratic practices, notably through the employment of participatory techniques. Beyond these political arguments, consolidationists look to economic reasoning to support the case for larger local governments.

The need for local governments to achieve allocative efficiency has provided the rationale for reform. Notwithstanding its political role, local government is more often seen as important for more instrumental reasons. Indeed, as for the south London citizen introduced earlier, his interest in local government extended only as far as whether it was an efficient refuse collection agency. (In fact, refuse collection is one of the more common services to be privatized.) Achieving greater efficiency in the allocative functions of local government has been a major impetus underlying boundary reform, though its achievement in practice has been as problematic as the theoretical definitions given to it have been difficult to measure. Oates's (1972) decentralization theorem can be taken as a starting point arguing that local government boundaries should be drawn so that differences of preference and need are minimized within the jurisdiction but vary significantly between jurisdictions.[9] Whereas Oates's theorem appeals to the political implications of boundary-drawing preferences, service provision typically takes into account the "technical efficiency" achievable through harnessing scale economies. As in Oates's theorem, measurement problems are severe; in spite of considerable research, the identification of scale economies has proven elusive. Typically, though, the argument of scale economies has pointed in the direction of consolidation or at least toward larger units and hence the need for boundary revision. Furthermore, concern for achieving greater allocative efficiency has led to substantial reductions in the number of local governments in many states. Thus, among twenty-three European countries between 1950 and 1992, three reduced the number of their local governments by 80 percent or more and a further five by 40 percent (Council of Europe 1995), often on economic grounds.

As significant as economic theories have been for boundary reorganization, planning has also provided an important impetus for reform. This has been more evident in Europe than in North America or Australia. Particularly in northern Europe, physical planning as part of a wider project of state intervention to steer urban growth became deeply embedded in systems of local governance. Planning and state intervention (as in the provision of social housing) became vital components of the overall processes of postwar modernization. Small wonder, then, that planning theories have had an influence on boundary reform, the more so because planning ideas have often been placed within scalar frameworks. Furthermore, because the (re)planning of cities has been part of state welfarism, and because local government has become a major agency (the major agency in the case of Britain) for the delivery of state welfarism locally, the influence of planning has been profound, reaching its apotheosis in cases such as the Scottish reform in which, after 1975, regional authorities[10] were established to meet the then fashionable ideas of the city-region.

These theories and counter-theories identify the debates surrounding the most basic question confronting local boundary reform: whether it should be undertaken in the first place. The proposition suggested here is that, regardless of whether reform is accepted as necessary, a principal objective of local government should be that it is capable of properly addressing local preferences and needs. The rationale here is to suggest that local governments be smaller rather than larger. But a fuller assessment would need to take into account issues of finance, including taxation and equity; both point toward consolidation to reduce those effects that fragmentation would tend to exaggerate, the divisions of the city between rich and poor. Ultimately, reconciliation between the two "positions" may not be possible because of the different value positions on which they are based, emphasizing the importance of the second proposition outlined below. Even so, mechanisms exist (e.g., through joint working arrangements; see Chapter 6 in this volume) that act to a degree as palliatives to the otherwise fissiparous trend within contemporary urban governance.

Proposition 2: How Local Government Boundary Revision Is Undertaken Should Be a Fair, Transparent, and Relatively Accessible Process

Boundary revision is a politically fraught exercise; because of the "absolute" nature of political boundaries, their reorganization has zero-sum outcomes with clear winners and losers. Not surprisingly then, local government boundary reform is politically contentious, and the stakes of either maintaining the status quo or redrawing the map along preferred lines are high. Hence, the procedures used to determine boundary revision can (and do) easily become a source of conflict. Precisely because, as the first proposition demonstrated, the meanings of local preferences (how and whether boundaries should be redrawn) are often contested, the need for transparency and accessibility in decision-making procedures is the more obvious.

As John Meligrana indicates in the introductory chapter, boundary revision is achieved through a variety of different methods, with particular types being favoured in particular countries. In Canada, quasi-judicial tribunals are used, as they have been in Britain, while annexation methods may or may not involve the use of local participation, including local referendums, to help determine boundary revision. Each has its advantages and disadvantages, but it is not my intention to discuss them here. Rather, my intention is to chart the implications that need to be taken into account in a set of practices that aims to be fair, transparent, and accessible. These practices are taken to be the basic criteria of a system in which, for "losing parties," the claim that there are built-in biases toward how boundary revisions have been debated is minimized.[11]

Orthodox accounts of policy making suggest that there are several different "phases" in which power relations play a critical role. These phases include policy initiation, agenda setting, non-decision making, and the processes involved in coming to a decision. These segments provide a framework in which to understand the boundary revision process. The first three relate to how issues become considered as amenable to policy (initiation); how, once it has been decided that the issue should become the concern of public policy, the details of it should be broached (agenda setting); and indeed which issues should not be on the agenda for consideration (non-decision making). Clearly, actors able to influence what is or is not on the agenda are powerful players in any policy-making process.

Finally, there are the procedures used to decide how the issue should be resolved, the outcome of which is the policy decision. Within these procedures, there are ample opportunities for power inequalities to become apparent, particularly since it is possible for the policy-making process to be relatively opaque and conducted in arenas not accessible to all the interests likely to be affected by the outcome. At each stage, bias is possible and a likely source of conflict.

Whether boundary reorganization becomes accepted (or not) as a proper issue for public concern is by no means as clear-cut as it may appear. Simply because boundaries have become in some sense anachronistic does not necessarily mean that their revision will become part of the political agenda. There are historical examples in which the need for revision was so apparent that the issue could not be ignored. The "mess of boundaries" and the multiplicity of local institutions serving English cities by the end of the nineteenth century were such that the standardization of boundaries, achieved through the network of counties and county boroughs, was, if not inevitable, a wholly rational policy to adopt. But the entangled administrative map of late-nineteenth-century London was no more a mess of boundaries than some contemporary American cities, yet their reform is nowhere near the political agenda. There are reasons that explain the difference, but the point here is that whether or not boundary reform becomes a policy issue is highly contingent.

Once boundary reform is considered suitable for policy amelioration, how the agenda for revision is set (or not set in the case of non-decision making) highlights the power of the "agenda setters." Which existing boundaries/local government units should be drawn into the reform process? Will reform be partial or comprehensive? Will it affect all local government boundaries? In the case of non-decision making, which local boundaries are not to be revised? Obviously, the agenda for reform is a vital stage in which elites will occupy key positions. Ostensibly, political elites hold such positions, particularly those at the centre rather than those in the localities themselves (see Proposition 3). But, given the costs and benefits of territorial reorganization, economic interests (and their elites) influence the agenda-setting process. This need not be just the interests of (local) capital, but, where labour unions are strong, they too may play a part in the process.[12] At the other end of the spectrum, agenda setting in local government systems may be decided locally through petition.

The procedures to be used in deciding how (and whether) boundaries need revision, as indicated previously, involve a variety of types. By looking at a specific example, we can begin to identify how fair, transparent, and accessible is the process.

In Scotland, minor local boundary reform is considered by a boundary commission. (By minor, I mean the small-scale revision to existing boundaries. The commission does not amalgamate existing divisions or create new ones.) Three boundary commissioners are charged with looking at the case for boundary revisions, amassing evidence, holding a local hearing at which interested parties can speak, and then deliberating in private and reaching a preferred outcome, which is communicated to the minister, the final adjudicator. It is an approach that is followed elsewhere in Britain in considering boundary reform, as in the case of constituency revision. It is a favoured process by the state in that, it is argued, opportunities are given for interested parties to participate, experts (the boundary commissioners) come to a considered decision, but the final decision is made by an elected representative who is politically accountable to Parliament for the resolution adopted. But the procedures may be less defensible than might appear. While the commissioners are more likely to be politically independent, partisanship may play a critical role in the final decision-making stage. How the hearings are conducted is more courtlike than informal, favouring certain witnesses over others. No procedures for assessing local opinion (through a referendum) are included. Whether such a system meets the criteria is at least debatable.

Consistent throughout the decision-making process is that power inequalities privilege some interests over others. Procedures (as Lindsey demonstrates clearly in the case of the United States) can have direct implications on outcomes. The final proposition takes this argument further by looking at the interplay between political elites.

Proposition 3: Boundary Reform Should Not Be Wholly Decided by Either Central or Local Political Elites

Central and local political elites, in particular elected representatives of both levels, are key actors in the process of local boundary reform. I have already touched on the reasons for this. For local elites, revision threatens their power base (or, alternatively, enhances it), implications that might also affect the electoral chances of politicians being reelected to the national assembly.[13] For the centre, revision may be necessary to the achievement of some other national policy. Both centre and locality have their own agendas in favouring (or not) reform. The point argued here is that neither should be allowed to achieve dominance, a position that might seem to be less obvious applied to the local rather than the centre. We will look at both arguments in turn.

Central imposition of boundary reform, in privileging its interests, will be prone to engendering, and disregarding, local opposition. In democratic states, such outright imposition is relatively exceptional and is a measure of the imbalance in, and strains of, central-local relations. Abolition of the Greater London Council in 1985 by the Thatcher government is an example of the problems to which central imposition can give rise. As noted earlier, the Labour-led council became a target for hatred by the centre, which was determined to press ahead with abolition. The move, spearheaded by the prime minister herself, was opposed by other cabinet members because of its implications for the governance of the city, yet it was pushed ahead. Partisan factors were allowed to dominate over the governance needs of the capital, while a network of ad hoc agencies, which lacked the political accountability of the former structure, assumed its administration. Unlike other major cities, London had no single political voice able to represent it either domestically or internationally. Demands for reinstatement of the Greater London Council have recently been met through the establishment of the elected London Assembly. In different degrees, such central imposition has encountered considerable local opposition in a number of cases elsewhere (e.g., Metro Toronto, Melbourne).

Central imposition being a signifier of authoritarianism, the countries covered in this volume illustrate examples at different positions in the spectrum of authoritarian/democratic decision making. As Jianfa Shen shows in the case of China, there are few opportunities for public participation in the city designation process. As experience from other developing countries shows, central imposition is more common (and necessary?) early in the state-building process. In contrast, in a majority of states in the United States, annexation is decided by popular determination. Other countries occupy a transitional position. In South Africa, municipal demarcation has been left to appointed boards, but the criteria for designation are articulated to take account of local factors (and presumably preferences). Yet, as Eran Razin shows in the case of Israel, the relationships between central determination (of boundary restructuring) and democracy are far from clear-cut; in that country, ministerial control (along with other factors) has been a powerful brake on reform.

Nor should boundary revision be wholly a matter of local concern, particularly of local elites. Of the latter, (party) political bias will tend to dominate how the reform process is conducted and its territorial outcomes. Overprivileging the position of local interests may lay the foundation for ossification; as the discussion of Spain here demonstrates, local (municipal) elites are unlikely to vote for territorial suicide, though the resistance to change has had popular support. Local civic pride in Spain (as in many other countries) provides a "politics of place" that central elites may be unable to ignore. Nor, given the nature of *local* government, should such politics be overruled. Yet, in part, the arguments are not unlike those of the dangers of political decentralization – namely, that local autonomy can be (and has been) used as a mask to serve the interests of particular groups and to provide a brake on reforms that serve the wider interest. Thus, where in the first proposition I argued that reorganization should address local preferences and needs, I also argued that they should not be allowed to dominate. Thus, for example, metropolitan areas are important economic engines for the national economy, the governance of which is key. Certainly, there is a case for preventing localism from overriding the wider interest.

Within the power games in which boundary reform is constructed, it is perhaps only "natural" that elites occupy powerful positions. As Bhabha (1990) has observed somewhat ironically, boundaries are created in the centre – presumably by elites. That is, boundaries are constructed to serve the imaginations and interests of those at the centre. For those living at the "edge" the boundary inevitably has a greater impact on everyday life. The reality of the impact of living close to the boundary has provided the basic rationale why boundary redrawing should not be left exclusively to elites, those of either central or local government. The boundary gives those who live within it particular reason to fully participate in its reconstruction.

Conclusion

This chapter has charted some of the major assumptions underlying the process of local government boundary reform and presented some key propositions delimiting an equitable reform process. For a political geographer, the latter task is perhaps unusual. Normative analysis, though historically part of the subdiscipline, is eschewed in favour of explanatory, more critical forms of analysis. Yet, in the "tradition" of applied geography, both forms of analysis can be considered together to inform issues of public concern. What is a more doubtful (dubious?) aspiration is that such analyses will resolve problems rather than inform debates.

Given the zero-sum nature of reform, such a conclusion has particular relevance to the problem of boundary revision. It may be possible to lay out the basis of a fair system for boundary reform – this would be a much larger exercise than the one presented here – but the influence of it on praxis is an entirely different issue. It is perhaps the case that policy makers, here the "boundary drawers," need to adopt a different mindset toward (local) political boundaries. While interested in different facets of the city – its economic governance and the nature of social life within it – recent (postmodern) accounts have talked in terms of the flexibly bounded city (Frug 1999). Flexibility here is not the same as Rusk's (1995) elastic city (see Chapter 1 of this book) but embraces the fluidities and mobilities of economic and social processes of the postindustrial city.[14] "Fixed" boundaries belong to an earlier phase of urban development and have become anachronistic. Analyses emphasizing the decentred postmodern subject point to multiple political configurations conforming more closely to the complex de facto social geographies constitutive of postmodern urban living.

Clearly, for boundary reform processes to incorporate such radically different ideas of the boundary requires not just a transformation in the mindsets of elites but also the winning of political legitimacy at large.

Notes

1. The exceptions include microstates such as Monaco and Andorra.
2. The trauma of the Victorian city, the juxtaposition of rich and poor, the prevalence of dirt and disease, became an obsession with writers such as Dickens and the object of early social reformers and social analysts.
3. The territorial divisions of Fascist Germany and of the Soviet Union provide clear examples of the trend.
4. Emergent cyberdemocratic practices may help to democratize local political processes unachievable through reliance on elections and other orthodox methods of political participation.
5. There is an argument here that local political territories and boundaries are of no consequence to citizens when it comes to local government. During the poll tax crisis in the United Kingdom (1990), residents on one side of a street in an inner-city borough found themselves paying different local tax bills from those on the other side. In spite of the difference, as one citizen-taxpayer put it, he didn't really care which side of the boundary he was on as long as his dustbins were emptied every week. Neither the boundary nor a sense of local political identity was of much significance in his case. This instrumental view of local government is possibly widespread precisely because of the mundane, yet important, services that it provides.
6. This is effectively the local counterpart to the fitting of state to nation.
7. During the Whitlam government (1972-75), the Commonwealth government sought to promote its welfarist program using local governments as the vehicles for delivery. In fact, the number of local councils, over 900, was too numerous, and the federal government advocated an "embryonic regionalization" of the local structure. The policies were opposed by the states as a constitutional invasion, while local councils were wary of what appeared to be a "backdoor" (if partial) method of reorganizing local boundaries.
8. Among Australian cities, the major exception here is Brisbane.
9. The theorem "assumes away" several factors usually observable in the real world. Even so, an empirical assessment of it would involve significant methodological problems quite apart from assuming the availability of appropriate data.
10. In some of the Scottish regions, reform resulted in extremely large local governments – in the case of Strathclyde, to an authority of over two million.
11. They are unlikely to be eliminated. Given the contentiousness of local boundary revision, "losing parties" are always likely to make some claim that the procedures were "unfair."
12. In Britain, for example, trade unions were considerably more important in the 1960s and early 1970s than they are today and played an important role in the reform process of that period.
13. This arises primarily because of the close connection between local government boundaries and constituencies for the national assembly in a number of countries.
14. Exemplars of the argument are provided in Lefèvre (1998) and Frug (1999).

References

Bailey, S.J. 1999. *Local Government Economics: Principles and Practice*. London: Macmillan.
Bhabha, H. 1990. *DissemiNation: Time, Narrative, and the Margins of Modern Nations*. In H.K. Bhabha, ed., *Nation and Narration*, 291-322. London: Routledge.
Council of Europe. 1995. *Regional and Local Government in Europe*. Strasbourg: Council of Europe.
Crick, B. 1983. *In Defence of Politics*. Harmondsworth: Penguin.
Frug, G.E. 1999. *City-Making: Building Communities without Walls*. Princeton: Princeton University Press.

Hart, T. 2001. "Transport and the City." In R. Paddison, ed., *Handbook of Urban Studies*, 102-23. London: Sage.
Hooghe, L., and G. Marks. 2001. *Multi-Level Governance and European Integration*. Lanham, MD: Rowman and Littlefield.
Lefèvre, C. 1998. "Metropolitan Government and Governance in Western Countries: A Critical Review." *International Journal of Urban and Regional Research* 22, 1: 9-25.
Oates, W.E. 1972. *Fiscal Federalism*. New York: Harcourt Brace Jovanovich.
Rusk, D. 1995. *Cities without Suburbs*. 2nd ed. Washington, DC: Woodrow Wilson Center Press.
Sack, R. 1986. *Human Territoriality: Its Theory and History*. Cambridge, UK: Cambridge University Press.
Simmel, G. 1908/1950. "The Stranger." In K.H. Wolff, ed., *The Sociology of George Simmel*, 402-8. New York: Free Press.
Storey, D. 2001. *Territoriality: The Claiming of Space*. Harlow: Pearson Educational.
Tiebout, C.M. 1956. "A Pure Theory of Local Expenditure." *Journal of Political Economy* 64: 416-24.
Wirth, L. 1938. "Urbanism as a Way of Life." *American Journal of Sociology* 44, 1: 1-24.

3
Goals for Municipal Restructuring Plans
Andrejs Skaburskis

This chapter draws on the international literature to examine the goals that may be pursued through the amalgamation, annexation, or incorporation of local governments. Practical, political, and economic dimensions are explored. The chapter shows the ways in which boundary restructure planning can make a difference to the character and efficiency of local government. It starts by looking at the inherent contradiction in the senior government's goal of creating and then maintaining viable and autonomous local governments. Political, functional, and administrative goals are discussed, and an attempt is made to show the ways in which boundary changes can affect the structure of local government and the cost and quality of decision making. Both practical and theoretical issues are discussed. Process issues are raised briefly, and the conclusions finish the chapter.

Viability and Autonomy

If there was a plan when a municipality's boundary was first drawn, then it is likely that the plan has been made obsolete by the changing environment. If a system of local governments was developed to suit the conditions of an earlier century, then surely changes in the nature and level of urbanization, globalization, social and gender relations, technology, income, demography, economy, preferences, consumer expectations, and citizen aspirations would make the old boundaries and structures of local governments obsolete. Cox (1974, 126) relates the need to change boundaries to "the change in the parameters affecting the intensity and distance decay of movement over space," and this fundamental condition, which shapes space and is the key determinant in all neoclassical economic models of the urban structure, changes the size of the territory that functions as an urban region as well as the interrelationships among its natural areas. The increasing size of cities with the spread of low-density suburban development increases the costs of uninternalized externalities and the importance of metropolitan area planning and region-wide coordination of policies. Increasing household income leads to more value being placed on the environmental resources being diminished by unplanned city growth and increases the spread of cities seen to spoil the environmental attributes being sought. The problems of the "postmodern metropolis" require region-wide planning. Sprawl, growth management, smart growth, jobs-housing balance, gridlock, and watersheds are at the forefront of many planners' minds, and their work may be eased by changing old structures of local governments.

The reduced costs of travel and communication at a global level change the relationship between municipal and senior governments and make the cities' welfare more dependent on changes that are well outside the nation but have to be mediated by local governments (Peirce 1993). The changes have meant that urban governments have lost control over their economies (Kearns and Paddison 2000). Local government restructure plans are seen as necessary if the urban region or even the nation is to maintain its competitive edge in a world of footloose international corporations. Cities can no longer be seen as though they are tucked into their regions, which themselves are within the nation, which is then involved in the international economy, the way that smaller Russian dolls are sequentially tucked into larger ones. Cities are not just parts of a larger geographic unit but also nodes in an international urban system that, to an extent, function independently of their national context (Magnusson 1996, 286; Ohmae 1995; Lever 1997). The changes have increased competition between cities, and such competition affects their policies on and approaches toward economic development (Haider 1992; Short and Kim 1999). Rusk (1993, 1998) suggests that "elastic" cities, those that can adjust their boundaries and local governments, can best defend their market shares of growth and bring prosperity to their residents. If the central municipalities cannot expand their boundaries, the region will lose market share and its place in the world order, with adverse social, economic, and fiscal consequences, with accelerated urban sprawl, and with segregated housing markets. Central cities need to adjust their land and fiscal resources to maintain their economies (Lefèvre 1998, 22). Restructure plans may be needed to keep the region vital in the global market.

The senior government, in creating local governments, has the task of creating viable and autonomous local entities, but then its continuing involvement as an overseer of local governments and as an adjudicator, instigator, or legislator of boundary changes is contradictory in a sense. The senior government is infringing on the autonomy of some local entity when it requires its amalgamation into a larger municipality, or when it sides with one jurisdiction to prevent its annexation by another, or when it goes along with the wishes of some residents to prevent rural areas from being incorporated as local governments. The significance of the contradiction is attenuated in a number of ways. Autonomy is not a discrete property but can be varied in degree; local units may be seen as "mostly autonomous" or autonomous to the point at which they start to impinge on their neighbours' freedom. The senior government, in advancing the autonomy of one unit, may curb that of another.

Local governments create local power bases that are resilient and can recover the valued attributes associated with autonomy. The identity of the local government and the identification of its residents with their municipality will reemerge in the future, after boundaries have been changed. "Once a particular set of local boundaries has been staked out and a local government is placed over these boundaries, whatever interests exist within the boundaries will find their political expression through this government" (Dupré, quoted in Cameron 1980, 230). But resilience is a double-edged sword, since the reemergence of local interests can form a ratchet against future changes. "Once an area has been defined and jurisdiction given, the space takes on a legitimacy of its own and community identification with and loyalty to that space to accommodate societal values and technological inventiveness is not regarded with any great favour, as may be seen by responses to proposals for amalgamations" (Chapman and Wood 1984, 142).

Wheeler (2002, 275) recognizes the changes in the postmodern metropolis and the need for regional planning but sees this as being unrealistic: "Clearly, new regional planning agencies with broad mandates are not likely to be created in most places, and those that are formed may not be effective in solving many regional problems ... Fundamental political difficulties work against the creation and success of new regional governments, including strong opposition from local, state, and provincial governments unwilling to give up power, the hostility of suburban voters unable to see how their interests are tied to the well-being of central cities, and the reluctance of central-city constituencies to see their progressive voting blocs diluted."

The emergence of local power helps to preserve the autonomy of municipalities and can affect their relative strengths and bargaining positions in later boundary disputes. Increasing differences in the size and strength of local governments may create the need for the senior government to help preserve the autonomy of the weaker municipalities at the expense of occasionally impinging on the territorial desires of stronger municipalities. The original goal of establishing a system of viable and autonomous local governments may require senior government involvement in restructure planning to help the region maintain its viability in the changing world.

Politics and Ideals

Changing municipal boundaries implies that the size or alignment of current municipalities is not optimal from the point of view of governance, the economy, the service delivery functions, the administrative ease, and the responsiveness of the local governments to the global changes as well as to their constituents' needs. The political issues can be addressed in at least two ways: one refers to the partisan and ideological interests of the senior government politicians and their ministries, while the other examines the more abstract notions of good government and the democratic aspirations of the region's residents. The functional and administrative issues will be discussed in the following sections of this chapter. Austin (1998) shows that the political goals are more important than the stated economic or fiscal objectives that usually provide the official rationale for restructure plans.

Amalgamation reduces the number of politicians whom the senior government has to deal with and can, therefore, be alleged to reduce the size of government and its cost to taxpayers. Eliminating local politicians may reduce the amount and vehemence of criticism directed to a senior government in the hands of a different political party. Boundary changes can influence the marginal voter in the municipality to favour a particular party. However, the strategy can lead to amalgamation, as in Toronto, or attempts to fragment local government, as in Los Angeles (Keil 2000). In Toronto, it is said, the Conservative government amalgamated the suburbs with the central city to do away with the troublesome and spendthrift politicians of the old City of Toronto and infuse the new entity with the sensible values of the middle-class suburban voters (Sewell 1998). Others suggest that the furor over amalgamation deflected attention from the property tax assessment reform that was concurrently instituted and would help the downtown office sector at the expense of inner-city homeowners (Sancton 2000, 150). Sancton points out that the left, centre, and right parties in Ontario have at one time or another promoted amalgamation plans. Keil (2000) shows that the boundary issues are not politically one-dimensional or ideologically unidirectional and quotes Keating (1995, 132): "Generally speaking, people with a beneficial view of government will support consolidation ... People who regard government as a necessary evil ... will tend to favour small scale, fragmented local governments. This includes conservatives, European 'liberals' (that is, supporters of the free market) ... anarchists and utopian left such as Greens and communitarian socialists."

On a more idealistic level, a senior government forms local governments to bring about the aerial division of power to promote the valued attributes of federalism and democracy. The division of power is a "device by which the federal qualities of the society are articulated and protected" (Livingston 1971, 22). Power "is divided in all societies and it is divided because such division can realize the basic objectives or values of a political community" (Maass 1959, 9). However, making the goals operational is either trivial or nearly impossible. The trivial approach simply points to the existence of local governments as the attainment of the objectives. The difficult approach would consider the manner in which liberty, equality, and welfare are advanced by changing local boundaries. It would, at the least, define the criteria for determining the optimal size of a local jurisdiction. Are larger or smaller municipalities better able to achieve the goals of federalism and democracy?

The concept of "political distance" has encouraged some political scientists to set the optimal size of a municipality between 100,000 and 250,000 people. Others say that smaller cities are better because they offer their voters a chance to know personally their politicians living in the community (Elezar 1973). The optimal size might respect the functions that the local government is to perform. "In many countries governmental threshold size is rather low. This may be a direct consequence of low functional expectations in those countries. Therefore, the question of ascribing the appropriate mix of population, area and financial resources is also one of defining the anticipated functional capacities. It may be quite reasonable to prescribe a large territory with small population and limited financial resources, so long as the expectation about functional capacity is extremely limited. It makes nonsense to expect such an authority to provide the same range of services as, say, a provincial town" (Recke, quoted in Chapman and Wood 1984, 146).

The optimal size should be expected to change over time with changes in the preference and need for public goods and environmental regulation, with the increasing complexity of urban systems, and with advances and changes in the cost of and need for commuting. The Internet affects views of community and the need to find satisfaction in any particular local area. Moreover, communities are not homogeneous entities but overlap and have competing interests (Burns 2000, 968). Communities of identity are formed with no reference to locality (Barnes 1997, 157). Increases in the size of local firms and changes in the structure of the local economy are also factors that determine the optimum size of local government jurisdictions. That size can be defined with reference to the potential for political integration in terms of the "sense of community, common identity, common interests, effective division of labour, complementary habits of and facilities for communication" (Merritt 1974, 187). The optimum size as defined by the "community of interests" may range from "small" in the case of remote hamlets to "large" in the case of urban regions. The reference to local residents' homogeneity and sense of community may yield an "optimum" well below the size of the governments involved in a boundary dispute, as pointed out by Ylvisaker and later by Chapman and Wood:

> No other has demonstrated ... that participation, loyalty and interest increases as political boundaries more nearly coincide with "natural" social groupings or economic areas ... The fact may well be otherwise, as conflict arouses interest. And as we sometimes too painfully have experienced, loyalty is as much *generated* by the very creation and symbolism of boundary lines, as it is by whatever elements of alikeness these lines may happen to include. (Ylvisaker 1959, 37; emphasis in original)

> It is necessary to distinguish between concepts relating to identity, participation and representation. They cannot be so easily tied together to support a local government system. The question of identification with place has been shown to bear no relation to place as defined by local government boundaries. In Britain, Hampton found that residents in various areas of Sheffield identified much more steadily with an area which he called a "home area," smaller than that covered by their local government. (Chapman and Wood 1984, 154)

Preservation of community identity and values is often raised by smaller municipalities facing amalgamation threats (Preston 2001; Danby and Mackenzie 1997). The sense of identity might emerge at times of duress (Hillier 1997). The goal of "preserving local identity" or "gaining local control" is at times advanced to coalesce opposition to restructure plans or to legitimize and disguise the materialism motivating quests for lower taxes. Miller (1981, 35) suggests that these goals are too vague to be satisfactory: "What aspects of local governance," he asks, "are so crucial that some people will devote hundreds of hours a year, for as many as ten years, to ensure that the local community be incorporated rather than annexed?"

Function and Structure

The optimal size of a municipality also depends on the functions that the government is to serve, the social characteristics of the area, the nature of the local economy, the size and interests of surrounding municipalities, the local residents' view of themselves as a community, and the nature of the existing local government. After these factors have been accounted for in the definition of optimal size, other issues need to be considered: "The component areas should be constituted of a sufficient diversity of interests to ensure effective debate within each component and transcending communities of interest among the several components. This criterion marks the point beyond which one should not press the search for 'natural' (i.e., homogeneous) communities to serve as jurisdictions for the component areas. This maxim ... implies that *debate* has a higher priority than either *efficiency* (as conventionally talked about in the literature of administration) or *participation, loyalty,* and *interest* (as thought to be more assured if governmental and especially social boundaries coincide)" (Ylvisaker 1959, 37; emphasis in original).

The value of debate and the benefits of diversity favour boundary restructure plans that enlarge small municipalities. The reduction of "political distance" as a goal is challenged by the benefits gained by the larger government units being better able to resist the parochial concerns of their residents. Officials in larger local governments are more prone to "unilateral action" that can advance more generous views of social welfare. The larger municipality may be in a better position to reach for some "'higher goal' such as the 'public interest' rather than simply 'maximizing' the preference schedules of individuals" (Tullock 1970, 32). As Chapman and Wood (1984, 146) point out, "Larger units will have a credibility and independence derived from their externally conceded legitimacy. The expectation of independent action will reinforce the fact of such action."

Small municipalities within a fragmented system of local government are more likely to house similar people with similar preferences and demands for local services. In a sense, this is good because it lets people move to the areas that offer the best mix of services and tax rates to suit their interests (Tiebout 1956). However, the fragmentation "allows powerful groups to impose their criteria and practices discretely and often unchallenged (Mabbott 1993)" (Davoudi 1995, 227). Fragmentation can do harm by accentuating the differences between people, distorting their perceptions of one another, and reducing the potential for integration, growth, and equity. It can cause class differences to develop within the disparate groups' reciprocal fears, myths, and prejudices. "'Separate and unequal,' the communities of the metropolitan areas have transformed the Jeffersonian ideal of grass-roots local democracy into a barbed-wire wall of municipal regulations which prevents redistribution of income through the public delivery of goods and services" (Castells 1982, 580).

Separation of the production of local services from their distribution has focused attention on the ability of local governments to gauge the needs and interests of their constituents. Small local governments can gain scale economies by buying services from larger municipalities or private firms. Once service production and distribution have been separated, few economic arguments remain to distinguish between the services that should be provided by a particular level of government, but this issue is not that simple. Local and senior government services may be distinguished by considering the size of the region benefiting from the services. However, the distinction is blurred by the many local services that also benefit the state or nation. The "decision as to the category into which any service is to be placed is itself arbitrary" (Cameron 1980, 224). If the allocation of responsibility for services across the government levels is based on judgment, then boundary changes justified by the service delivery arguments are based on prior beliefs about the nature of the services to be delivered by the local government. The quest for an optimum size based on ability to meet service requirements is circular when the selection of services is determined by the size of the jurisdiction. Nevertheless, technical arguments regarding boundary delineation can be offered after the mix of services that will be left for the local government has been determined.

> Street lighting, cemeteries, recreation grounds, community halls, curbing and guttering are matters that require no uniformity as between one community and another. Others, such as public health services or sewage, may be the subjects of a set of standards which have to be defined for the whole state but which can be better provided locally since the demand is locally based. Yet others, such as town and land-use planning and building regulations, may fall into the second group of local services and yet be regarded as a matter of such vital importance that another sphere of government should control it. (Chapman and Wood 1984, 162)

Choice and Control

Given the set of functions to be performed by local governments, boundaries can be based on decision-making costs: the cost of coming to a collective agreement and the costs imposed on people not favouring the agreement. In general, increasing the number of municipalities reduces these costs. The more uniform a local area, the lower the chance that the collective decisions will impose costs on cultural, ethnic, or lifestyle minorities. The larger the number of small municipalities, the greater the chance that a minority can move to be in a jurisdiction with people of similar background. But the more homogeneous the municipalities are, the less likely they are to have policies that redistribute income, and the system of segregated cities is likely to have the disadvantaged groups confined to the places that offer the least support and opportunity for advancement (Kearns and Forrest 2000, 1002).

The functionalist goal seeks a welfare-maximizing nexus between the supply of public services and the demand for them. The more small municipalities divide up a region, the more choices can be offered in theory, and the better they can meet the needs of their constituents (Fisher and Wassmer 1998). The fragmentation of boundaries and the possibility of changing boundaries reduce property tax burdens as households and firms move or change boundaries to equalize their taxes with the benefits that they gain from local services (Garasky and Haurin 1997; Henderson

1985). Thus, fragmented local governments eliminate property tax burdens. Tiebout (1956) develops the marginal conditions that would define the optimal size of local jurisdictions and shows that "voting with your feet" is welfare maximizing.

However, spreading responsibility across special-purpose districts to gain scale economies threatens the viability of local governance and passes the responsibility for the coordination of local services to the senior government. "From this perspective, the municipalities are one case among many: their councils attract realtors, builders, developers and, lately, activists in residents' and ratepayers' associations; school boards attract teachers and parents of school children; hospital boards attract health professionals and volunteers; and so on. These tendencies are not necessarily sinister, but they provide reason for the public to be suspicious of municipal claims to control over other special purpose authorities. Why should one sort of special purpose agency be predominant? Should the responsibility for regulating such agencies not fall to a general purpose government – namely, the province?" (Magnusson 1985, 588).

Peterson (1981, 20) points to the lack of a plausible mechanism in the Tiebout model for determining the optimal size or for making the needed boundary changes: "Any time that social interactions come to be structured into recurring patterns, the structure thus formed develops an interest in its own maintenance and enhancement." The sense of shared identity develops an interest that is not the summation of individual interests or the quest for a technically derived optimum. Mostly, the interest is in being bigger, gaining market share, having the competitive edge, or lowering current or future tax burdens. After all, services are more or less the same everywhere. Fostering exclusive municipalities will lead to economic loss unless neighbouring municipalities accept the lower-income residents or discordant land uses. And the changing role of local governments in negotiating with "supraregional and multinational capital, and the effectiveness with which they tailor the particular set of local conditions of production, have become the decisive factors shaping a city's profile as well as its place in the international hierarchy" (Mayer 1995, 232). Small cities do not have the talent to entice multinationals and may not have the will to resist the political, fiscal, and social contributions of big business and, thereby, reject the advances of big business. Contracting out services can erode governance functions, "hollowing out ... the state," and reduce the public sector's control of service delivery, its implementation and monitoring (Rhodes 1996, 663). Privatization aggravates the effects of globalization in undermining local government (Castells 1998). Large local governments are not just scaled-up small ones. A benefit-cost treatment of the trade-off between scale economies and decision-making costs is valid only when structural conditions remain unchanged.

There is a disjuncture between theoretical deductions showing that a highly decentralized system of government can best help people achieve their own ends and the real-world outcome that has small governments in the hands of big companies or real estate interests. But staying at the conceptual level, the value of reducing decision-making costs has to be weighed against the value of the debate generated within larger and more diverse municipalities. Cox and Reynolds (1974, 32) relate "homogeneity or heterogeneity of socialization ... to the geographic variation of cultural values." Sharpe (1981, 113) raises a number of other concerns:

> The public choice case is buttressed by some large assumptions. These include – implicitly or explicitly – that local government services will determine the individual's domicile; that the coordination of cognate services or of adjacent areas is unnecessary, or can be achieved by inter-authority bargaining; that land-use planning is of no importance; that redistributive services should be left to senior government; that the abuse of power in local government is largely a function of scale; that there is no need for more integrated government as population density increases; and that in the absence of a market test, public bureaucrats are virtually autonomous.

Environmental considerations also support amalgamation plans that would create a larger and more diverse municipality. Cox (1979, 212) notes that local politicians need "financial backers" and are, therefore, more likely to represent business and labour interests that "are frequently in coalition against environmental interests." In a more diverse jurisdiction, the wealthier residents are more likely to support environmental conservation and may be "more willing to forgo tax base and job advantages in order to preserve the environment." In a more diverse community, the wealthy can pay more for the environmental protection that may benefit everyone. Increasing concern for environmental issues increases the optimum size of local government jurisdictions. Fragmentation of local government into a large number of small units increases the difficulty and cost of the decision making needed to overcome problems with spillovers. The main conclusion points to the narrowness of the goals put forward by public choice advocates and the need to consider a broad range of economic factors and objectives.

Administration and Governance
The senior government, in reviewing applications for boundary changes or for incorporating new municipalities, considers the fiscal capacity of the new entity, its power to govern, and its ability to resist the special interests that may counter the public interest. New jurisdictions require

the fiscal capacity to pay for the services that they provide. Linking service-benefiting areas to the tax base that pays for the service helps to ensure that decisions on service provision yield net social benefits. The need for an adequate local tax base is established, in part, by the desire to make local officials accountable for their service delivery decisions. In part, the local tax base assures the autonomy of municipalities. Local governments relying on earmarked funds are, in a sense, only administering senior government programs. Senior governments can use their revenue-sharing programs, such as the Rate Support Grant in the United Kingdom, to manipulate local governments (Johnston 1979; Kirby 1982). Senior administrators reviewing local boundary proposals may assess the adequacy of the tax and will consider factors that can erode the base or keep it from growing at the rate of growth of service needs. The objective of creating fiscally sound local government units tends to favour larger units with more diverse economies. Other administrative objectives may include the need to simplify existing organizational structures. Local government officials should have control over a range of instruments that is wide enough to allow them the freedom to make policy decisions. The ability to govern requires that local officials have choices and that they have responsibility over a relatively wide range of services and functions.

The fragmentation of local government units through ad hoc restructuring decisions can erode the federal qualities described earlier. Increasing the senior government's responsibility for a larger number of "somewhat" solvent local areas weakens the local public sector and, thereby, increases the ease with which it can be manipulated by special-interest groups. Magnusson (1981, 577) points to the history of local government reform to show how the US executives who were "impatient with government" proposed to consolidate local authorities to eliminate unnecessary duplication and reduce the cost of government. The effect of consolidation, however, created the potential for more government control and interference in the market. Larger local governments could pursue goals uncongenial to business, such as the environmental goals mentioned earlier. Under a fragmented system of local government, Magnusson notes, "business corporations have been able to play one authority off against another, to secure tax concessions and relief from offensive regulations." However, amalgamation of small local governments is not necessarily bad for business: the sophisticated joint public-private real estate development ventures that have helped to revitalize many US inner cities are probably not possible in small areas. Big firms sometimes want large governments dominated by a few politicians who can resolve problems over large territories (Sancton 2000, 147). Amalgamation may be a prelude to downloading of senior government services and a strategy to downsize government (Quesnel 2000, 115), but the theoretical arguments for connecting overall size of government and degree of fragmentation or consolidation go both ways (Nelson 1992, 40). The administrative talent, experience, and fiscal sophistication required to implement such plans are less likely to be found in small towns. A reduction in the number of politicians at the local level should improve the quality of the "marginal" politician drawn from a fixed population.

Goals and Process

A senior government has a range of options for dealing with boundaries beyond setting up a legal process under which local areas implement boundary changes or the imposition of centrally conceived plans (see Table 3.1) (Carr and Feiock 2001; Aryeety-Attoh et al. 1998; Liner and McGregor 1996; Liner 1990; Sengstock 1960). The very decision to make plans based on the functional and administrative arguments presented in the above paragraphs has welfare consequences, as pointed out by leading planning theorists: "The critical view of the 'economization' of public policy represents it as an attempt to establish a dominant hegemony which crowds out the voices of other systems of meaning, while privileging capital and particularly big capital" (Healey 1995, 257; see also Fischer 1990; Freidmann 1992; and Mingione 1991).

The senior government's approach may depend on the degree to which local governments are seen as independent entities that can articulate their residents' interests, on the extent to which all levels of government are committed to open processes, and on the nature of the relationship between local and senior government politicians. The choice of option will also depend on the magnitude of the perceived problems, on the level of conflict that the issues are raising at the local level, and on beliefs regarding its potential resolution through open participatory processes. If differences or conflicts are great, then the senior government may unilaterally proceed to restructure local government boundaries and functions, but it does so at its peril. If the real reasons for making the changes cannot be promulgated, if politicians are able to pursue hidden agendas, then again a centrally imposed solution will be found, with the resulting discord and anguish until time reestablishes allegiances. If the boundary changes aim to bring about income redistributions by changing property tax assessments or rates, then the imposed boundary change may be the only way to achieve the goal.

Alternatively, the senior government may try to form efficient, responsive, and adaptive municipalities through a gradual process determined by the rate at which requests for changes are made by local residents and their elected officials. It may consider the objective of local autonomy very important, more important than administrative efficiency or short-term viability, and help to bring about a participatory process that lets local governments and their constituents find their own solutions. The senior government may further viability and autonomy goals by acting as a facilitator or by setting the rules for conflict resolution whenever incorporation, annexation, or amalgamation issues arise. It may adopt, or threaten to adopt, a parental role to help resolve local disputes in ways that balance the competing jurisdictions' rights to act independently and be free from

Table 3.1

Summary of goals for boundary restructuring plans

Viability and autonomy goals	• internalize externalities • global competition • intermunicipal coordination • dispute resolution, mediation
Political objectives	• division of power and goals of federalism • local power, locally responsible governments • local capacity to govern • unilateral decision-making capability • stimulation of political debate • stimulation of viewpoints beyond self-interest
Functionalist goals	• capture of scale economies • locally responsive decision making • reduction of intermunicipal spillovers • reduction of "free-rider" problems • promotion of socially desirable redistribution • social mix objectives • environmental considerations
Administrative goals	• financial solvency of incorporated areas • financial independence and responsibility • adequate, stable, and nonerodable tax base • growth elasticity of tax base • power-to-govern objectives • broad range of functions and instruments • distinction of intergovernmental responsibilities • effective intergovernmental relations • promote executive's accountability • streamline organizational structures
Process goals	• preserve degree of local autonomy • preserve flexibility of the restructuring process • effect gradual change • guided change with clear objectives • opportunity for local participation • recognize the uniqueness of the problem environment • promote intergovernmental cooperation

the dominance of larger municipalities. It can offer its "good offices" or mediate the dispute or help local jurisdictions to develop "objective" information about the likely consequences of alternative plans. The "fact-finding" function may be financed by the senior government to help maintain a nonfractious decision-making process at the local level. The senior government can pay for the process that ensures the thoughtful participation of affected people. It can ensure that relevant issues are raised and that local participants are aware of the consequences of their proposals.

A continuous process of adjustment may be instituted with formal procedures for dispute resolution. Some cases will require the senior government to redesign the rules for annexation, amalgamation, and incorporation and make hard decisions regarding process. Magnusson (1987) has suggested that the senior government can serve a useful function by becoming the scapegoat that helps to coalesce the disputing parties, draw away their attention, give rest to their discord, and then let the local residents and firms resolve their own boundary problems. But open processes do have costs and consequences that, in practice, may not be as emancipatory as theorists might want to believe. Boundary changes and overall restructure plans may, at times, have to be implemented unilaterally for reasons of expediency. "The struggle for civilization – all the way from building sidewalks to containing the Russians – places a premium on action, performance and decisions. Not all of these can or should wait the infinitely elongated process of 'multiple consensus' to which we have been forced in our rabbit-hutch tradition of breeding governmental agencies" (Ylvisaker 1959, 47).

Conclusions

Restructure problems emerge as a result of changes in the economic, physical, and social environments of municipalities and unincorporated areas. The choice of issues to be dealt with when boundary disputes emerge depends, in part, on the senior government's evaluation of the situation and its politicians' interest in improving the structure of local government through processes that are transparent and accepted by the affected parties. The province or state gives local governments the power to govern in ways that help to ensure their autonomy. This devolution of power, in turn, makes boundary changes difficult and may counter the general goal of maintaining an open process by which boundaries are adjusted in light of changing environments. The need to ensure that the system of local government can change to maintain viable and competitive economies in the face of globalization will impinge on the autonomy of some jurisdictions and often leads to conflict – and, hopefully, the senior government's quest for sensitive solutions.

The contentiousness of situations in which requests for incorporation, annexation, or amalgamation arise may be eased if the senior government has already established a set of clear guidelines and can point to the objectives that can be pursued through the restructure process to eventually benefit all of the parties involved. Setting forth the objectives, however, may be the most problematic part of the restructure exercise for at least three reasons.

The first difficulty is due to the need for transparency of and then agreement on goals if they are to guide the formation of plans through an open process. The goals and consequences discussed will guide the final decisions and are not just devices to legitimize some other purpose. The difficulty is in developing the setting in which the relative value of ends and means can be discussed, with the hope that the discussion is part of the decision-making process.

The second problem with the focus on goals is in the presuppositions that would have goals and criteria proposed before starting the restructure process. The dominant quest by planning theorists today appears to look for ways in which the decision process can be made more democratic by being decentralized and open to a variety of outlooks. The quest, it seems, is for an emancipated and empowered public. The normative premises look much like the ones motivating the public choice theorists, and the prescriptions of both might be open to some of the same critiques. Case studies might shed light on the dynamics by which boundaries are changed and on the importance of legislative constraint and meaningful participation.

The third and last difficulty discussed here is raised by the range of goals and outcomes that might be achieved by restructure planning and both their contradictions and their ephemeral nature. Political distance, value of participation, and quality of the sense of identity are hard to grasp in a way that lets these values be put on the table in trade-off discussions. The tendency is to grasp an intangible goal and evangelically promote it at the expense of not seeing the other issues. Autonomy was an example that ran against viability and forced us to accept the weaker view, "more or less autonomy," a concept that is inherently contradictory. The public choice arguments for representation and for a local government that can best respond to the wishes of its constituents have to be weighed against the impacts of changes on the constituents and the possible loss of control due to the political interests being absorbed by big business, real estate concerns, or pressure groups. The ideal setup for democratic welfare-maximizing choice works well under ideal conditions, but the environment in which choices are made changes along with the structure of local government, and the new interests that come into play in the local arena may, in the very terms of public choice welfare-maximization language, reduce the well-being of the citizens, as they themselves would see it if they could know the alternative. Other examples were also presented in this chapter to place the benefit-cost assessment on nebulous ground and to challenge any process for arriving at a restructure plan. How should debate, not the airing of conflicting viewpoints but the exchange that leads to an enlarging of viewpoints, be traded off against either the potential for a better fit between demand and supply of local services or the costs and loss of control due to fragmenting service delivery across special-purpose, non-accountable agencies? How do participatory decision-making processes deal with redistributive policies? Will the residents of a jurisdiction about to be annexed accept the "greater good" as just compensation for higher property taxes? As in most planning problems, the difficulty is in grappling with the open-endedness of consequences, their emotive spark, their direct link to individual interests, and their indirect connection to broader societal goals. The following case studies may show how some of these issues are played out in the real world.

References
Aryeety-Attoh, S., F.J. Costa, H.A. Morrow-Jones, C. Monroe, and G.G. Sommer. 1998. "Central-City Distress in Ohio's Elastic Cities: Regional and Local Policy Responses." *Urban Geography* 19, 8: 735-56.
Austin, D.A. 1998. "Politics vs Economics: Evidence from Municipal Annexation." *Journal of Urban Economics* 45: 501-32.
Barnes, M. 1997. *Care, Communities, and Citizens*. London: Longman.
Burns, D. 2000. "Can Local Democracy Survive Governance?" *Urban Studies* 37, 5-6: 963-73.
Cameron, D. 1980. "Provincial Responsibilities or Municipal Government." *Canadian Public Administration* 13: 220-35.
Carr, J.B., and R.C. Feiock. 2001. "Tax Annexation 'Constraints' and the Frequency of Municipal Annexation." *Political Research Quarterly* 54, 2: 459-70.
Castells, M. 1982. "The Wild City." In L.D. Bourne, ed., *Internal Structure of the City*, 573-84. New York: Oxford University Press.
–. 1998. *End of Millennium*. Oxford: Blackwell.
Chapman, R., and M. Wood. 1984. *Australian Local Government: The Federal Dimension*. Sydney: Allen and Unwin.
Cox, K.R. 1974. "Territorial Organization, Optimal Scale, and Conflict." In K.R. Cox and D.R. Reynolds, eds., *Locational Approaches to Power and Conflict*, 109-40. New York: John Wiley.
–. 1979. *Location and Public Problems: A Political Geography of the Contemporary World*. Chicago: Maaroufa Press.
Cox, K.R., and D.R. Reynolds, eds. 1974. *Locational Approaches to Power and Conflict*. New York: John Wiley.
Danby, S., and F. Mackenzie. 1997. "Reconceptualizing Local Community. Environment, Identity, and Threat." *Area* 29, 2: 99-108.
Davoudi, S. 1995. "Dilemmas of Urban Governance." In P. Healey, S. Cameron, S. Davoudi, S. Graham, and A. Madani-Pour, eds., *Managing Cities: The New Urban Context*, 225-30. New York: John Wiley.
Elezar, D. 1973. "Cursed by Bigness: Or, Toward a Post-Technocratic Federation." *Federal Policy* 3: 240-98.
Fischer, F. 1990. *Technology and the Politics of Expertise*. London: Sage.

Fisher, R.C., and R.W. Wassmer. 1998. "Economic Influences on the Structure of Local Government in U.S. Metropolitan Areas." *Journal of Urban Economics* 43: 444-71.

Friedmann, J. 1992. *Empowerment: The Politics of Alternative Development*. Oxford: Blackwell.

Garasky, S., and D.R. Haurin. 1997. "Tiebout Revisited: Redrawing Jurisdictional Boundaries." *Journal of Urban Economics* 42: 366-76.

Haider, D. 1992. "Place Wars: New Realities of the 1990s." *Economic Development Quarterly* 6: 127-34.

Healey, P. 1995. "Discourses of Integration: Making Frameworks for Democratic Urban Planning." In P. Healey, S. Cameron, S. Davoudi, S. Graham, and A. Madani-Pour, eds., *Managing Cities: The New Urban Context*, 251-72. New York: John Wiley.

Henderson, J.V. 1985. "The Tiebout Model: Bring Back the Entrepreneurs." *Journal of Political Economy* 93: 248-64.

Hillier, J. 1997. "Values, Images, Identities: Cultural Influences in Public Participation." *Geography Research Forum* 17: 18-36.

Johnston, R.J. 1979. *Electoral, Political, and Spatial Systems*. Oxford: Oxford University Press.

Kearns, A., and R. Forrest. 2000. "Social Cohesion and Multilevel Urban Governance." *Urban Studies* 37, 5-6: 995-1017.

Kearns, A., and R. Paddison. 2000. "New Challenges for Urban Governance." *Urban Studies* 37, 5-6: 845-50.

Keating, M. 1995. "Size, Efficiency, and Democracy: Consolidation, Fragmentation, and Public Choice." In D. Judge, G. Stoker, and H. Wolman, eds., *Theories of Urban Politics*, 135-59. Thousand Oaks, CA: Sage Publications.

Keil, R. 2000. "Governance Restructuring in Los Angeles and Toronto: Amalgamation or Secession?" *International Journal of Urban and Regional Research* 24, 4: 758-81.

Kirby, A. 1982. "The External Relations of the Local State in Britain: Some Empirical Examples." In R.K. Cox and R.J. Johnston, eds., *Conflict, Politics, and the Urban Scene*, 88-106. New York: St. Martin's Press.

Lefèvre, C. 1998. "Metropolitan Government and Governance in Western Countries: A Critical Review." *Journal of Urban and Regional Research* 18, 1: 9-25.

Lever, W.F. 1997. "Delinking Urban Economies: The European Experience." *Journal of Urban Affairs* 19, 2: 227-38.

Liner, G.H. 1990. "Annexation Rates and Institutional Constraints." *Growth and Change: A Journal of Urban and Regional Policy* 21, 4: 80-94.

Liner, G.H., and R.R. McGregor. 1996. "Institutions and the Market for Annexable Land." *Growth and Change* 27: 55-74.

Livingston, W.S. 1971. "A Note on the Nature of Federalism." In J. Meelcison, ed., *Canadian Federalism: Myth or Reality*, 19-29. Toronto: Methuen.

Maass, A., ed. 1959. *Area and Power: A Theory of Local Government*. Glencoe, IL: Free Press.

Magnusson, W. 1981. "Metropolitan Reform in the Capitalist City." *Canadian Journal of Political Science* 14: 557-85.

–. 1985. "The Local State in Perspective." *Canadian Public Administration* 28: 575-99.

–. 1987. Personal communication.

–. 1996. *The Search for Political Space: Globalization, Social Movements, and the Urban Political Experience*. Toronto: University of Toronto Press.

Mayer, M. 1995. "Urban Governance in the Post-Fordist City." In P. Healey, S. Cameron, S. Davoudi, S. Graham, and A. Madani-Pour, eds., *Managing Cities: The New Urban Context*, 231-50. New York: John Wiley.

Merritt, R.L. 1974. "Locational Aspects of Political Integration." In R.K. Cox, D.R. Reynolds, and S. Rokkan, eds., *Locational Approaches to Power and Conflict*, 187-212. New York: John Wiley.

Miller, G.J. 1981. *Cities by Contract: The Politics of Municipal Incorporation*. Boston: MIT Press.

Mingione, E. 1991. *Fragmented Societies: A Sociology of Economic Life beyond the Market Paradigm*. Oxford: Blackwell.

Nelson, M.A. 1992. "Municipal Amalgamation and the Growth of the Local Public Sector in Sweden." *Journal of Regional Science* 32, 1: 39-53.

Ohmae, K. 1995. *The End of the Nation-State: The Rise of Regional Economies*. New York: Free Press.

Peirce, N.R. 1993. *Citistates: How Urban America Can Prosper in a Competitive World*. Washington, DC: Seven Locks Press.

Peterson, P.E. 1981. *City Limits*. Chicago: University of Chicago Press.

Preston, S.M. 2001. "Tracing the Connections among Municipal Amalgamation, Community Identity, and Planning for the Niagara Escarpment in Ontario." *Environments* 29, 2: 91-103.

Quesnel, L. 2000. "Municipal Reorganization in Quebec." *Canadian Journal of Regional Science* 23, 1: 115-34.

Rhodes, R.A.W. 1996. "The New Governance: Governing without Government." *Political Studies* 614: 652-67.

Rusk, D. 1993. *Cities without suburbs*. Baltimore: Johns Hopkins University Press.

–. 1998. "America's Urban Problem/America's Race Problem." *Urban Geography* 19, 8: 757-76.

Sancton, A. 2000. "Amalgamations, Service Realignment, and Property Taxes: Did the Harris Government Have a Plan for Ontario's Municipalities?" *Canadian Journal of Regional Science* 23, 1: 135-56.

Savitch, H.V., and R.K. Vogel. 2000. "Metropolitan Consolidation Versus Metropolitan Governance in Louisville." *State and Local Government Review* 32, 3: 198-212.

Sengstock, F. 1960/1985. *Annexation: A Solution to the Metropolitan Area Problem*. New York: William S. Hein.

Sewell, J. 1998. "Thinking about Mike Harris: Speech to the National Interest, OISE Auditorium, October 20, 1998." <www.johnsewell.org/issues/harris-speech-oct29.html>.

Sharpe, L.J. 1981. "The Failure of Local Government Modernization in Britain: A Critique of Functionalism." *Canadian Public Administration* 24: 92-115.

Short, J.R., and Y.H. Kim. 1999. *Globalization and the City*. Harlow: Addison Wesley Longman.

Tiebout, C. 1956. "A Pure Theory of Local Expenditure." *Journal of Political Economy* 64: 416-24.

Tullock, G. 1970. *Private Wants and Public Needs*. New York: Basic Books.

Wheeler, S.M. 2002. "The New Regionalism: Key Characteristics of an Emerging Movement." *Journal of the American Planning Association* 68, 3: 267-78.

Ylvisaker, P. 1959. "Some Criteria for a 'Proper' Areal Division of Government Powers." In A. Maass, ed., *Area and Power: A Theory of Local Government*, 122-49. Glencoe, IL: Free Press.

4
Annexation Activity and Policy in the United States
Greg Lindsey

In the federalist system of government in the United States, powers not ceded to the national government in the Constitution are reserved for the states. The states did not cede the federal government authority for adjusting municipal boundaries; hence, state legislatures either directly adjust municipal boundaries or establish procedures that local units of government must follow when changing them. A consequence of this dimension of federalism is that procedures for annexation and other methods of changing boundaries differ from state to state. Moreover, most states have authorized multiple methods for annexation and periodically change them, in response to either perceived local needs or, in some cases, the power of local lobbies. Although these factors complicate analyses of approaches to annexation, scholars have developed general frameworks for classifying them and for testing their effects on rates of annexation. Knowledge of the details of state law governing annexation is essential for understanding how municipalities craft strategies to annex land and grow.

This chapter provides an overview of annexation policy and activity in the United States. It begins with a general description of annexation procedures used there and then summarizes rates of annexation in different states using data from the US Bureau of the Census. Findings related to the effects of annexation policy on rates of annexation are described, policy debates over annexation procedures are summarized, and issues in annexation are illustrated with a case study. The chapter concludes with an assessment of priorities for research related to annexation policy in the United States.

Approaches to Annexation in the United States
Scholars and policy analysts interested in municipal government have studied processes of annexation in the United States for more than fifty years (McQuillin 1949; Dixon and Kerstetter 1959; Sengstock 1960; National League of Cities 1966; Hill 1978; US ACIR 1993; Adams and

Freese 1995; Palmer and Lindsey 2001). During this period, they have developed and refined several schemes for classifying and analyzing approaches to annexation. These schemes generally have been based on legal authority for approval of boundary changes, although other schemes based on procedural requirements such as those for public hearing or for referenda among property owners in territories to be annexed have also been proposed. The most commonly used system of classification, known as the Sengstock typology, identifies five general approaches that can be differentiated on the basis of the level or branch of government that has statutory authority for determining the outcome of annexation proposals or whether public referenda are required as a condition of annexation (Sengstock 1960; Palmer and Lindsey 2001). Short descriptions or explanations of these approaches, including the number of states where the approach is used and predominates, are presented in Table 4.1. Figure 4.1 is a map of the states that illustrates where different approaches are used. Forty-four states authorize annexation by municipalities. The six that do not, most of which are in northeastern United States, are classified as legislative determination (i.e., these states have retained authority for making boundary changes). In most of these states, all land has already been allocated to local jurisdictions.

Popular Determination

Consistent with historic American traditions of democratic self-rule, a majority of states have established procedures for annexation that provide for some type of popular determination in which residents of territories to be annexed have the right to vote to determine the outcome of an annexation proposal. Popular determination is the primary method used in twenty-nine states, while thirty-eight provide for some form of self-determination such as initiating annexation by petition (Table 4.1). Analyses of statutes indicate that twenty-eight states require referenda in areas to be annexed, while fourteen and seven, respectively, require referenda in municipalities or the county that is diminished (Lindsey and Palmer 1998).

The basic rationale for popular determination is political: requirements for referenda provide for self-determination and serve as a check on actions by aggressive municipal governments. Critics of popular determination argue, however, that referenda are costly and time consuming, that they can frustrate initiatives to increase efficiency in administration of municipal services, and that, to the extent that referenda deter annexation, they permit small population groups to consume municipal amenities as "free riders."

Although some form of popular determination predominates in the United States, state procedures differ considerably on the public groups eligible to vote and on the relevant technical criteria, such as the majority of electors required to affirm a proposal. In addition to people who

Table 4.1

Annexation methods used in the United States

Annexation method	Definition/explanation	Number of states[1]	
		Primary method used[2]	Methods used commonly
Judicial determination	Courts rule on annexation proposals. Few states require judicial review of all proposals. Courts typically become involved after opponents file remonstrances or appeals.	1	20
Legislative determination	Special act of state legislature required to change municipal boundaries.	8	18
Municipal determination	Municipal legislative bodies can annex land unilaterally by majority vote.	8	22
Popular determination	Public referendum required prior to annexation. Voting groups include (1) property owners or residents of territory to be annexed, (2) municipal residents, or (3) residents of diminished jurisdiction (township or county).	29	38
Quasi-legislative determination	State-authorized independent, nonjudicial tribunal (e.g., boundary commission) rules on annexation proposals.	7	12

1 Based on survey of representatives of state municipal associations (Palmer and Lindsey 2001).
2 Total is fifty-three because three states report that two methods are used approximately equally.

own land or reside in the territory to be annexed, groups eligible to vote include, as noted previously, the entire populations of the municipality initiating the annexation or the territory to be diminished. The effects of enfranchising these populations generally are predictable, although circumstances peculiar to particular proposals matter. That is, municipal populations typically favour annexation as a way to expand the local tax base, while county populations typically oppose it because of concerns about loss of the tax base. These general positions vary, however, depending on fiscal and other effects of a proposal and how well voting populations understand them. Many fiscal impact analyses have shown, for example, that the costs of services to residential neighbourhoods exceed potential tax revenues and that annexation may adversely affect a

Figure 4.1

Primary annexation method and average annual number of annexations, USA, 1990-98

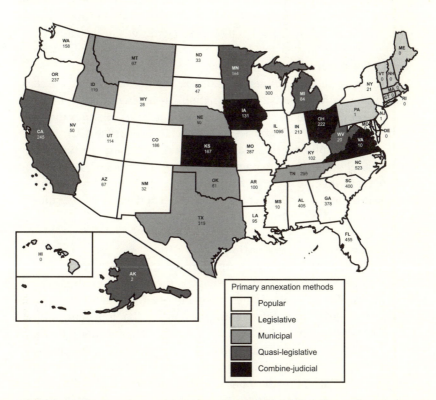

Source: Center for Urban Policy and Environment, School of Public and Environmental Affairs, Indiana University–Purdue University, Indianapolis, 2002.

municipality financially. To the extent that voting publics understand and care about these issues, the outcomes of referenda depend on the details of proposals.

Municipal Determination

Although thirty-four states authorize municipalities to initiate annexation proceedings (Palmer and Lindsey 2001), municipal determination is used commonly in only twenty-two states, and it is the primary method of annexation in just eight of them (Table 4.1). From an administrative perspective, municipal determination is the most efficient approach because referenda or hearings before tribunals are not required. Advocates of municipal determination suggest that it is necessary to eliminate the free-rider problem and duplication or inefficient delivery of services between municipalities and counties (Reynolds 1992). They also argue that municipal determination is essential to maintain the economic growth and vibrancy of municipalities (Rusk 1993). Critics of this approach point out that residents of areas to be annexed have not voted for the municipal officials pursuing annexation and argue that municipal determination is inconsistent with principles of self-determination. They also argue that this approach enables poorly thought-out land grabbing by aggressive municipalities.

Legislative Determination

Eight states, including the six where annexation does not occur, are classified as states with legislative determination. Such determination distances decisions from the people most affected by outcomes of annexation proposals. This approach is attractive theoretically because legislators represent large geographic areas and are in a position to balance the interests of municipalities and property owners in areas to be annexed. Criticisms of this approach include the argument that decisions about annexation may become intertwined with other legislative issues and reflect neither municipal priorities and needs nor the interests of property owners.

Quasi-Legislative Determination

Quasi-legislative determination, an approach in which independent tribunals adjudicate annexation proposals, is the primary method used in seven states. This approach, which grows out of reform traditions in American government, is predicated on the assumption that independent, nonpolitical bodies can base decisions on the merits of annexation proposals rather than on political or parochial considerations. Other arguments in favour of this approach are that it provides for balanced representation and development of institutional expertise and memory. Criticisms are that it involves the creation of another layer of government or bureaucracy and that appointees are not really free from political influence.

Judicial Determination

Judicial determination is the primary method of authorizing annexation in only one state, although courts play important roles in hearing appeals and remonstrances in many states. Judicial determination provides for impartiality in the resolution of disagreements over annexation, but reliance on this approach raises issues related to the separation of powers among branches of government and whether reliance on the judicial branch represents unconstitutional delegation of legislative authority.

Trends in Annexation Law and Policy

Recent analyses of trends in annexation indicate that laws and policies are becoming more complex and that state lawmakers are using procedural requirements to balance the interests of municipalities and property owners affected by annexation. Although one study (Adams and Freese 1995) concluded that state legislatures were increasing opportunities for municipal determination, another study (Palmer and Lindsey 2001) found that, between the 1970s and 1997, the number of popular determination states (according to the Sengstock typology) increased from sixteen to twenty, while the number of municipal determination states decreased from eleven to eight. With respect to changes in specific procedures, the number of states that allow property owners to initiate annexation increased from thirty-three to thirty-seven from 1978 to 1997, while the number of states that allow municipalities to initiate annexation increased from twenty-four to thirty-four. For the same period, the number of states that require public hearings and referenda on annexation proposals increased, respectively, from twenty to thirty-one and from twenty-three to twenty-eight. Thus, legislatures increased opportunities both for municipalities to act and for property owners in areas to be annexed to participate in and influence annexation proceedings.

Changes in annexation law in the state of Indiana, historically a municipal determination state, provide a useful example that illustrates the increasing complexity of annexation law. Until 1999, municipalities in Indiana could annex land essentially unilaterally provided that they met minimum contiguity requirements and procedural requirements for hearings and fiscal impact analyses. Specifically, state law directed that courts decide remonstrances on behalf of municipalities if one of two conditions were met (Indiana Code 36-4-3): "The area is 1/8 contiguous; the density of the territory is at least 3 persons/acre; 60 percent of the territory is subdivided; or the territory is zoned commercial, industrial, or business; OR the territory is contiguous, except that at least one-fourth (1/4) rather than one-eighth (1/8) of the boundary must coincide with municipal boundaries; and the land is needed and can be used by the municipality for its development in the reasonably near future."

In one county in Indiana, however, because of a piece of special-purpose legislation, the court was required to grant remonstrances on behalf of *remonstrators* if "services provided by other units of government were adequate, if the annexation would have a significant financial effect on residents, and if a majority of property owners or owners of more than 75 percent of total assessed valuation in the territory to be annexed signed a petition opposing the annexation" (Palmer and Lindsey 2001, 13). From a pragmatic, political perspective, this provision gave property owners in outlying areas effective veto power over annexation proposals – provided that they could obtain a majority of signatures on petitions.

In 1999, in response to controversies over "forced annexations" in a number of rapidly growing communities, state legislators extended versions of these provisions for judicial review to the other ninety-one counties in the state but, at the same time, made remonstrance more difficult by requiring a supermajority rather than a simple majority of signatures for remonstrance. This legislative action has limited the ability of municipalities in Indiana to annex territory unilaterally, thereby changing the state from one characterized by municipal determination to one with elements of municipal, popular, and judicial determination. More generally, this action illustrates national trends. Even as states in the United States are providing increased opportunities for people affected by annexation to participate in local decision-making processes, they are also making the processes more complex. Scrutiny of procedural requirements is essential in understanding how statutory checks and balances function in particular annexation proceedings.

Rates of Annexation in the United States

Annexation is common in most states: hundreds of municipalities have annexed land during the past thirty years. Table 4.2 presents the number, area, population, and average population density of individual annexations in the United States for each of the three decades since the 1970s. Figure 4.1 includes the average annual number of annexations by state for the 1990s. By decade, the number of annexations has ranged from more than 61,300 in the 1970s to more than 75,300 in the 1980s. These numbers correspond to annual averages by state of 123 and 151, respectively. Illinois, a state with 102 counties and approximately 1,300 cities, towns, and villages, has led the nation in annexations, with more than 26,500 separate boundary changes since 1970. Nonetheless, Illinois has not led the nation in area annexed. During the 1970s and 1980s, more area was annexed in Texas than in any other state; in the 1990s, municipalities in Montana annexed more land.

Although rates and area of land annexed have remained roughly constant over time, the population and therefore density of the land annexed

Table 4.2

Frequency and characteristics of annexation in the United States

	1970-79	1980-89	1990-98
Number of states where annexation occurred	45	45	44
Total number of annexations in US	61,356	75,337	66,578
Square miles annexed	8,771	9,196	8,568[1]
Estimated population annexed	3,168,000	2,575,000	723,467
Average population density (people/miles^2)	361	280	82[2]
Mean number of annexations per state per year	123	151	148
Maximum annexations in one state in decade	11,415 (Illinois)	9,560 (Illinois)	9,855 (Illinois)
Maximum area annexed in one state (miles^2)	1,472 (Texas)	1,515 (Texas)	1,137 (Montana)
Maximum average density in one state (people/miles^2)	940 (N. Carolina)	1,525 (Nebraska)	632 (Texas)

1 Area of land annexed is reported only for forty-two states and therefore is an underestimate.
2 Among forty-two states.

has decreased consistently and substantially during each of the past three decades. While the average density of land annexed during the 1970s was more than 360 persons per square mile, the average density during the 1990s was only about 80 persons per square mile. It is clear that municipalities are increasingly annexing land that is less populated. This change is consistent with trends toward increased use of popular determination and findings of scholars that methods of annexation authorized by state legislatures affect rates of annexation.

Annexation Procedures and Rates of Annexation
Scholars have completed a series of studies exploring the relationship between annexation procedures and rates of annexation (Dye 1964; Wheeler 1965; McManus and Thomas 1979; Galloway and Landis 1986; Liner 1990, 1993; Liner and McGregor 1996; Feiock and Carr 1996). Although earlier studies found no clear relationship, more recent studies have found that expected theoretical and intuitive relationships hold. That is, scholars have found that municipalities with authority to annex land more or less unilaterally exercise that authority, that more annexations occur in states classified as municipal determination states, and that annexation is less frequent in popular determination states where annexation statutes require the consent of property owners or residents of the territory being annexed. These findings are robust because they are based on multiple tests, including tests of the Sengstock typology (Liner 1990, 1993; Liner and McGregor 1996) and tests of specific procedural requirements (Feiock and Carr 1996). Feiock and Carr (1996), for example, found that requirements for public hearings, approval by county commissions (i.e., the diminished jurisdiction), and referenda for electors in areas to be annexed all deterred annexation. These findings are important because they provide insights into ways that states can use their authority to adapt procedures to address substantive issues raised by annexation.

Substantive Issues in Annexation
Annexation is important as a policy issue because of its role in the growth of American cities and towns and its effects on the level and quality of services offered to urban residents. Political issues and issues of governance are at the heart of the continuing debate over annexation policy at the state level, but substantive issues, including issues related to administrative efficiency, local government finance, public health, the environment, and quality of life, are also important. Although these issues can be separated for the purposes of discussion, they are practically inseparable. For example, property owners raise political issues related to representation in part because of fiscal issues related to taxation for municipal services. Similarly, annexation is often proposed as a way to rationalize extensions of

water and sewer lines and solve public health and environmental problems. Infrastructure issues, however, also cannot be separated from fiscal issues. The following discussion summarizes some of the most important issues debated in annexation proposals.

Political Issues

Political issues associated with annexation include, as indicated previously, issues of self-governance and representation. An important issue for people who have been annexed or face annexation is the right to participate in, and particularly to vote on, proposed annexations. In municipal determination states, property owners who lack the opportunity to vote on annexation proposals are often vocal about forced annexation and, to the extent that annexation increases taxes, the issue of "taxation without representation." Property owners also argue that they lose the right to self-governance through homeowners associations and access to township and county officials. Municipal leaders, however, argue that annexation provides residents in outlying areas with opportunities to vote for officials who set policies in the urban areas where they live and that referenda requirements hinder their ability to provide for the health of the communities that they serve. They contend that referenda make it difficult, if not impossible, to redress inequities that develop when residents in suburban areas consume municipal services but pay no municipal taxes. The primary issue at the state level, then, is balance, specifically how to balance the rights of property owners with the needs of municipalities.

Some experts believe that states should, in fact, make it easier for municipalities to annex. Prominent urbanist David Rusk, the former mayor of Albuquerque, has decried the decline of cities and the continued economic and racial segregation accelerated through suburbanization. He argues that states must act to "improve annexation laws to facilitate continuous central city expansion into urbanizing areas" (1993, 124). Laurie Reynolds, a professor of law at the University of Illinois College of Law, who acknowledges that the "strongest motivating force in determining the shape of state annexation statutes is the notion that individuals should have the right to choose the government under which they live," nonetheless concludes that

> Close examination, however, reveals that the principle simply does not justify granting virtual veto power to residents in outlying areas who object to municipal annexation. Those who live on the fringe of a municipality have in fact exercised their right of self-determination; they have chosen to live in and be part of an urban area. Having made that choice, the municipality's exercise of its annexation power would merely confirm the reality that this land already is urban. The nonresidents on the fringe

should no more have the power to opt out of the responsibilities of urban life than should city residents be able to claim an exemption from taxes to support services they do not use. In many instances, then, the self-determination principle merely provides nonresidents a way to protect themselves from assuming the burdens, while letting them enjoy the benefits, of being part of a municipality. (1992, 266)

These types of political issues can be mitigated partly through procedural requirements such as different contiguity or density requirements for parcels or tracts to be annexed, improved notice, mandatory periods of time between public hearings and votes on referenda, and longer periods for remonstrance. The choice among these types of options is value laden, dependent on political beliefs and judgments, and only partially amenable to technical analysis. Thus, depending on how state legislatures craft annexation law, they can either fuel or moderate controversy at the local level.

Fiscal and Economic Issues
In the United States, issues related to taxes are nearly as contentious as the issue of one's right to choose the government under which one lives. No one contests the fact that taxes will increase for property owners who are annexed, but many people who are annexed neither want services nor believe that they need them, and they therefore resent paying taxes for them. The critical issue from the state's perspective is again balance, specifically whether increases in taxes are reasonable given the services provided. Compared to the fundamental political issue of the right to self-determination, the state's interests in this issue seem to be narrower, and greater deference to the judgments of local elected officials seems to be warranted. It is clear, however, that states create significant incentives for annexation through their tax and fiscal policies. In particular, local governments annex because the property tax remains a primary source of revenue. If a state undertakes significant tax reform, such as capping or eliminating the property tax, motivations for and against annexation change dramatically.

One of the state's main interests with respect to economic and fiscal issues is to ensure that municipalities have the capacity to provide services promised to property owners who will be annexed. To this end, some states require that fiscal impact analyses or plans be prepared as a prerequisite to annexation. Even when states require fiscal analyses, however, other issues may emerge. Without statutory language that prohibits annexation if fiscal impacts appear to be negative, municipalities may annex land anyway. And, without specific guidance and third-party review, fiscal analyses are unlikely to include a complete accounting of all fiscal effects, let alone all economic effects.

The magnitude of tax increases associated with annexation is another important fiscal issue. The questions of whether taxes are too high for particular services and whether taxes paid by property owners cover the costs of all services are complex. In general, the answers to these questions are that costs are site specific and dependent on local factors. The planning literature generally suggests that the taxes paid by the residential sector do not cover all costs of services and that commercial and industrial sectors are important for moderating taxes on individuals. Controlling for characteristics of service delivery, taxes tend to be higher in places with proportionately less commercial and industrial development. States can address these types of issues by enabling municipalities to use tax abatement authority more frequently or to phase in tax increases for property owners who are annexed. The desirability of this latter option is limited, however: its approach reduces the revenues available to municipalities to finance capital and other services necessary to serve the annexed territory.

Administrative Issues

Although administrative issues are intertwined with both political and economic concerns, they can be distinguished because of their relative specificity. Among important administrative issues are those related to criteria for annexation, requirements for service delivery, and the right of property owners to remonstrate. States that authorize municipalities to annex land typically establish both specific and general prerequisites for annexation. Examples of specific criteria include those for contiguity and density, such as those described earlier for the state of Indiana. More subjective criteria, such as the criterion in Indiana that required municipal officials simply to determine that the land is needed for the continued growth and development of the municipality, have greater potential for abuse.

Equity in service delivery is an important administrative issue. An example related to equity is a requirement that services in an annexed area be equivalent to services in comparable areas of the city. Although this type of provision seems to be reasonable at face value, municipalities can use it to justify decisions not to deliver certain services. For example, municipal officials could determine that undeveloped areas do not need a particular service because other undeveloped areas within the municipality do not receive it. Clarification of requirements related to service delivery can eliminate potentially contentious issues.

Another administrative issue involves the property owners' right to remonstrate. Developers who want land to be annexed sometimes waive the right to remonstrate when negotiating an extension of services. They then include these waivers as covenants on property when it is resold, thus precluding individuals who purchase lots from remonstrating. Although this practice can frustrate property owners, the constitutionality of restricting developers from engaging in it is debatable. If municipalities and developers were precluded from entering into these types of agreements, then the flexibility that developers and municipalities have to negotiate would be reduced.

Other Issues

Although public health, environmental, and other issues tend to be overshadowed by political, economic, and administrative issues, some of them constitute some of the most important rationales for annexation. It is a cliché that environmental problems do not respect political boundaries, but in fact problems related to the management of water and air resources constitute a strong argument for annexation. For example, municipalities that rely on groundwater for public drinking water must comply with federal and state requirements to protect their wells from contamination. Often the recharge areas that supply municipal water systems extend beyond municipal boundaries. Annexation is thus one way that municipalities can gain control over the territory required to protect drinking water. Similarly, municipalities are often responsible for managing stormwater runoff and drainage. Failure to manage stormwater can increase flooding in urban rivers and streams. Developments in suburban unincorporated areas are often not subject to the same requirements for stormwater management as are developments within municipal areas. To the extent that municipal managers must contend with runoff generated in outlying areas, municipal residents subsidize suburban residents. Carefully planned annexation can help to remedy this type of inequity and improve the environment. Issues related to identity and sense of place are also important. Many long-term residents of unincorporated areas simply do not want to be part of a municipality. They may want to retain the rural character of their home or prefer the status of living in a separate place. If people hold these values dearly, then they are likely to oppose annexation strongly.

State Statutes Shape Municipal Annexation Strategies: The Case of Fort Wayne, Indiana

Case studies can illustrate the importance of these issues and how municipalities craft annexation strategies in response to state laws. The history of annexation in Fort Wayne, a small city (population 206,000) in Indiana, provides a useful example because its approach to annexation has been planned, systematic, and aggressive. During the 1980s and 1990s, as a result of careful planning that took advantage of particular provisions of state statutes, Fort Wayne annexed more land than any other city in the state.

The city's annexation strategy can be traced to a comprehensive annexation study completed by its Department of Community Development and Planning in 1975. This study recommended that all urban land contiguous to the city be annexed, as well as all non-urban land needed to control and manage future growth (Department of Community Development and Planning 1975). The study specifically recommended annexation of three large suburban parcels at the city's northeast, north, and southwest borders. In 1988, after the election of a new mayor, the city adopted an aggressive, large-scale annexation strategy to annex these areas in three separate but related ordinances. The overall strategy comprised the tactic of annexing large suburban areas in successive phases, a neighbourhood negotiation program incorporating innovative tax abatements, and the commitment of high-level staff and legal resources in preparation for remonstrances and legal challenges.

The geographical target of highest priority was a suburban area to the northeast, where the heaviest development had occurred and residents had remonstrated successfully against piecemeal annexations for two decades. When developing their strategy, city officials recognized that they could not annex all areas simultaneously because they lacked the administrative and financial wherewithal to deliver a package of municipal services in an equitable time frame acceptable to the court. To deal with this problem, they phased in the annexations, taking advantage of provisions in the state annexation statute that allow for the deferral of the effective date on which an annexation is completed. Planners prepared a single ordinance that annexed the entire northeast area but staged the effective date in four phases (Table 4.3). Implementation of the new strategy resulted in significant growth of the city, ultimately adding more than 22,600 people, 5,000 acres, and property assessed at more than $109 million.

The strategy of phasing in the annexation had financial and political, as well as administrative, dimensions. From an administrative perspective, the strategy relied on the contiguity requirement that one-eighth of the annexed territory boundary be contiguous with the annexing city's current boundary. Each new phase provided the contiguity base for the next phase. From a financial perspective, this strategy allowed the city to incorporate Phase I revenues in the fiscal plan for Phase II and so on for successive phases. From a political perspective, officials believed that this approach might help to mitigate the concerns of some residents. Because a larger number of residents lived in Phases III and IV rather than in Phases I and II (see Table 4.3), they were thought to be less likely to sign a remonstrance petition or to contribute to a legal fund for a court challenge to the annexation.

At the same time that the city announced the phased strategy, municipal officials began a series of negotiations with people in the neighbourhoods

Table 4.3

Annexation schedule and characteristics of four northeast annexations

Annexation	Passed by council	Effective date	Population (1990)	Size (acres)	Dwelling units	Assessment (dollars)
NE Phase 1	02/14/89	09/21/91	5,091	1,290	1,697	35,649,500
NE Phase 2	02/14/89	12/31/91	3,470	880	1,388	21,440,410
NE Phase 3	02/14/89	12/31/94	6,703	1,168	2,370	19,000,000
NE Phase 4	02/14/89	12/31/97	7,400	1,690	2,187	33,000,000
Totals			22,664	5,028	7,642	109,089,910

to be annexed to mitigate opposition. One tactic involved a series of town meetings with neighbourhood associations in which citizens were able to negotiate for specific improvements that exceeded the standard package of municipal services or for tax abatements. Although most neighbourhoods were not offered or did not negotiate for different levels of service, Fort Wayne ultimately phased in new municipal property taxes over a two-year period for residents in Phases I and II. Residents in Phase I were abated 66 percent of their first year's tax bill and 33 percent in the second year. Phase II residents were only abated 50 percent of their first year's tax bill. Because the ordinance was passed in 1989, with an effective date set for 1991, this phasing meant that residents were not required to pay a full tax bill until 1994 – five years after the ordinance was passed.

Although the city planned its strategy carefully, it did not address the concerns of many people who opposed the annexations, and there was significant controversy over them. People campaigned vigorously against the annexation and organized an aggressive remonstrance petition drive. A judge, however, determined that the remonstrators had failed to secure the legally required number of valid signatures on their remonstrance petition and dismissed the case. Technical issues were never considered. Factors that contributed to the failure of the opponents to obtain the requisite number of signatures included the city's aggressive marketing of the rationale for annexation, the existence of waivers of rights to remonstrate that some property owners had signed when they accepted municipal sewer service, and the belief shared by some residents that annexation was a good or inevitable thing.

Annexation proposals for the north and southwest areas were comparable in scale to the northeast annexation and also involved phasing in of effective dates, but these annexations did not involve negotiations over additional services or tax abatements, and they generated significant controversy. The north annexation, which included three phases with two different effective dates up to four years from passage of the ordinance, ultimately added 9,959 persons, 6,764 acres, and more than $134 million in assessed value to the city. The third phase of the north annexation differed from the first two phases as well as from the northeast annexation in that it was annexed for future industrial growth, included few structures (67) and people (187), and relied on the second, more general criterion for annexation then applicable in Indiana. Although remonstrators worked actively to overturn the annexation, they too failed to obtain enough valid signatures for a court review. The southwest annexation did not include phasing or tax abatements but set the effective date for the entire area – 15,215 people and 8,228 acres – to be January 2006. Opponents were successful in obtaining the required number of signatures (51 percent) for remonstrating, and the case is now being heard in court.

Discussion and Priorities for Research

It is necessary at this point to tie together the preceding lines of inquiry. In the United States, states either control municipal boundary changes directly or establish procedures that local governments must follow when changing them. Most states provide for multiple approaches to annexation, with both provisions for municipalities to initiate annexation and provisions for referenda or opportunities for property owners to remonstrate against annexation. Comparatively few states have established independent tribunals or boundary commissions, and only one relies exclusively on the courts to approve boundary changes, although courts play important roles in many states in resolving disputed annexations. Over time, annexation laws have become more complex, and people affected by annexation have been given greater opportunities to participate in annexation proceedings.

Particular provisions in state laws influence rates of annexation. Annexation is more common in states considered municipal determination states and less common in states where referenda for people in areas to be annexed are required. Rates of annexation have remained relatively constant over the past three decades, although the population density of land annexed has declined significantly. This trend is consistent with changes in annexation laws that provide people with greater roles and power in annexation proceedings: municipal officials apparently are focusing on annexing more vacant land and may be initiating annexation earlier to avoid confrontations with people occupying developed land.

The state of Indiana and the city of Fort Wayne provide useful examples of both of these general trends and the complexity of the problem of annexation. Indiana law, which historically granted municipalities (in all but one county) the power to annex land virtually unilaterally, has been changed to provide for greater roles for the populations affected and the courts. The city of Fort Wayne, in a complex process that has unfolded over nearly thirty years, shrewdly used particular provisions in state enabling legislation to craft a long-term strategy that resulted in annexation of thousands of people and acres of land and increased the municipal tax base by hundreds of millions of dollars. Even as the courts are deciding the outcomes of Fort Wayne's historic annexation initiatives, new provisions in state law are changing the rules for future annexation.

The fact that annexation statutes are complex and evolving means that research is needed to understand the consequences of continuing changes. Research to monitor changes in annexation law is clearly needed. This research, although apparently straightforward, is deceptively complex. Modern information technology facilitates periodic reviews of state statutes, but statutory reviews without the benefit of other information about how laws work in practice can lead to erroneous interpretations of the laws.

Statutory analyses supported by expert evaluations and case studies provide the richest assessments of annexation policy.

Among other priorities, research to determine the consequences of increased opportunities for self-determination is important. While results of past research indicate that these changes will tend to deter annexation, they may not over time reduce annexation but cause municipalities to plan earlier and initiate annexation with developers and owners of land prior to development, thereby preventing the types of issues outlined in the Fort Wayne case associated with annexation of large tracts of populated land.

Studies that control for state and local fiscal systems when exploring the effects of annexation statutes would also be useful. I noted earlier that it is very difficult to sort out issues of governance and representation from fiscal issues. Research that focuses on the relative effects of municipal reliance on different taxes, such as property sales or taxes, and the distributive effects of annexation would shed light on this issue.

As illustrated by the Fort Wayne case, details of annexation law matter. Another priority for research involves analyses of ways that municipal officials adapt to and use criteria for annexation. Areas ripe for study include, for example, the effects of different contiguity and density requirements on rates of annexation or whether requirements for fiscal impact analyses lead to different outcomes. Another relevant research topic is whether subjective criteria, such as the requirement in Indiana that a municipality determine that annexation of an area is necessary for the growth and development of the community, lead to more frequent annexation or greater roles for the court.

This review has necessarily been brief and, as a consequence, has not addressed issues such as whether property owners actually initiate the majority of annexations – even in municipal determination states – or whether property owners initiate annexation because they see potential benefits or because they believe they have no alternative in the long run and think they are more likely to benefit from voluntary negotiation rather than remonstration. Studies that analyze local circumstances that lead to annexation can provide insights useful to scholars and analysts interested in the process of municipal boundary change.

References

Adams, Alicestyne, and B.P. Freese. 1995. *Mississippi Initiative Measure No. 6: A Comparative Study of Mississippi Municipal Annexation*. Starkville: John C. Stennis Institute of Government.

Department of Community Development and Planning. 1975. *Annexation Policy and Program Study*. Fort Wayne, IN: City of Fort Wayne.

Dixon, Robert G., and John R. Kerstetter. 1959. *Adjusting Municipal Boundaries: The Law and Practice in 48 States*. Washington, DC: American Municipal Association.

Dye, Thomas R. 1964. "Urban Political Integration: Conditions Associated with Annexation in American Cities." *Midwest Journal of Political Science* 8: 430-36.

Feiock, Richard C., and Jered B. Carr. 1996. "The Consequences of State Incentives and Constraints for Municipal Annexation." Paper presented at the annual meeting of the American Society for Public Administration.

Galloway, Thomas D., and John D. Landis. 1986. "How Cities Expand: Does State Law Make a Difference?" *Growth and Change* 17: 25-45.

Hill, Melvin B. 1978. *State Laws Governing Local Government Structure and Administration.* Athens, GA: Institute of Government.

Indiana Code, Title 36 Local Government, Article 4. Government of Cities and Towns Generally, Chapter 3. Municipal Annexation and Disannexation, 13. Remonstrances; hearing; order; requirements. <www.in.gov/legislative/ic/code/title36/ar4/ch3.html>

Lindsey, Greg, and Jamie Palmer. 1998. *Annexation in Indiana: Issues and Options.* Indianapolis: Indiana Advisory Commission on Intergovernmental Relations.

Liner, Gaines H. 1990. "Annexation Rates and Institutional Constraints." *Growth and Change* 21, 4: 80-94.

–. 1993. "Institutional Constraints and Annexation Activity in the U.S. in the 1970s." *Urban Studies* 30: 1371-80.

Liner, Gaines H., and R.R. McGregor. 1996. "Institutions and the Market for Annexable Land." *Growth and Change* 27, 1: 55-74.

McManus, S.A., and R.D. Thomas. 1979. "Expanding the Tax Base: Does Annexation Make a Difference?" *Urban Interest* 1: 15-28.

McQuillin, Eugene. 1949. *The Law of Municipal Corporations.* Chicago: Callaghan.

National League of Cities. 1966. *Adjusting Municipal Boundaries: Law and Practice.* Washington, DC: National League of Cities.

Palmer, Jamie L., and Greg Lindsey. 2001. "Classifying State Approaches to Annexation." *State and Local Government Review* 33, 1: 60-73.

Reynolds, Laurie. 1992. "Rethinking Municipal Annexation Powers." *Urban Lawyer* 24: 247-303.

Rusk, David. 1993. *Cities without Suburbs.* Washington, DC: Woodrow Wilson Center Press.

Sengstock, Frank S. 1960. *Annexation: A Solution to the Metropolitan Area Problem.* Ann Arbor: University of Michigan Press.

US Advisory Commission on Intergovernmental Relations (US ACIR). 1993. *State Laws Governing Local Government Structure and Administration.* Washington, DC: Government Printing Office.

US Bureau of the Census. 1980. *Boundary and Annexation Survey 1970-1979, Report GE-30-4.* Washington, DC: Government Printing Office.

–. 1990. *Boundary and Annexation Survey 1980-1989.* Produced by the Geography Division, 2 August 1999. CD-ROM.

Wheeler, Raymond H. 1965. "Annexation Law and Annexation Success." *Land Economics* 41: 354-60.

5
Canadian Experiences of Local Government Boundary Reform: A Comparison of Quebec and Ontario

Raphaël Fischler, John Meligrana, and Jeanne M. Wolfe

Canada is a federal state consisting of ten provinces and three territories, in which the federal and provincial governments have complementary roles. The division of powers and responsibilities between the two levels is outlined in the Constitution Act of 1982, which embodies the British North America Act of 1867. While there are many areas of overlap or uncertainty, since many fields of competence were not even thought of in 1867 (for instance, airports or telecommunications), the provinces have exclusive power over all local matters. These include local government, education, health, and land management. All local authorities and municipalities, as well as any other sub-provincial units of government, obtain their powers and jurisdiction from the provinces, which is legislatively delegated, usually in the form of a municipal act or a planning act. Since the size, form, structure, duties, and rights of municipalities are highly controlled, local governments are commonly referred to as "creatures of the provinces." In other words, they are not recognized by the Constitution as a distinct and separate form or level of government.

The provinces are thus free to create, alter, or eliminate any aspect of their local government system. This important point has clear implications for the restructuring of local government boundaries. The provincial governments set the area of jurisdiction of local governments, establish the procedures for their redrawing, and are the ultimate arbitrators of any request to change the territories of local governments. Since each province has a somewhat different geography, culture, and traditions, issues and procedures regarding local government boundary changes vary across the country.

This chapter examines local government boundary restructuring undertaken in Canada over the last half-century, using as examples the two most populous and urban provinces, Ontario and Quebec. They have contrasting legal foundations: common law in Ontario and civil law in Quebec.

A note on Canadian terminology is in order at this point. Annexation refers to the taking over of a part of a municipality by another; it most often occurs when a rapidly growing urban municipality requires more space for development and "annexes" part of an adjacent rural municipality. Amalgamation refers to the fusion or merger of two or more municipalities in their entirety.

For the purposes of this analysis, three distinct phases of boundary reform are identified for each province. In Quebec, they are: first, the 1960s and early 1970s, a time of starts and stops; second, the period of great municipal reforms introduced at the end of the 1970s and implemented during the 1980s; and third, another time of major transformation in the late 1990s, including forced amalgamations. Each period is characterized both by major interventions by the provincial government, and by ongoing programs to encourage municipal amalgamations, the latter being a matter of public policy since the late 1960s. In Ontario, institutions and legislation governing annexation divide the province's procedures for redrawing municipal boundaries into three phases. The first and longest phase covered the period between the 1950s and 1982, when a quasi-judicial agency, the Ontario Municipal Board (OMB), had virtually complete jurisdiction over annexations as granted to it by the province. The second phase, from 1982 to 1995, began with new legislation to enlarge the role of locally elected officials and the provincial Ministry of Municipal Affairs to resolve boundary disputes without recourse to the OMB. The last phase, from 1995 to the present, has been characterized by more streamlined annexation and amalgamation procedures to restructure the territories of local governments and to facilitate amalgamations. As in Quebec, recent public policy favours the reduction of the number of local municipalities through the merger of small units.

The following account provides a brief introduction to the local government system in each province before comparing procedures and changes in the three periods identified for each province.

Local Governments in Ontario and Quebec: An Introduction

Ontario
In Ontario, the contemporary seeds of local boundary problems can, to a degree, be traced to the original survey of local government territories as well as the original governing legislation set by the provincial government over a hundred years ago. The Ontario government's passage of the Municipal Act in 1849 caused both counties and townships, surveyed during the early 1790s, to become municipal units of government. The act created a strong legislative distinction between rural and urban by separating cities, and some towns, from the direct political operation of county government. The county was to be an upper-tier local government with a

governing board represented by members appointed from the elected council of the lower-tier municipalities, that is, villages, towns, or townships. The board was entrusted to make policies and regulations with respect to, for example, the administration of justice, the construction and maintenance of county roads, and the distribution of general welfare funds. The cities, although physically located within a county, were not politically part of the county government. The cities were to be the centres of urban-economic development. In other words, they were to contain the urban land uses, while the counties and their townships were to manage rural land uses.

This underlying spatial principle embedded in the Municipal Act and the physical structure of the county system were not fundamentally disturbed or altered between its passage in 1849 and the early 1970s and again during the late 1990s.

Quebec

Municipal government in Quebec during the French regime (1608-1763) was relatively rudimentary. Local institutions were largely ecclesiastical: parishes, districts, and *fabriques*. Two cities, Quebec and Montreal, had special status, but apart from them, local society was governed by the intendant of New France, the seigneurs (large land holders), and the church (Harris 1966). In fact, the Durham Report of 1840, enquiring into the roots of discontent following rebellions in the colony, lamented the absence of municipal government in Quebec and attributed many of the problems to a lack of local autonomy.

A Municipal Act was passed in 1855, to be replaced by the Municipal Code in 1870, a piece of legislation that, though often modified, still remains one of the two major laws governing municipalities in the province today. The Municipal Code recognized parishes and townships, the former being the early ecclesiastical domains and the latter having been laid out and surveyed in the parts of Quebec not settled under the seigneurial regime after it was ceded to Britain through the Treaty of Paris in 1763. At the same time, counties, then also electoral districts, were demarcated, many on the basis of the old seigneuries. They assumed responsibility for rural roads and water courses.

It was soon realized that the Municipal Code did not cover the needs of the growing towns, and consequently in 1876 an act dealing with cities *(Corporations de ville, clauses générales)* was adopted. This was replaced by the Cities and Towns Act *(Loi des cités et villes)* in 1903. As in Ontario, cities and towns did not form part of the county administrations. The Municipal Code, laying out the rights and duties of rural municipalities, and the Cities and Towns Act, which does so for urban municipalities, remain the most important legislation for local government today. Both contain provisions for the annexation, amalgamation, or establishment of municipal territories (Baccigalupo 1984). Indeed, the period 1880-1914 saw the multiplication of speculative subdivisions on the fringes of large cities and their incorporation as independent municipalities. Many of them assumed high levels of debt in order to develop a full set of urban infrastructure and facilities, leading in many cases to bankruptcy and, consequently, to annexation by the central city (e.g., Hochelaga, Maisonneuve, and Saint-Henri in the Montreal area). Wealthier suburban municipalities, whose fiscal and social assets attracted the interest of the central city, managed to stave off attempts at annexation (e.g., Outremont, Westmount, and Hampstead) (Linteau 2000).

By the end of the First World War, rapid population growth (both through natural increase and immigration), industrialization, the continued multiplication of the number of municipalities, the financial failure of many, and the increasing complexity of their administration led to the founding of the Ministry of Municipal Affairs in 1918 *(Loi du Ministère des Affaires municipales)*. The department was set up to control and oversee the activities of municipalities and to provide technical advice and assistance to their councils. The Depression of the 1930s, when many municipalities encountered financial difficulties, led to the establishment of a second provincial institution in 1932, the Quebec Municipal Commission *(Loi sur la Commission municipale)*. The commission, whose members were appointed by the lieutenant-governor-in-council, was initially responsible for the fiscal health of municipalities, especially in relationship to borrowing.

After the Second World War, extraordinary suburban growth occurred on the fringes of most towns and cities. In some cases, real estate developers petitioned to set up a new municipality in order to service part of a rural parish for urban purposes. This was the case for Lorraine and for Candiac on the fringes of Montreal. In other cases, the urbanizing hamlet part of a parish, wishing to provide itself with modern water and sewer services, for which the rural rest of the population did not wish to pay, separated itself from the parish as a village. In addition, a settlement in a non-incorporated part of the province (usually a mining or logging centre) could apply to become incorporated as a municipality.

Since before the so-called Quiet Revolution of the 1960s, the question of the number of municipalities in Quebec, and their often illogical shape, small size, and limited capacity to deliver services to their population has been widely debated and the subject of numerous enquiries and commission reports.[1] The approaches tried have been both gradualist and abrupt and of course intertwined with the question of second-tier, regional government.

Phase 1: 1950s-70s

Judicial Determination by the Ontario Municipal Board

The immediate postwar years brought tremendous growth pressures. Townships on the edges of cities found it impossible to adequately service the expanding urban growth, the result of "spillover" from the cities. Although intermunicipal agencies and commissions to coordinate communication and planning between townships and adjacent cities were attempted, the usual response was either for a township to reincorporate as a city or for a city to annex the urban portions of a township. This situation sowed the seeds of many fierce battles between townships and cities over the control and management of urban development. In the middle, of course, sat the provincial government, which, on the one hand, wanted to avoid being drawn into local boundary disputes but, on the other hand, was responsible for the orderly development of the entire province as well as the manner by which its local government system adjusted to such development pressures. The provincial government solution was to delegate the responsibility to decide to a quasi-judicial tribunal known as the Ontario Municipal Board (OMB).

The OMB is made up of provincially appointed members to approve, among other things, the alteration of municipal boundaries (Adler 1971; Makuch 1983; Ross 1962). The OMB acts like a judicial tribunal by holding public hearings to receive, review, and judge annexation applications. This board can be compared and contrasted with South Africa's Municipal Demarcation Board (see Chapter 11).

There are three ways to initiate an OMB hearing on annexation. First, application by a municipal council can be made by passing a bylaw requesting an increase in municipal territory. This bylaw may arise from petitions by residents within the municipality or the municipality's own determination of its additional land needs. Second, the minister of municipal affairs can petition the OMB to hear a case regarding municipal boundary extensions, presumably in the provincial interest and not necessarily of local origins. Third, at least 150 electors of a town, village, or township, or 500 electors of a city of a given area, can petition their councils to have their collective properties annexed to another municipality. Once a petition is made, the municipality must pass an annexation bylaw.

During the hearing, the OMB can make substantial requests for information, indicating the types of information required and their methods of presentation. The board also has the power to call evidence from local or provincial government departments or to retain experts to provide assistance. Based on the circumstances of each application, the conduct of each hearing may vary by application and over time, at the discretion of the board. In general, the hearings of the board are conducted in a judicial-like manner; the board allows written statements of claim or defence by municipalities or local planning boards having jurisdiction over the affected area. Lawyers usually write these statements and present them to the board. Counsel representing other jurisdictions examine these statements.

The board judges the prevailing merits of each individual application, comparing it to the broader public good, based on stated provincial policies. If no provincial policy exists, the board works on the premise of preserving the greatest common good. In effect, the board formulates provincial policy in local governance. The board has ruled that the "burden of proof" in establishing the "need" for annexation rests with the municipality making the application. Hence, the annexing municipality needs to make a *prima facie* case for annexation. The annexing municipality has to present evidence, meeting OMB standards of proof, viewed either in the light of provincial policy or existing or antecedent legislation. But exact standards or reasons for annexation are not readily forthcoming from provincial regulations or policies.

The OMB operates under the principle that urban municipalities are under no obligation to provide water and other services to developments beyond their borders. Furthermore, the board is reluctant to rule on potential solutions other than the relocation of municipal territory, because this ruling could be interpreted as a substantial creation or alteration of existing provincial policies. Thus, the board has changed its conservative or narrow interpretation of overseeing issues of municipal governance to simply determining the territorial dimensions of municipalities.

Furthermore, the burden of proof resting with the annexing municipality has to contain factual evidence of the estimated growth and development, not only in the areas to be annexed, but also in the existing boundaries of a municipality. Here the basis of any annexation claim rests on forecasts of urban growth and development. In refuting the "need" for annexation, many townships facing a potential loss in territory have challenged the accuracy of the urban growth forecast put forward by the annexing municipality.

During the 1950s and 1960s, the OMB awarded substantial land gains to urban municipalities. The board, however, guarded against premature annexations through reductions in the amount of land requested in several rulings based on the evidence of likely future directions and amount of geographical growth. However, not all OMB activities involved solely a determination of annexation applications. Some resulted in more creative solutions to the governance of city-regions in Ontario. The most noteworthy is the board's involvement in the creation of Metropolitan Toronto in 1954, the first two-tiered local government in North America. But this was an anomaly, since the board preferred the traditional solution of annexation to reform local governments across southern Ontario.

Quebec's Boundary Reform during the 1960s and Early 1970s: Starts and Stops

In Quebec, the enormous suburban growth of the postwar years led, as elsewhere, to the fragmentation of urban areas as more and more municipalities were created. By 1963, there were 1,751 municipalities, 1,000 of them with fewer than 1,000 people. During this period, there were two approaches to boundary reform: one top-down, legislated, in response to some specific problem, the other bottom-up, relying on action from the municipalities themselves.

Legislated interventions themselves were of two types. One was simply to consolidate a group of municipalities forming a functional though fragmented urban area, or an area subject to a major development initiative. The other was to create a second tier of local government to ensure coordination of development in the major urban regions. For instance, in 1966, the consolidation approach led to the Ministry of Municipal Affairs amalgamating the fourteen municipalities of Île Jésus, lying just north of the Island of Montreal, to form the new Ville de Laval to help solve the problems of servicing extraordinarily rapid suburbanization. In 1971, the government also legislated the amalgamation of eleven rural municipalities to contain the site of the new Mirabel airport, located just north of Montreal. Eleven municipalities were amalgamated at Becancour on the south side of the St. Lawrence River to accommodate a heavy industrial complex. Mergers at Sainte-Anne-des-Monts were aimed at facilitating the development of a ski resort and at Gaspé a national park. The Municipality of James Bay, an area larger than Switzerland, was carved out of the wilderness to facilitate hydro development. In some cases, contiguous towns with inequitable distributions of resources were amalgamated by law to ensure redistribution. This was the case with Rouyn-Noranda and Haute Rive–Baie Comeau in northern Quebec.[2]

The second legislative approach was to introduce a form of regional government for the three major conurbations, which were to be responsible for major urban infrastructure. After years of debate, and finally triggered by a police strike in Montreal in 1969, the Montreal Urban Community (Figure 5.1), along with the Quebec Urban Community and the Outaouais (Hull-Gatineau) Regional Community were created, thus introducing a second tier of local government.[3] They operated by indirect representation and taxation, and, in the cases of Montreal and Quebec, their territory did not cover the whole of the urbanizing area, just the central parts. In Montreal, for instance, this area was just the Island of Montreal, representing about two-thirds of the metropolitan population. The acts creating this tier of government also provided for future boundary changes as operations became rationalized. For instance, the Montreal Urban Community Act of 1969 stated that, "Within five years after the coming into force of this act, the Community shall prepare and submit to the Minister a project for rearranging the territorial limits of the municipalities" (p. 20). Despite various studies, this was not done, although some consolidation took place within the Quebec Urban Community.

While these top-down decisions were being made, there were also more gentle programs to encourage municipal amalgamations. The first was the 1965 Voluntary Amalgamation of Municipalities Act *(Loi des fusions volontaires, S.Q. 1965, c.56)*. It envisioned the amalgamation of two or more contiguous municipalities to consolidate their revenues and to improve the quality and variety of services offered to their populations. Councils had to be in agreement: mergers could not be instigated by the provincial government. Appropriate studies regarding the transition had to be prepared and application made to the Ministry of Municipal Affairs for ratification.

Figure 5.1

Municipalities in the Montreal metropolitan area

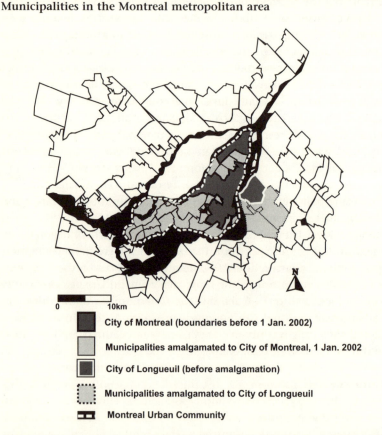

Source: Based on Statistics Canada profile of census subdivisions in Montreal (2001 Census of Canada).

This initiative was considered to have limited success since between 1965 and 1971 only forty-two amalgamations were registered. One interesting part of this legislation was that it permitted only the amalgamation of whole municipalities; the splitting of municipal territory by annexation of a part was disallowed (Glenn 1977).

The slow rate of change to the local government map resulted in further studies. In 1971, the Ministry of Municipal Affairs proposed a province-wide redrafting of municipal structures (Tessier 1971). This proposition suggested grouping municipal structures together into *secteurs d'aménagement* (planning districts). The whole of the settled parts of the province would be divided into sectors based on physical and socioeconomic criteria for planning purposes, and the old county councils would be disbanded in favour of these new units. The whole question was thrown open to public debate, but largely because the existing municipalities read it as the first step toward their disappearance through future amalgamations, and because the Union of County Councils protested vigorously, the proposal was abandoned.

The government then tried another tack that seemed to hold more promise. In 1971, a revised act was passed, an Act to Promote the Grouping of Municipalities *(Loi favorisant le regroupement des municipalités, L.Q. 1971, c.53)*. Its main new provisions were that the minister of municipal affairs could define "regroupment units" if it was believed that it was advantageous to an area and order that studies be made to that end. Municipalities were then supposed to make application for merger. In addition, the law allowed that "The Minister may make any new municipality constituted under this act a grant not exceeding fifteen dollars per capita payable in five annual and consecutive instalments."

With the introduction of both a stick and a carrot, many more municipalities were soon engaged in joint studies. A three-pronged implementation program was devised by the ministry to expedite the process of boundary reform: (1) the re-amalgamation of parishes and villages; (2) the reorganization of municipalities within the urban and regional communities of Montreal, Quebec, and the Outaouais, as set out in the legislation that created them, although this approach to boundary reform had no success in Montreal; and (3) the rationalization of municipal boundaries for other urban centres. This approach met with little success: between 1972 and 1979 only seventy-two amalgamations occurred. By 1981, there were still over 1,500 local municipalities.

Ontario's Regional Reform

Sweeping changes to Ontario's municipal structure surfaced in the late 1960s with the province's white paper, *Design for Development*. Such reforms altered the traditional spatial model of Ontario's local government system: they created regional municipalities that bound together rural and urban government units under one political umbrella. This approach created a two-tier system of local government: regional and local units. Regional municipalities, to a degree, were an adaptation of the former counties to provide for a "better" local administrative structure over the most urbanized and urbanizing portions of the province. They were achieved by radically reducing the number of local municipalities and expanding the territories of the remaining ones. Oddly, the spatial configurations of county boundaries were left unaltered.

Three key points emerge from this period of regional reform. First, it represented the earliest instance of direct and dramatic provincial government action to alter the territorial configuration of its local government system. In the past, the province was content to let local governments fight out boundary disputes within the quasi-judicial forum of the Ontario Municipal Board, as discussed above. It therefore reveals the tremendous power that the province has over its local government system. How it uses this power to change the areal jurisdiction of local governments is thus critical in understanding the issue of local government boundaries within the Canadian context.

Second, by this action, as mentioned above, the province altered the centuries-old model of a local government system strictly divided into rural and urban units of government. A new model emerged that sought to join rural and urban land uses and development issues within one unit of local government, the regional municipality. In this way, the stage was set for even more dramatic changes to local government boundaries in the late 1990s as discussed later in this paper.

Third, the creation of regional municipalities occurred only in the most urbanized portion of the province; it was not an all-inclusive project. Thus, many potential annexation applications were placed on hold pending the outcomes or recommendations of studies, reports, and decisions regarding the creation of regional municipalities by the province. But as the "final" regional municipality was created in 1974, cities in counties unaffected by regional reform could potentially have swamped the OMB with an overload of annexation applications. In short, if the remaining counties were not going to be reformed into regional municipalities, then annexation at the local level was the only other alternative. Thus, if the province was unwilling to extend regional reform across the entire county system, it would be forced, at the least, to reform the process for deciding annexations.

Phase 2: 1970s-80s

Ontario's Municipal Boundary Negotiations Act
The pressure to reform the annexation procedure came from both the Association of Counties and Regions of Ontario (ACRO) and the Association

of Municipalities of Ontario (AMO). In May 1979, AMO drafted a position paper that outlined five steps to settling boundary disputes: notice to adjust boundaries, negotiations between municipalities, conciliation by a fact finder, arbitration by a permanent boundary commission and the option of appeal to the cabinet. The provincial response, through the Ministry of Intergovernmental Affairs, was to establish an interassociation working group to devise a procedure that was more political and less legal for resolving boundary disputes and amalgamations. An experience in Barrie had revealed the flaws of the legalistic and adversarial OMB procedures and supported greater involvement of locally elected representatives (Ontario 1980).

This inclination toward new annexation and amalgamation procedures revealed divergent interests in the province and the municipalities. Both ACRO and AMO wanted to secure a more political procedure that was not in the provincial interest. Apparently, since the turn of the century, the province had been content to see the OMB act as a lightning rod for any hotly contested political disputes and thus was reluctant to see a new procedure that might have allowed annexation disputes to enter the provincial political forum. A compromise had to be found allowing annexation to remain a local political issue but, at the same time, insulating the province from direct political accountability.

In 1979, the minister of intergovernmental affairs announced a provincial-local agreement on new boundary procedures. The province premised the new agreement on a cooperative approach, with annexation decisions reached through negotiation and mediation. The dispute mechanism was, in part, modelled after labour negotiation techniques, in which a "neutral" fact finder creates a background report that forms the basis of discussions for a negotiating committee. This committee would be comprised of locally elected council members affected by a municipality's annexation request.

Ontario's Municipal Boundary Negotiations Act was proclaimed as law early in 1981, thus ending the Ontario Municipal Board's long history of deciding annexation disputes. It also marked the first provincial legislation devoted entirely to resolving municipal boundary disputes in Canada, as opposed to measures and procedures within sections of various provincial municipal or planning acts.

The Municipal Boundary Negotiations Act simplified the initiation of an annexation procedure to a simple bylaw of the annexing municipality. This procedure closed the option to fringe developments or to residents who could potentially start an annexation procedure, as noted previously. Public involvement would also be limited to the requirement for passing any bylaw by a municipal council. Passage of the bylaw represented the annexation application which was forwarded directly to the Ministry of

Municipal Affairs. There was no legal requirement that the annexation bylaw be forwarded to other provincial ministries or departments, such as those of the environment or agriculture.

The permissible reasons for annexation are not found in the legislation. However, provincial guidelines to annexations under the Municipal Boundary Negotiations Act offer some clues. Accordingly, consideration of annexation should arise regarding service problems associated with fringe developments, issues concerning a particular site, such as an institution or factory, and municipal boundaries requiring "housekeeping" (Ontario 1994). These considerations, as enumerated in the guidelines of the Ministry of Municipal Affairs, suggest that the act will only deal with small-scale annexations focussing on a particular area. The large-scale annexations decided by the OMB during the 1950s and 1960s are assumed not to occur in the future, especially since the province just restructured its most urban counties.

Receipt of the bylaws by the minister reveals the central position of the province in the new procedures. It thus falls to the minister and the ministry of municipal affairs to collect the facts, make inquiries, and determine party municipalities. Right from the start, the minister identifies the stakeholders in the dispute and the issues to be addressed, all apparently with no formal requirement of public participation. The law only instructs the ministry to seek the opinions of school boards. This directive reveals the political sensitivity that can occur from any boundary adjustment resulting in the transfer of pupils from county school boards to city school boards.

This initial power to investigate or make inquiries required the restructuring of the ministry to create a new division called the Municipal Boundaries Branch. This branch would assist the minister in applying the requirements of the new act. Bureaucrats within the branch play a key role in guiding the annexation application through the legislative procedure. They provide a neutral "clearing house" for the collection and distribution of information about any annexation application. A municipality will commonly consult the branch prior to passing the necessary annexation bylaw. Here the branch has an informal opportunity to deal with the boundary problem. The Municipal Boundaries Branch can also perform the role of a messenger or "go-between" among party municipalities. In particular the minister of municipal affairs relies on the branch for key advice on annexation matters. Thus, the bureaucrats have a strong capacity to shape and influence the outcome of an annexation application.

After making an inquiry, the minister has four divergent options at his or her disposal. Two are premised on the idea that, through inquiries made by the minister, an agreement among party municipalities is reached, thus requiring either legislation or an order-in-council to give legal effect to an annexation agreement. Again the assumption is that only minor boundary adjustments will be contemplated. An annexation agreement to be enacted by an order-in-council has a legal requirement of public notice. If any objections are voiced, then the minister must weigh them against the broader provincial interest contained in the order. Thus, this function is no different from the OMB's role in deciding on an annexation based on the merits of the greatest common good. Whatever objections are recorded, the act gives the minister several options.

The other two options create avenues if no annexation agreement is reached during the initial inquiry or if the minister wishes to seek any other remedy. With no agreement, the minister can form a negotiating committee, the central institution in the new legislation. The committee brings together local politicians of the disagreeing party municipalities in a nonjudicial setting. The committee is left with the task of discussing the "facts" of the annexation application as well as trying to reach an amicable arrangement regarding municipal boundaries and related matters. The involvement of local elected officials and the flexibility of the committee have both been touted as strengths of the new boundary procedures. These strengths contrast with the quasi-judicial hearings of the OMB, which were adversarial and confrontational.

The minister, however, has tremendous overt and covert power to shape the workings and outcomes of any negotiations committee. For example, because the minister decides the committee membership (i.e., party municipalities), inclusion or exclusion of municipalities and their elected officials, with known and expressed views regarding annexation, can work to favour an outcome. Certainly, the minister is obliged to appoint members to the committee from the annexing municipality and the municipality facing a loss of territory. However, the minister can be more flexible in appointing members from the county or the surrounding townships. Furthermore, the minister appoints the chief negotiator, usually the director of the Municipal Boundaries Branch, who will ultimately draft a report on any recommendations made by the committee and/or of discussions undertaken. Finally, the minister can set conditions on the committee, such as deadlines and topic areas of discussion, which surely can create bias in the procedures. The committee is not legally obliged to be open to the public, unlike OMB hearings, which are held in public.

To assist the negotiation committee, the minister can establish a three-member issues review panel, presumably at the request of the committee. This panel's role is to deal with questions beyond the normal expertise of the negotiating committee. Such questions may derive from municipal engineering or budgetary matters. In turn, these particulars arise from the perceived cost benefits of various annexation proposals explored by the committee. Instead of the committee stalling negotiations on a specific and technical issue, it can refer the issue to the panel. Then the committee can continue deliberating on the broader or more fundamental issue of local government restructuring. The issues review panel only provides advice and has no power to make any decisions.

The chief negotiator's report is the outcome of the negotiation committee. Presumably, the report will contain recommendations agreed to by the party municipalities or, in the case of no agreement, an analysis of outstanding issues. The act imposes no legal requirement on the contents or format of the report. There is thus a measure of flexibility to accommodate or address the conditions specific to a given city-region.

The agreement of the negotiating committee or the report of the chief negotiator is then sent to the minister and the party municipalities. At this stage, the report is a public document widely circulated to groups outside the party municipalities (i.e., school boards, ratepayers, property owners, and other public agencies). However, there is no explicit requirement within the Municipal Boundary Negotiations Act to furnish other groups with copies. Once the chief negotiator's report is received, the party municipalities are legally required to hold one or more information meetings and to discuss the matter within a council meeting. This is the first opportunity for the public to learn of and express opinions on the report's contents and related matters. The new boundary procedures may afford an expanded role for local politicians, but they do not ensure direct public involvement.

From the required council meeting, a resolution or opinion of council on the report is sent to the minister. The act's stipulation of an opinion by the municipal council gives an opportunity to other elected officials to enter the process. The opinion of the local council ensures that the municipal representatives on the negotiating committee have been acting in concert with the wishes of the entire council.

The opinions give the minister the basis to decide on the next step. The minister may determine that any disagreements are mild and correctable with further discussion of the negotiations committee or through advice from the issues review panel. If the collective opinions of the party municipalities are in general agreement, then the minister can give effect to the agreement through an order-in-council or through legislation. If the opinions are too divergent, then the minister can end any further discussion, thus maintaining the status quo on governance of the city-region. Or the minister can take any other measure that he or she considers appropriate. The exact form of these measures is not mentioned in the act. Therefore, the minister retains the ultimate power to resolve the dispute.

Between 1981 and 1995, over 100 boundary adjustments were made under the requirements of the Municipal Boundary and Negotiations Act. The majority of these adjustments were resolved without the establishment of a statutory negotiating committee. As noted above, these resolutions suggest the act's utility regarding small-scale annexations or annexations with all-party agreement. In fact, the spirit of the act assumes that party municipalities are willing to negotiate an amicable resolution.

Quebec's Municipal Reform, 1977-90

The Parti Québécois had municipal reform as a major plank in its platform, so its election in 1976 ushered in a period of change that completely altered the face of local government in Quebec along with the geography of place names. With the objectives of decentralizing public administration and strengthening local government in order to promote the economic development of the province, a secretariat for planning and decentralization was set up to spearhead the work (Québec 1977). A four-pronged attack was adopted, each prong introduced through systematic consultations with municipal leaders and the public. They were (1) agricultural zoning, both to protect agriculture and to control the spread of urban growth; (2) better fiscal arrangements for municipalities to enable them to become more autonomous; (3) a land use planning and development act; and (4) an act respecting municipal democracy aiming to strengthen local government and make it more transparent and responsive.

While only the land use planning and development act directly related to boundary changes (namely, the abolition of the county councils and their replacement by regional county municipalities [RCMs]), it is important to understand them in order to follow subsequent events.

The first prong was passage in 1979 of an act to preserve agricultural land *(Loi sur la protection du territoire agricole, L.Q. 1979, c.10)*. Introduced by the minister of agriculture, this legislation protected good agricultural land from development. All the settled areas of the province were mapped, and farmland was classified according to its biophysical characteristics and economic potential. After negotiations with municipalities, limits were set. The act is administered by a provincial commission *(La Commission de protection des territoires agricoles)*, which hears petitions for changes in limits and uses, in conjunction with the municipalities involved. Land zoned for agriculture has a lower effective tax rate and is eligible for a number of programs directed at agricultural improvement. The zoning also established a perimeter of urbanization for each municipality affected. When drawn, it allowed for urban growth for at least twenty years at the then current rates of urbanization. Since 1979, the limits have been modified many times, but the intent is still the same.

The second prong was to make local governments more autonomous. To this end, an act to reform municipal taxation *(Loi sur la fiscalité municipale et modifiant certaines dispositions législatives, L.Q. 1979, c.72)* was passed in 1979, and it removed school taxes from property tax rolls, leaving the field of direct taxation open only to municipalities. Schools were to be financed from the provincial treasury. It was thus hoped that education would improve in the poorer parts of the province and that municipal governments would have larger, more secure sources of revenue, become capable of making long-range investment plans, and have greater freedom of action. (In fact, the school boards retained the right to tax up to twenty-five cents per hundred dollars of evaluation for special extras. Today, this is a subject of hot debate because proposals have been made to increase this figure in the interest of aiding provincial finances.) The act also abolished all special grants to municipalities, with the exception of equalization grants to very small and impoverished localities. Conditional grants had tended to make long-term budgeting very chancy because municipalities were never sure of what they might receive. The law further permitted the taxation of all provincial government properties at par instead of receiving grants in lieu of taxes, the traditional practice which had paid about 40 percent of assessed value. Finally, the act provided for standardized evaluation, budgeting, accounting, and reporting procedures (Québec 1979). (The province had moved to standardized property assessment rules in 1972. Property is supposed to be assessed at 100 percent market value throughout Quebec, although municipalities can of course set their own mill rates).

With municipalities on a firm financial footing, the third prong was to pass an act respecting land use planning and development *(Loi sur l'aménagement et l'urbanisme, L.Q. 1979, c.A-19.1)*. This act was the first general and direct planning legislation in Quebec (both the Municipal Code and the Cities and Towns Act had only permissive provisions for planning) and gave instructions on the preparation of both regional development plans *(schéma d'aménagement)* and municipal plans *(plan d'urbanisme)* (Québec 1980a). However, the really interesting part from the point of view of boundary changes was the new delimitation of space. County councils were abolished, and municipalities were directed to group themselves into regional county municipalities (RCMs) for planning purposes, on the basis of affinity. Municipalities were to ask where their populations worked, went to school, shopped, and banked and with which neighbours they shared services. They then had to decide on how to form a council, how to achieve representativeness (by population, area, tax base, or other), whether any municipality should have power of veto, and the like (Québec 1980b).

The new RCMs were to take over the role of the former county councils regarding property assessment rolls for rural municipalities, rural roads, water courses, and solid waste management. This process was to be completed within seven years, and then each member municipality had two years in which to prepare a detailed plan within the regional framework. Land use control, zoning, building, conservation, and environmental bylaws remained the responsibility of the local government (Léveillée 1982).

While there was anxiety at the start, by 1983, ninety-four RCMs had been created, replacing the seventy-four old county councils, often with very different configurations. (The Urban and Regional Communities of Montreal, Quebec, and the Outaouais, and amalgamated towns such as Ville de Laval and Mirabel, were each considered an RCM.) The map of Quebec had been redrawn. The former UCCQ *(Union des conseils de comté du Québec)* became the UMRCQ *(Union des municipalités régionales de comté et des municipalités locales du Québec)*, representing the RCMs and the smaller rural municipalities.

The fourth and final prong of the reform was to prepare the ground for improved local democracy. An act to modify certain legislation concerning democracy and renumeration of elected officials in municipalities *(Loi modifiant certaines dispositions législatives concernant la démocratie et la rémunération des élus dans les municipalités, 1980, c.16)* aimed to rid municipal councils of cronyism and make local politics more open. Elected officials were to be paid on a sliding scale according to the size of the municipality. This meant that people could devote much more time to council matters and, it was hoped, that new people would be attracted into the municipal arena who could not otherwise afford the time. Council members were to declare their work and property interests on election to avoid conflict of interest situations. Municipal political parties were encouraged, large municipalities were to divide themselves into wards for electoral purposes, and information to citizens was to be made freely (Québec 1980b).

Most of the 1980s in the municipal world was spent in getting these new structures and procedures established and working. But the question of possible amalgamations did not go away. Most local politicians, and indeed residents, resisted the idea of boundary changes, whether by annexation, amalgamation, or consolidation. They cited the loss of local democracy, the responsiveness of small government, the shared sense of belonging, and the usually lower tax rates of little units, in fact all the reasons advanced by the public choice school of thought, which also maintained that competition, especially between suburban municipalities, keeps costs low.

By the mid-1980s, the Union of Municipalities of Quebec (UMQ) believed that the future of cities and towns, which it represented, was uncertain. Did creation of the RCMs represent a template for future radical changes? Talk of alternative means of service delivery, user pay, contracting out, and privatization was in the air. Senior governments were beginning to debate restructuring, deficit reduction, and downloading. Despite all the reforms, the future of the municipal system seemed to be insecure. The UMQ argued that municipalities are governments in that their leaders are elected by universal suffrage and that they have the right to tax, but on the other hand they have no constitutional rights and operate by policies and rules handed down by the provincial level of government. Having promised decentralization, Quebec seemed to be gradually recentralizing (UMQ 1986).

Further, toward the end of the 1980s municipalities began to fear that amalgamation policies were directed to another end – that the provincial government wanted larger municipal units in order to download services to well-staffed administrations in order to balance its own budget. The laws governing municipal boundaries were rewritten in 1988 as the Act Respecting Municipal Territorial Organization *(Loi sur l'organisation territoriale municipale, L.Q.R. 1988, c.0-9)*, and in 1990 discussions were begun with the municipalities on new ways of sharing costs (Québec 1990). In 1991, the Liberal government adopted a policy to transfer responsibilities and costs for police and local roads to rural municipalities (services that had essentially been provided by the provincial police and road crews) and public transit. The "Réforme Ryan," named after the Minister of Municipal Affairs, Claude Ryan, was not kindly received.

Phase 3: 1990s and Beyond

Ontario's Streamlined Approach

Ontario's third phase of boundary reform has its roots in the "common-sense revolution," the 1995 election platform that returned the Progressive Conservative Party to power after more than 10 years in opposition. Throughout the election campaign, the Progressive Conservatives, under the leadership of Mike Harris, asserted their commitment to local government reform based on the need to "rationalize the regional and municipal levels to avoid the overlap and duplication that now exists."[4] This rationalization process was at its most extreme between 1996 and 1998. Bill 26, the Savings and Restructuring Act, speedily passed in January 1996, was the highlight of these changes. Referred to as the "Omnibus Bill," it addressed numerous issues, such as toll highways, health services, physician services, disclosure of public sector salaries, and municipal restructuring; in all, it proposed over 160 amendments to over forty different provincial statutes.

Furthermore, the Local Services Realignment initiative – what the municipalities called "downloading" – announced in May 1997 furthered the province's common-sense rationalization. Based partly on the recommendations of the "Who Does What?" panel, the initiative began the realignment of provincial and municipal responsibilities, which saw municipalities assuming full responsibility for key services such as social housing, municipal transit, and property assessment, primarily in exchange for a greater provincial responsibility in education. With this drastically altered provincial-municipal relationship, in addition to the trend of decreasing provincial transfer payments and the overhaul of the property tax system in 1997, municipalities were left in quite a different situation than they were in 1995.

To deal with the changes, the province repeatedly emphasized municipal restructuring as a solution. The province's framework for municipal restructuring was presented in Bill 26, included as Schedule M, Amendments to the Municipal Act and Various Other Statutes Related to Municipalities, Conservation Authorities, and Transportation. Essentially, Bill 26 gave permissive restructuring powers to the province's municipalities, counties, and unorganized territories. The purpose of these amendments was to facilitate large-scale municipal restructuring of a significant magnitude, in a prompt and efficient manner.[5]

In this regard, the Schedule M amendments and the Municipal Boundary Negotiations Act differed primarily on three points. First, Schedule M was geared toward a "large geographic area," a scale that the Municipal Boundary Negotiations Act (MBNA) had failed to effect. Second, Schedule M was not confined to the narrow issue of boundaries but was to "facilitate municipal restructuring of a *significant* nature" (Municipal Act 2001, S.O. 2001, c.25, s.171[1], emphasis added), which could include the transfers of powers or responsibilities among municipalities. Third, the procedures outlined in the amended Municipal Act were more basic than the elaborate options and institutions found in the Municipal Boundary Negotiations Act.

Throughout its restructuring crusade, the province repeatedly emphasized its commitment to allowing municipalities to develop local solutions to municipal restructuring and its hesitance toward provincially imposed solutions. Section 25.2 of the Municipal Act gives municipalities the authority to develop their own restructuring proposals. Proposals are required to contain both a detailed description of the restructuring, usually a copy of the restructuring proposal report, and proof that the support mechanism was adhered to, generally in the form of a copy of the municipal bylaws or resolutions. Ontario Regulation 216/96 established this mechanism for determining support for restructuring proposals. It established the required degree of support and the prescribed manner of achieving this support. Specifically, the regulation requires a double majority of support: the support of the majority of the municipalities and the support of more than half of the total number of electors in the affected municipalities. When the affected municipalities are in a county, a triple majority of support is required, involving the additional support of the county council.

Proposals achieving the prescribed level of support and adhering to the prescribed method of support are submitted to the minister of municipal affairs and housing, who then must implement the proposal, by order, subject to any regulations made by the lieutenant-governor-in-council.

This order of implementation must be published in the *Ontario Gazette*, and a copy of the order must be filed with the clerk of each municipality involved, who then makes the order available to the public. In implementing restructuring proposals, the minister's powers are established by Ontario Regulation 143/96. This regulation gives the minister a range of powers in implementing proposals, including the power to create, amalgamate, or dissolve municipalities' local boards; the power to establish a municipal council's composition and voting structures; the power to transfer assets and liabilities, rights, and responsibilities between municipalities; and the power to provide for the continuance or termination of municipal documents, such as official plans or zoning bylaws.

To assist municipalities in investigating restructuring alternatives and developing restructuring proposals, the minister of municipal affairs and housing, in accordance with the power permitted by Section 25.4 of the Municipal Act, developed guiding principles for restructuring proposals, which appeared in the ministry's *Guide to Municipal Restructuring* published in August 1996. It proposes five principles that municipalities must strive for: (1) less government resulting from fewer municipalities and fewer politicians; (2) an accessible and accountable representation system; (3) efficient service delivery, including reduced overlap and captured spillovers; (4) municipal self-sufficiency by delivering municipal services funded by municipal sources; and (5) sustainable economic growth and development.[6] It is the responsibility of the municipalities to determine if they have met these criteria.

The provincial government also established an alternative for municipal restructuring. Under Section 25.3 of the Municipal Act, a municipality or a group of seventy-five inhabitants in an unorganized territory can request that the minister appoint a commission to develop and implement a restructuring proposal "in the locality or in such greater area as the Minister may prescribe."[7] The aim of this alternative is to permit an independent party to make recommendations for regions where local consensus cannot be achieved.

When developing a restructuring proposal, a commission must consult with each municipality involved and may consult with other bodies or persons that it deems appropriate and necessary. Unlike the MBNA, there is no determination of party municipalities, and the commission is free to meet with any municipality, or other body, that requests consultation. However, it does not have the power of the Court of Queen's Bench – that is, it cannot call witnesses. After consultation, the commission must provide the draft proposal to municipalities and the public and invite written submissions. At least one public meeting regarding the draft proposal and the written submissions is required, during which time the commission must hear the concerns or opinions of those in attendance. Following the public meeting, the commission revises the draft based on the written submissions and public input and then releases its final restructuring proposal. A copy of the final draft must be filed with each municipality, and a notice must be put in a general-circulation local newspaper or through another appropriate method.

Thirty days after the last public meeting or the deadline for written submissions, whichever is later, the commission may order implementation of the restructuring proposal. Again this order must be published in the *Ontario Gazette* and a copy filed with the clerk of each municipality. This fact is given public notice, but no further public meetings are required. In implementing a proposal under Section 25.3, a commission has powers similar to those of the minister established by Ontario Regulation 143/96. It is important to note that, once a commission is established, a final recommendation will be forthcoming. This expectation provides the motivation for municipalities to come to their own agreements or risk having the commission thrust proposals on them.

There have been dramatic exceptions to these two routes of municipal restructuring, exceptions that have received much attention from local government reform critics, since they are seen as "forced amalgamations." The amalgamation of Metropolitan Toronto on 1 January 1998, through the City of Toronto Act (Bill 103), was the most prominent example. Much of the criticism emerged against the passing of Bill 103 so quickly, despite the overwhelming disapproval of Metropolitan Toronto's residents, the lack of public participation in the process, and past studies (namely, the *Golden Report*) emphasizing that amalgamation was not a suitable approach.

Similar events unfolded in four other regions in Ontario. After a history of unsuccessful local government reform efforts in the regions, in September 1999 the minister of municipal affairs and housing appointed four special advisors to develop a report of recommendations concerning local government reform in Ottawa-Carleton (Glenn Shortliffe), Hamilton-Wentworth (David O'Brien), Sudbury (Hugh Thomas), and Haldimand-Norfolk (Milt Farrow). The mandate of these special advisors was to determine the best alternative for achieving the province's five restructuring principles in each region. The special advisors conducted extensive public meetings and received numerous submissions from the public throughout a ninety-day consultation process, and each submitted a report in November 1999. All four advisors recommended the establishment of a "megacity" through the amalgamation of the regional government and the area municipalities. These recommendations culminated in the passing of the Fewer Municipal Politicians Act (Bill 25), which established the cities of Greater Sudbury, Hamilton, and Ottawa and the towns of Haldimand and Norfolk, commencing 1 January 2001.

The key to the amalgamation of both Metropolitan Toronto and the regional governments of Sudbury, Hamilton-Wentworth, Ottawa-Carleton, and Haldimand-Norfolk was that the restructuring was instigated and legislated by the provincial parliament and not by the municipalities themselves. In doing so, the province did not remain true to its own commitment of assisting municipalities in developing locally driven, locally satisfactory restructuring proposals, instead imposing provincial solutions.

However, while these exceptions have received much attention, the majority of restructuring proposals within Ontario have been developed under the first route of restructuring, Section 25.2. According to the Ministry of Municipal Affairs and Housing, over 85 percent of the total number of municipalities (about 230) restructured by May 2001 had been achieved in this manner. The remaining proposals were provincially imposed solutions, structured by either commissioners or special advisors. However, while the vast majority of municipal restructuring in Ontario has been the result of locally driven initiatives, the focus of public attention remains primarily on these larger and more populous urban centres.

Quebec's Merger Mania
While the 1980s had represented a period of formation and consolidation of the RCMs, the fragmentation of local government remained an issue. In 1993, the Organization of Municipal Territories act *(Loi sur l'organisation territoriale municipale, L.R.Q. 1993, c.0-9)* was revised, and a guidebook was prepared for municipalities, describing very precisely the steps to be followed in pursuing an amalgamation. Furthermore, it provided an attractive new schedule of grants to help municipalities to do so (Québec 1994). This new policy promised that amalgamations would continue to be voluntary and that their effects would be financially neutral on local taxpayers for a period of five years.

This initiative was supported by research. While earlier studies (e.g., Carter 1986), in true public choice theory mode, showed that smaller municipalities achieve low costs for services to residents, Brisson (1996) was able to show the benefits of mergers. He chose a sample of 163 small municipalities – mostly with populations under 2,000, of which 21 were the result of amalgamations and of which all offered the same range of services – and used a longitudinal analysis (1986-93) to study changes over time. He showed that costs per capita for merged municipalities increased by 53 percent over the eight-year period but that those for the nonmerged increased by 67 percent, a major difference of 14 percent. Not only did financial performance improve, but other performance indicators were extremely positive.

This study added credibility to the Ministry of Municipal Affairs' quest for bigger municipal governments. In May 1996, the minister unveiled yet another initiative to promote consolidation. Villages, parishes, and unorganized settlements totalling fewer than 10,000 people were to be amalgamated; if they did not amalgamate, then they would lose their equalization grants (allowances were made for small municipalities). By March 2000, only 162 of the 407 municipalities targeted had merged, although another 19 had filed joint applications. The minister gave a slight stay of execution. Communities that failed to comply would be penalized in a progressive manner: as of 1 January 2001, they would receive only half of their grant and after 1 January 2002, none of it (Québec 2000). This threat evidently brought results. In the calendar year 2001, 212 old local governments disappeared and were replaced by 49 amalgamated municipalities; of these, 22 are reunited villages and parishes (Québec 2002).

Meanwhile, the problems of the region of Montreal, the home of half the population of Quebec, began to receive more attention. In 1992, the Liberal government launched an enquiry into Greater Montreal, defined essentially as the Census Metropolitan Area, containing over 100 municipalities, distributed between twelve RCMs and the Montreal Urban Community (Task Force on Greater Montreal 1993a) (Figure 5.2). Popularly known as the Pichette Task Force, after its chairman, the commission received the mandate to discuss the conditions under which municipal services and administration should be carried out in the years ahead.

The final report of the task force was a document true to the "new regionalist" school of thought. New regionalists, unlike the proponents of metropolitan government of the 1960s and 1970s, do not base their arguments solely on economies of scale in service delivery, integrated spatial planning for land use and transportation to control growth and foster public transit, the promotion of regional environmental policy, and the containment of externalities. Rather, they stress economic development, the necessity for a city-region to be competitive in the global economy by providing an environment attractive to investment, one-stop shopping, and the elimination of petty jostling for business between fragmented municipalities (Keating 1998; Lefèvre 1998; Norris 2001). Inter-municipal cooperation and new forms of governance, based on partnerships and collaboration between the public, private, and third sectors, are advocated.

The task force proposed the creation of a regional council to govern the city-region, composed of members from area municipalities, the abolition of the twelve RCMs, and the formation of four territory-wide service boards. The cover page of the final report sums it up: "Montreal, a city-region; efficient, prosperous and vibrant; international by vocation; at the service of its citizens" (Task Force on Greater Montreal 1993b).

The provincial government, by this time headed by the Parti Québécois, toyed with the idea of setting up a metropolitan development commission, but this idea did not find favour with the UMRCQ *(Union des municipalités régionales de comté du Québec)* or with the suburban municipalities.

But, in its desire to balance the provincial budget, the government did impose an annual contribution totalling $375 million on all municipalities for the period 1997-2000, arguing that all had to tighten their belts and do their part in confronting the deficit. The municipalities were furious. Opposition from the UMRCQ was largely ignored, but, after much debate, the UMQ *(Union des municipalities du Québec)* agreed to cooperate, though only on the condition that the government would create a commission to study the thorny question of local finances and taxation.

That body, the *Commission nationale sur les finances et la fiscalité locale,* reported in 1999 (Québec 1999). In a large and wide-ranging report, the Bédard Commission recommended, among many other things, increasing local financial autonomy, but it also found that existing local government structures, with the multiplicity of local units, interwoven intermunicipal

Figure 5.2

Amalgamated municipalities and regional county municipalities, Montreal metropolitan area

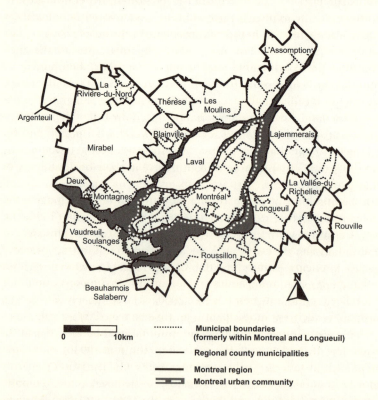

Source: Based on Statistics Canada profile of census subdivisions in Montreal (2001 Census of Canada).

agreements, duplication of effort, and fiscal inequities, were not suitable for the modern world. In urban agglomerations, poor planning, daunting intermunicipal competition, excessive commuting, and externalities required urgent attention. Metropolitan entities were needed for the regions of Montreal and Quebec City, regions within which municipalities should be amalgamated into a maximum of twenty for greater Montreal and six for greater Quebec City. The municipalities in the other four metropolitan areas, Chicoutimi, Hull-Gatineau, Trois-Rivières, and Sherbrooke, should either agree to a form of metropolitan government or amalgamate. The RCMs should be reinforced by transferring to them more local municipal functions. All new metropolitan structures and the RCMs should have direct election of their representatives and their own taxing powers in order to improve accountability and transparency.

Most reactions by municipal politicians to the Bédard report were hostile: they had not anticipated that municipal finances and municipal territorial extents and structures would be so linked. The UMQ was particularly against the idea of the direct election of leaders and the prospect of losing the municipal monopoly on direct taxation to a second tier of local government. However, the approach of the Bédard Commission in using fiscal indicators as analytic tools, in performing detailed critiques of taxation practices and public sector spending, and in addressing equity questions through an accountant's lens evidently found favour in the government's eyes.

Despite all the heated debate that followed, in March 2000 Louise Harel, the minister of municipal affairs, launched a new white paper on municipal reorganization, closely based on the findings of the Bédard report, titled *Municipal Reorganization: Changing Our Ways to Better Serve the Public* (Québec 2000). This paper had two thrusts: the amalgamation of local municipalities, including rural ones, and a frontal attack on the problems of urban areas and the RCMs.

The program of municipal amalgamations in the more rural parts of the province was mainly an evolution of policies already adopted in 1994. The two new initiatives were the penalties for municipalities not choosing to move ahead, as already mentioned, and an enlargement of the powers of the Quebec Municipal Commission (QMC) to permit it to intervene in cases where a majority of municipalities and a majority of the population in a given locality support a request (Québec 2000, 61). Presumably, this means that a small, recalcitrant municipality can thus be reeled into a consolidation, which seems more like forced annexation. Furthermore, the QMC will intervene in any case at the request of the minister of municipal affairs. In such instances, it will examine possible amalgamation scenarios and may hold public hearings or have studies undertaken before it reports back to the ministry, which will then act on its recommendation. The legislation was amended to empower the minister to demand that certain local municipalities submit a joint amalgamation request within a set deadline.[8] Thus, although a facade of voluntary amalgamation is preserved, mergers are, in fact, forced.

The second thrust of the white paper referred to urban areas. First, metropolitan communities were to be established for the regions of Montreal, Quebec City, and the Outaouais (Hull-Gatineau) to replace the existing urban communities, but they would be of much greater territorial extent, essentially covering the census-defined metropolitan area in each case. The existing RCMs would not be called into question, except in the case of municipal amalgamations. In addition, reorganization was to include the amalgamation of municipalities in metropolitan cores, and advisory committees were set up, consisting of one administrator and selected local politicians, to examine ways of instituting tax-base sharing and to recommend possible merger scenarios. These scenarios seemed to vary from that espoused by the mayor of Montreal, "one island, one city," to that combining municipalities into geographic groups (Québec 2000). One thing that the white paper was clear about was that no new municipality must claim bilingual status, a right that has existed in Quebec municipalities if over 50 percent of the population has English as their mother tongue.

The legislation setting up the metropolitan communities (e.g., *Loi sur la Communauté métropolitaine de Montréal, L.Q. 2000, c.34*) came into effect on 1 January 2001. Each metropolitan community is responsible for land use planning, public transportation, funding for social housing, economic development, and tax-base sharing. The council is elected indirectly: it consists of the mayors of the largest municipalities and representatives of municipalities throughout the region. Funding comes through assessed shares of local municipalities, user fees, tax-base sharing, and (a new departure) some gasoline taxes and registration fees.

The next feature of the urban thrust was the amalgamation of all the core municipalities of the major urban centres. For Montreal, this meant the amalgamation of all the twenty-eight municipalities on the Island of Montreal to form the new city; on the south shore of the St. Lawrence, it meant the merger of all the former municipalities of the RCM of Champlain to form the new city of Longueuil (Figure 5.2). Similarly, in Quebec City, municipalities were amalgamated on the north shore of the river to form the new Quebec City and on the south shore to form the new Levis. In the Outaouais region, Hull, Gatineau, and surrounding municipalities were similarly amalgamated. The Act to Reform Municipal Territorial Organization in the Metropolitan Regions of Montreal, Quebec, and the Outaouais *(Loi portant réforme de l'organisation territoriale municipale des régions métropolitaines de Montréal, de Québec et de l'Outaouais, L.Q. 2000, c.56)* came into effect on 1 January 2001.

There were extensive public complaints about such draconian measures and unsuccessful court cases challenging the changes. Nevertheless, transition committees were put into place to oversee the changes, elections were held in November 2001, and the new cities became operative on 1 January 2002. The new City of Montreal, like that of Longueuil, was organized into boroughs, some of which were simply new incarnations of amalgamated municipalities. Others were carved out of the old City of Montreal, while yet others were the products of mergers among former suburbs (Figures 5.1 and 5.2). Thus, municipal boundary changes in Montreal involved both the enlargement of the city to the perimeter of the Island of Montreal and the redefinition of boundaries among former suburbs, now city boroughs.

In past decades, municipal boundary changes in Quebec occurred not through partial annexations but through wholesale mergers, whether voluntary or imposed, and through the creation of regional and metropolitan structures. In fact, most changes were imposed by provincial fiat, though quite a few were enacted under the influence of incentives and disincentives from the province. In the latest round of mergers, from 1 January 2001 to 30 June 2002, some 228 municipalities were merged into 50 new entities. Despite this effort and preceding ones, the municipal map of Quebec remains fragmented, with hundreds of very small municipalities. Officials at the Ministry of Municipal Affairs will certainly continue working to simplify this map.

Conclusion

This chapter provides an analysis of the various experiments in municipal boundary restructuring policies and procedures put in place by the governments of Ontario and Quebec between the 1950s and the present. Three distinct phases of experimentation with differing annexation laws and procedures were identified for each province: (1) judicial determination by the Ontario Municipal Board (1950-82) and Quebec's period of "starts and stops" (1960s-70s); (2) Ontario's popular determination (1982-94) and Quebec's period of great municipal reforms (late 1970s and 1980s); and (3) a streamlined approach in Ontario (1995 to present) and Quebec's period of major amalgamations (1990s to present). Each phase contains important lessons regarding the application of various techniques for solving the complex boundary problems experienced by many local government systems. Furthermore, the two provincial cases offer both divergent and convergent practices regarding municipal boundary reform within Canada.

In many respects, both Ontario and Quebec have convergent histories with regard to their treatment of the "boundary problem." Overall, the boundary reforms in both provinces reveal the nation's constitutional condition that municipalities are merely "creatures of the province." Both Ontario's and Quebec's Ministries of Municipal Affairs play central roles in shaping the debate and conditions under which municipal boundary restructuring could and can take place. Both provincial ministries have showed a capacity to bring tremendous changes to the territorial maps of their local government systems. However, the manner and degree by which each province used this power reveal the diverse approaches that can be taken within the same constitutional setting.

Even though both provinces have absolute power to redraw municipalities, neither used it exclusively. Both provinces sought to establish procedures whereby local municipalities could decide on, or have input into, revisions to the territorial status quo. Quebec's method was perhaps gentler than Ontario's since its emphasis was on voluntary boundary restructuring and on the use of more carrots than sticks to encourage boundary reform. Ontario, however, sought to establish boundary reforms that would insulate it from being drawn into what were usually fierce political contests over territory waged by neighbouring municipalities. When Ontario did act, it was usually swiftly and resulted in dramatic changes to its local government map.

The most obvious divergence was in the type of municipal boundary changes. Quebec firmly avoided annexations in favour of municipal amalgamations and consolidations. Quebec's strategy of municipal boundary reform was to group existing municipal governments into more "logical" territorial configurations. In Ontario, annexation was preferred; amalgamations were a last resort or a consequence of frequent and sustained annexations. In fact, the amalgamations undertaken to form regional municipalities during the late 1960s and early 1970s may have fanned the flames of annexation by municipalities untouched by this regional reform. Only toward the mid-1990s did amalgamation become more central to the Ontario government's campaign to reduce the number of municipalities in the province.

Furthermore, both provinces also diverged with respect to the reform of county boundaries. Ontario's municipal boundary reform did not disturb the historic county boundaries; instead, it carved regional municipalities out of the existing territorial dimensions of its historic county system. Quebec, however, abandoned the traditional county boundaries in its creation of regional county municipalities. The divergence is also evident in the fact that the creation of Ontario's regional municipalities was largely restricted to the urban areas of the province, while Quebec's institution of RCMs covered the whole of the settled part of the province.

The creation of regional municipalities in Ontario and regional county municipalities in Quebec represents an important convergence in the comparative experiences of boundary reform in these provinces. These reforms, which established a two-tier system of local government, created the template for the municipal amalgamations and the dramatic decline in the number of local governments. By the 1990s, provincial governments in both Quebec and Ontario sought to restructure municipalities within regional municipalities.

Unfortunately, it appears that neither Ontario nor Quebec has been able to solve the chronic boundary problems of its municipal governments. Both provinces are currently studying or actively pursuing further boundary reform. The provinces converge here on a crucial point: the inherent policy of the provincial governments was always to reduce the number and enlarge the size of local government units. It appears that no other strategy was considered.

Notes

1 For instance, *Commission d'enquête sur les problèmes métropolitains de Montréal* (Paquette Commission), 1953-55; *Commission d'étude du système administratif de Montréal* (Champagne Commission), 1960-61; *Commission d'étude des problèmes intermunicipaux dans l'île de Montréal* (Blier Commission), 1964; *Rapport de la commission d'étude des problèmes intermunicipaux sur la Rive-Sud* (Lemay Report), 1967.
2
- Charter of the City of Laval *(Charte de la Ville de Laval, S.Q. 1965, c.89).*
- Act Respecting the Vicinity of the New International Airport *(Loi concernant les environs du nouvel aéroport international, L.Q. 1970).*
- Act Respecting the Town of Becancour *(Loi concernant la ville de Bécancour, L.Q. 1966, c.23).*
- Act Respecting the Neighbourhood of Mont Sainte-Anne Park *(Loi concernant les environs du Parc Mont Sainte-Anne, L.Q. 1971, c.50).*
- Charter of the Town of Gaspé *(Charte de la Ville de Gaspé, L.Q. 1970, c.76).*
- James Bay Region Development Act *(Loi du développement de la Baie James, S.Q. 1971, c.34-35).*
- Act to Regroup the Towns of Baie-Comeau and Hautrive *(Loi regroupant les villes de Baie-Comeau et Hautrive, L.Q. 1982, c.23).*
- Act Concerning the Towns of Rouyn and Noranda *(Loi concernant les villes de Rouyn et de Noranda, L.Q. 1985, c.80).*
3
- Quebec Urban Community Act *(Loi de la Communauté urbaine de Québec, L.Q. 1969, c.83).*
- Montreal Urban Community Act *(Loi de la Communauté urbaine de Montréal, L.Q. 1969, c.84).*
- Outaouais Regional Community Act *(Loi de la Communauté régionale de l'Outaouais, L.Q. 1969, c.85).*
4 PC Party of Ontario, *Common Sense Revolution* (1995), 17.
5 Savings and Restructuring Act, 1996, Statutes of Ontario 1996, c.1, Sch. M, 25.1 (a)-(c).
6 Ontario Ministry of Municipal Affairs and Housing, *A Guide to Municipal Restructuring* (August 1996), ii-iii.
7 Bill 62, the Direct Democracy through Municipal Referendums Act, passed in 2000, eliminated the provision in the Municipal Act that allowed seventy-five electors in a municipality to petition the minister to establish a commission.
8 This means that there must be a statutory instrument, duly published in the *Official Gazette*. For example, "Authorization to the Minister of Municipal Affairs and Greater Montreal to require Village de Métis-sur-Mer and Municipalité des Boules to file a joint

application for amalgamation (An Act respecting municipal territorial organization, R.S.Q., c. O-9)," from the *Gazette officielle du Québec* 133, 42 (17 October 2001): 5749. Similarly, an amalgamation has to be ratified by the National Assembly (provincial parliament).

References

Adler, G. 1971. *Land Planning by Administrative Regulation: Policies of the Ontario Municipal Board*. Toronto: University of Toronto Press.

Baccigalupo, Alain. 1984. *Les Administrations municipales québécoises des origines à nos jours*. 2 vols. Montréal: Les Éditions Agence d'Arc.

Brisson, Gilbert. 1996. "Les Regroupements amélioreraient la performance des municipalités." *Municipalité* avril-mai: 20-23.

Carter, Richard. 1986. *La Diversification des revenues et le niveau des dépenses des municipalités du Québec*. Québec: Université Laval, École nationale d'administration publique et Groupe de recherche en organisation industrielle. (Rapport présenté à la Commission d'étude sur les municipalités.)

Glenn, Jane Matthews. 1977. "L'Aménagement du territoire en droit public québécois." *McGill Law Journal* 23, 2: 242-61.

Harris, Richard C. 1966. *The Seigneurial System in Early Canada*. Madison: University of Wisconsin Press.

Keating, Michael. 1998. *The New Regionalism in Western Europe: Territorial Restructuring and Political Change*. Northampton, MA: E. Elgar.

Lefèvre, Christian. 1998. "Metropolitan Government and Governance in Western Countries: A Critical Review." *International Journal of Urban Research* 22, 1: 9-25.

Léveillée, Jacques, éd. 1982. *L'Aménagement du territoire au Québec: Du rêve au compromis*. Montréal: Nouvelle optique.

Linteau, Paul-André. 2000. *Histoire de Montréal depuis la Confédération*. Nouvelle édition augmentée. Montréal: Boréal.

Makuch, S. 1983. *Canadian Municipal and Planning Law*. Toronto: Carswell.

Norris, Donald F. 2001. "Prospects for Regional Governance under the New Regionalism: Economic Imperatives versus Political Impediments." *Journal of Urban Affairs* 23, 5: 557-71.

Ontario. 1980. *An Examination of the Brantford-Brant Local Government Pilot Project: An Alternative Annexation Process*. Toronto: Local Government Division, Ministry of Intergovernmental Affairs, 1980.

–. 1994. *Guide to Annexations under the Municipal Boundary Negotiations Act*. Toronto: Municipal Boundaries Branch.

Québec. 1977. *La Décentralisation: Une perspective communautaire nouvelle*. Québec: Ministère du conseil exécutif, Secrétariat à l'aménagement et à la décentralisation.

–. 1979. *Reform of Municipal Taxation and the Financing of Urban and Regional Communities and of Public Transportation*. Québec: Ministère des Finances, Ministère des Affaires municipales, Ministère des Transports.

–. 1980a. *Les Grandes réformes du monde municipal 1977-1980*. Québec: Ministère des Affaires municipales.

–. 1980b. *Land Use Planning in Quebec: A Collective Project*. Québec: Secrétariat à l'aménagement et à la décentralisation.

–. 1990. *Partage des responsabilités Québec – Municipalités: Vers un nouvel équilibre*. Québec: Ministère des Affaires municipales.

–. 1994. *Guide du regroupement de municipalités*. Québec: Ministère des Affaires municipales.

–. 1999. Commission nationale sur les finances et la fiscalité. *Pacte 2000*. Québec: Les Publications du Québec.

–. 2000. *Municipal Reorganization: Changing Our Ways to Better Serve the Public*. Québec: Ministry of Municipal Affairs.

–. 2002. *Regroupements de municipalités, réalisés du 1 janvier 2001 au 31 décembre 2001*. Québec: Ministère des Affaires municipales.

Ross, R. 1962. *Local Government in Ontario*. 2nd ed. Toronto: Canada Law Book.
Task Force on Greater Montreal. 1993a (January). *Progress Report* (Pichette Report). Montreal: Task Force on Greater Montreal.
–. 1993b (December). *Montreal, a City-Region* (Pichette Report). Montreal: Task Force on Greater Monteal.
Tessier, Maurice. 1971. *Proposition de réforme des structures municipales*. Québec: Ministère des Affaires municipales.
UMQ. 1986. *Rapport de la Commission d'étude sur les municipalités* (Parizeau Commission). Montréal: Union des Municipalités du Québec.

6
The Two Waves of Territorial Reform of Local Government in Germany
Hellmut Wollmann

Germany has experienced two distinct periods of local government territorial reform. The first occurred in the "old" Federal Republic during the late 1960s and early 1970s, and the second, after German unification, occurred in East Germany starting in the early 1990s. This chapter will examine these two periods of boundary reform. The factors that drove the reforms during each period are identified and analyzed, and an assessment of their effects, within the limits of available empirical evidence, is undertaken.

A brief summary of Germany's intergovernmental setting is first presented in order to provide the institutional and political context in which local government territorial reforms were debated and ultimately decided. The first reform period in the "old" Federal Republic is then examined. This examination is followed by a discussion of the later territorial reforms in East Germany. The chapter concludes by presenting the German account of reforms to its local government territories within a comparative and speculative perspective.

Intergovernmental Setting

To put the account and analysis of the reform of local government territories in an appropriate perspective, an overview of the intergovernmental context is provided. This overview includes an introduction to the German federal system as well as the functional, political, and territorial model of German local governance. Thus, this section sorts out some of the terms and concepts used to describe Germany's local government system.

The Intergovernmental Status of Local Government

German local government consists of two tiers: the counties *(Kreise)* as the upper tier and the municipalities *(Gemeinden)* as the lower tier. The majority municipalities lie within counties (and are called in German *kreisangehörige Gemeinden*, which can be translated as "municipalities within counties"). However, the larger towns and cities exercise the responsibilities and powers of both levels and are known in German as *kreisfreie Städte*, which means "county-free towns." This is similar to the "county boroughs" or "county cities" in Britain and the "city-counties" division of local governments found in the United States (Norton 1994, 251).

Germany's federal system of government consists of the Federation *(Bund)* and the Federal States *(Länder)*, while the local governments do not constitute a self-standing third level within this federal structure. According to the German Constitution and legal doctrine, local governments are considered part of the *Länder* (Figure 6.1). They are, using American terminology, "creatures" of the *Länder*. Therefore, the territorial and institutional frameworks in which local governments operate are decided by the *Länder*. In other words, municipal charters as well as territorial boundaries of local governments are set by the *Länder*. The Federation has no say in these matters.

However, German constitutional tradition does afford a scope of autonomy over local responsibilities to local governments. These local responsibilities are protected against infringement and abolition by federal or *Land* legislation. The Federal Constitution of 1949 provides two key sections that furnish this legal protection to local governments.

First, Article 28 of the Federal Constitution (*Grundgesetz*, "Basic Law") states that the municipalities, and to a somewhat lesser degree the counties, have the responsibility to regulate "all matters of the local community *[örtliche Gemeinschaft]* within the frame of the existing [federal and *Länder*] legislation." This provision of the Federal Constitution is generally seen as an "institutional guarantee" of local self-government that the *Länder* are bound to respect in their legislation regarding local governments. Therefore, the Federal Constitution does, on the one hand, recognize the special status of local government in the entire constitutional system and thus binds or limits the action of the *Länder* vis-à-vis the local governments. But, on the other hand, the Constitution makes the qualification that the "right" of the municipalities (and counties) can only be exercised "within the frame of existing legislation." This qualification has opened the door for legislation, particularly passed by the *Länder*, that can curb local autonomy.

Article 28 of the Federal Constitution has been interpreted by the Federal Constitutional Court and by the entire judiciary as granting and ensuring an "institutional guarantee" to local governments that makes its "core" and "essence" immune to encroachment by both federal and *Länder* legislation. Yet an important qualification in this institutional guarantee pertains to local government territories. Article 28 of the Federal Constitution (and similar provisions in the *Länder* constitutions) do not provide any guarantee to the territories and boundaries of individual municipalities (or counties) from changes made by an act of *Land* legislation passed by the *Länder* (Stern 1981, 205). All in all, Article 28 gives some protection to municipalities against a legislative act of a *Länder* parliament that violates the basic postulates of "due process" in the *Länder's* dealing with the municipalities.

Second, any municipality (or county) that claims to have been violated in its rights under Article 28 of the Federal Constitution may file a complaint to the constitutional court of the respective *Land* or the Federal Constitutional Court. Thus, it should come as no surprise that such court proceedings were amply resorted to by municipalities in the conflicts about territorial reforms (see discussion below).

Figure 6.1

German *Länder* and municipal governments

Functional (and Political) Model of Local Government

Within this constitutional circumstance, in which local governments are not a self-standing (third) layer of the federal system but regarded as constituent parts of the *Länder,* the two-tier local governments have, in the German constitutional and administrative tradition, been characterized by a broad scope of tasks and responsibilities. The local governments' profile as a *multifunction and general purpose* government contains two conceptual strands that have converged and reinforced each other. First, the "general competence clause," constitutionally recognized by Article 28, as discussed above, provides a basis for the "general purpose" model encouraging and legitimating the municipalities and counties to take care of "all matters relevant to the local community."

Second, the counties and (to a lesser degree) the municipalities have, in addition to their local self-government matters, been responsible for carrying out public functions "delegated" to them by the state. This is known as the "dual function" principle (Wollmann 2000a, 46; Marcou and Verebelyi 1993, 79) in which the local authorities have come to be administratively responsible for a gamut of public functions (e.g., the issuance of building permits or car and driver's licences, the civil registry) that in other countries are often carried out by (single-purpose) local field offices of the senior (central/state) government. In other words, the dual-function model refers to the local functions as well as the delegated functions carried out by local governments. Functional reforms have been discussed and pursued as a strategy to further (politically) *decentralize* or (administratively) *deconcentrate* the intergovernmental setting by transferring further public (administrative) functions from state *(Land)* agencies to the local authorities – with the traditional dual-function model providing the conceptual basis and "peg" for such delegation.

This functional prevalence of the local authorities as *territory-based, general purpose* local governments in the coverage of public activities and functions at the local level has its correspondence in the limited array of *special purpose* (sectoral) administrative units of state *(Land)* administration *(Sonderbehörden)* in Germany's intergovernmental system. This is the result of the federal level that is constitutionally enjoined from having administrative offices of its own on the sub-*Länder* level (except for a constitutionally enumerated minimal number of functions, such as customs and border police). As a result, the *Länder* have made use of (and further accentuated) the dual-function model of local government by "delegating" administrative functions to the general purpose local authorities.

Territorial Format of the Local Government Levels Up to the 1960s

The Second World War resulted in an unprecedented and extensive redrawing of Germany's territorial boundaries. One-quarter of the German

Reich's territories in the eastern provinces fell to Poland and the Soviet Union – with over ten million Germans fleeing or being expelled to West Germany. The remaining German territory was divided in 1949 into four occupational zones, the borders of which were sorted out by political bargaining among the four powers. Within this territory, ten (originally twelve) new *Länder* were created whose boundaries were also determined by the political will of the occupational forces rather than by the historical boundaries of the *Länder* in the (pre-Nazi) Weimar Republic.

Amid and despite this unprecedented upheaval and redrawing of territorial boundaries in the international, national, and state *(Länder)* scales, the territorial boundaries of the counties and municipalities in postwar West Germany remained conspicuously unchanged. The massive efforts of reconstructing the devastated cities, the housing of millions of refugees, and the legendary "miracle" of phenomenal economic recovery, in which the local level played a decisive part, took place largely within local government territories that dated from the nineteenth century or earlier. The attempts after the First World War to have the outdated boundaries of municipalities reformed were limited mainly to some of the country's largest cities. For example, in 1920 (Greater) Berlin was formed through amalgamation by a legislative fiat by the parliament of Prussia.

Thus, despite the unprecedented political, economic, and national/state territorial changes that (West) Germany underwent during the years immediately following the Second World War, the territorial boundaries of the counties and municipalities remained unchanged. The local government system consisted of 24,000 municipalities (with an average population of 2,000) and 425 counties (with an average of 60,000 inhabitants).

Territorial Reforms of Local Government in the ("Old") Federal Republic in the 1960s and 1970s

Factors and Discourses Shaping the Reform Agenda
Debate on the need for dramatic and radical reforms of the historically inherited territorial structure of local governments emerged and quickly gained momentum during the late 1960s. The following section highlights the factors and discourses that gave rise to and propelled this reform movement.

Massive Shifts in the Settlement Structure
Rapid postwar economic recovery and the influx of more than ten million refugees from Germany's former eastern provinces (which resulted in a one-quarter increase in West Germany's population) greatly contributed to large-scale urbanization and industrialization of West Germany. The ensuing new demographic and industrial agglomerations cut across the

old territorial boundaries of municipalities and counties and made them increasingly dysfunctional (Norton 1994, 37 ff.). In the rural regions, this national demographic and socioeconomic restructuring was accompanied by a dramatic decline of agricultural activities, resulting rural depopulation, and general thinning of the rural settlement structure.

Rising Debate on Regional Planning
In the face of advancing urban agglomerations and the progressive decline of rural regions, the discourse among regional planners was marked by the idea of having a functionally differentiated system of "central localities" (*zentralörtliches* system) as the essential guide to Germany's future settlement structure. Furthermore, regional planners demanded, during this time, that instruments of comprehensive "spatial planning" *(Raumordnung)* and *Land* as well as regional planning *(Landesplanung, Regionalplanung)* be put in place. Moreover, the professional discourse among public administration specialists increasingly addressed the issues of "reconstruction of public administration" (*Neubau der Verwaltung,* to quote the title of a then influential book written by a prominent public administration expert, Frido Wagener [1980]).

The growing discourse on regional planning and public administration reflected the rationalistic and scientific mood *(zeitgeist)* of the time that had important consequences and influences and the growing concern over local government territories. Planning and administrative discussions revolved, to a degree, around the attempt to define the "optimal sizes" of counties and municipalities according to (normative) criteria relating to the kinds of services (schools, social services, recreational facilities, etc.) that the different types of local governments, according to their degree of "centrality," should provide. This rationalistic approach to regional planning brought into sharper focus the need to inject a territorial concern regarding the relationship between "planning space" and "administrative space." This concern was a key tenet in the debate to replace the outdated territorial boundaries of local government with "rationally" planned ones (Mattenklodt 1981, 161).

Expansive ("Social Democratic") Welfare State
Still another powerful conceptual and policy push came from the expansion of the welfare and intervention state that, as in other Western European countries, was embarked on in the Federal Republic in the late 1960s and particularly after the election of the Social Democrat-led federal government under Chancellor Willy Brandt. In view of the salient role that the local authorities had, premised on the traditional territory-based, multifunctional model, played in policy implementation and law application in Germany's intergovernmental system, their administrative capacity now

became crucial, when it came to administratively coping with and executing the broad array of reform policies and new legislation that came out of this period of "reform policies." Hence, the territorial reforms of local governments were an almost logical precursor needed to ensure and enhance the administrative capacities of the local authorities to put into practice new policies dealing with, for example, infrastructure, environment, and social issues.

Functional Reform

Finally, a further impulse for local territorial restructuring came from a reform debate and discussion regarding the "overhauling" of the Federal Republic's intergovernmental system to further (politically) decentralize and (administratively) deconcentrate the decision-making and administrative functions (Seibel 2001, 79). To prepare the ground for *functional reforms* by way of transferring further public functions from state *(Land)* agencies to the (general purpose) local authorities, the territorial reforms of local governments were seen as mandatory (Norton 1994, 253).

Reform Debates and Measures in the (West) German *Länder*

Processes and Conflicts

Recall that in the Federal Republic's constitutional setting the power to alter the territorial boundaries and format of the local government units lies exclusively with the *Länder* governments. In formal terms, under the existing legal provisions, an explicit consent of the local population, say, by way of referendum, is not required. In the last resort, the *Länder* parliaments decide by legislative fiat.

The *Länder* governments embarked on extensive territorial reforms between 1965 and 1968 that were completed between 1974 and 1979. On average, it took about eight years to put the new territorial format of local government in place. The long duration of the process reflects the political controversies that the territorial reforms aroused and probably also the caution with which the *Land* governments chose to proceed.

Reflecting the rationalist and scientific *zeitgeist* of the period, a reform commission was set up by most *Land* governments or *Land* parliaments (Mattenklodt 1981, 166). Composed of practitioners as well as academic experts, the commissions were to prepare recommendations regarding reforms. The commission's main challenge was to find a balance between the (possibly tension-fraught) goal of enhancing the administrative capacities of the newly created local governments and the goal of retaining, if not enhancing, their democratic potential. In their practical work, much attention was given to the future map of the counties and municipalities based on functional criteria and the system of central localities. In

Nordrhein-Westfalen (Figure 6.1), for instance, the optimal size of the ("unitary") municipality was defined by the reform commission as having approximately 8,000 inhabitants, viewed as the minimum threshold needed to support the provision of a primary school, retirement home, and pharmacy (Norton 1994, 252).

After the *Land* government put forward its recommended territorial reform, a kind of "voluntary phase" *(Freiwilligkeitsphase)* was entered in most *Länder*. In this phase, the *Land* government tried to get the affected municipalities and counties to "voluntarily" go along with the commission's reform proposal. The *Land* government's method of "persuasion" often included financial incentives such as "merger bonuses" *(Eheprämien)* to sweeten the bitter pill of amalgamation.

However, in many cases, the territorial reform proposal put forth by the *Land* governments encountered heavy resistance from local politicians as well as local residents. In fact, in most *Länder,* fewer than half of the municipalities "voluntarily" agreed. Thus, in the majority of cases, legislative fiat, a "finalizing act" *(Schlussgesetz),* by the *Land* parliament was required to put the new territorial map of local governments into binding legal force.

In several cases, the municipalities resorted to their right, laid down in the Federal Constitution as well as in the *Länder* constitutions, as discussed above, to file a complaint with the constitutional court of the *Land* (or, in default, with the Federal Constitutional Court) on the claim that the constitutionally guaranteed status of the municipality was violated by the legislatively imposed amalgamation (Stern 1981, 205 ff.; Stüer 1978; Gunst 1990, 190, with references to such court cases). Yet the constitutional courts (as well as the legal doctrine) have been unanimous in assuming that, while Article 28 of the Federal Constitution contains an "institutional guarantee" of local self-government, it does not afford any constitutional warrant for ensuring the existing territorial boundary and format of the individual municipality. So, in most cases, the judicial complaints of municipalities have been dismissed by the constitutional courts. Only in a few instances has the legislatively imposed amalgamation been nullified for largely procedural reasons.

Patterns of Municipal Territorial Reforms
Two strategies, along a continuum, can be discerned from the reorganization of municipal governments. At one end of the continuum is the strategy ("Strategy I") to redraw the boundaries of all existing municipalities by way of merging (amalgamating) them and forming (territorially and demographically enlarged) "unitary municipalities" *(Einheitsgemeinden).* At the other end of the continuum is the strategy ("Strategy II") in which all existing municipalities, even the small ones, are retained as *political*

local government units (with an elected local council and a mayor [possibly part-time] and exercising the political rights and responsibilities of local self-government), while a set of *joint authorities* is created of which the municipalities are members and that serve them as their *administrative* support unit. The joint authorities are typically run by a board appointed by the councils of the member municipalities, have (small) full-time administrative staffs, and are headed by a director accountable to the board (Table 6.1).

In the choice and the putting in place of the new territorial and organizational scheme and map for *municipal* local government, the *Länder* have shown a remarkable degree of variance in which the aforementioned two strategies have been translated into practice. At least three distinct patterns can be distinguished.

The "purest" realization of Strategy I can be found in *Land Nordrhein-Westfalen* and *Land Hessen* (Figure 6.1), where, without exception, new unitary municipalities were formed. This brought the average local government population to 14,000 in Hessen and to as high as 45,000 in Nordrhein-Westfalen. There may be two reasons for these "radical" amalgamations in these two *Länder*. First, their levels of urbanization (indicated by the population density; see Table 6.1, column 2) likely lessened the call and pressure for having joint authorities as a way to allow for the survival of small municipalities. Second, a political motive can be surmised in the fact that both *Länder* were run, during the crucial reform period, by Social Democrat-led governments. Social Democrats on the federal, *Länder,* and municipal levels were the political party that, more than the others, appeared to be ideologically and politically committed to wholesale administrative modernization as well as to the then dominant rationalist planning creed.

In contrast, *Land Schleswig-Holstein* and *Land Rhein-Pfalz* have largely followed Strategy II. Only about 20 percent of the municipalities have disappeared by way of amalgamation, while over 90 percent have become members of joint authorities, and just 10 percent continue to exist as unitary municipalities. The reason for this reform trajectory can plausibly be related to the comparatively distinct rural settlement pattern (indicated by a low population density). Furthermore, particularly in Schleswig-Holstein, the reformers have drawn on (and been bound by) the past experience that this *Land* had with a variant of the joint authority model of local government *(Amt)*.

Land Baden-Württemberg and *Land Bayern* (Figure 6.1) show a "mixed" reform approach in that each reduced the number of existing municipalities by about two-thirds through amalgamation (reaching an average population of 6,000 and 9,000, respectively), while a significant share of municipalities (in Bayern, about 40 percent) formed unitary municipalities,

Table 6.1

Demographic changes between 1968 and 1978 (German Federal Republic)

Länder	Population	Population density (km²)	Total no. of municipalities in 1968	Total no. of municipalities in 1978	Reduction (%)	Average population (after reform)	% of municipalities having joint authorities
Baden-Württemberg	10.4	294	3,379	1,111	67.1	9,000	84
Bayern	12	173	7,077	2,052	71.0	6,000	62
Hessen	6	287	2,684	423	84.3	14,000	0
Niedersachsen	7.8	166	4,231	1,030	75	7,800	73
Nordrhein-Westfalen	18	528	2,277	396	82.6	45,000	0
Rheinland-Pfalz	4	203	2,905	2,320	20.1	1,700	95
Schleswig-Holstein	2.7	176	1,378	1,132	17.9	2,400	91
German Federal Republic	60.9	230	23,931	8,464	64.9	7,000	75

Sources: Mattenklodt (1981, 156 ff.); Laux (1993, 140); author's own calculations.

and more than half were linked to joint authorities. This middle-of-the-road course is probably accounted for by the number of rural areas in these *Länder*. It may also be accounted for by the political climate since both *Länder* had Christian Democrat-led governments and majority parties that were sensitive to their traditional electorates in the rural areas and their small localities (Table 6.2).

Territorial Reforms of County Local Government

In contrast to the various territorial reforms to municipal governments, as discussed above, the *Länder* proceeded uniformly with regard to the territorial reforms of the counties (Table 6.2). Overall, the number of counties was reduced by approximately half, bringing the average county population to about 170,000 inhabitants.

Functional Reforms

In most *Länder*, completion of the territorial reforms was followed by *functional reforms* in which, as it was originally envisaged, the enhanced administrative capacities of the (territorially and organizationally enlarged) unitary local governments as well as of the joint authorities were seen as the viable basis for transferring further administrative tasks from state authorities to local authorities (Mattenklodt 1981, 176, for the example of Nordrhein-Westfalen). This transfer of administrative tasks further expanded and reinforced the status and role of the territory-based, multi-functional model of local government in Germany's intergovernmental setting and shrinking and curbing the realm of local-level, single purpose (sectoral) state agencies outside local governments. Yet the range of functional reforms has remained limited (Mattenklodt 1981, 181).

The ("Old") Federal Republic's Territorial Reforms of Local Government in International Perspective

The German experience can be placed in a broader European comparative perspective. In many northern European countries, similar debates and activities on local territorial reforms emerged during the 1960s and 1970s. The lead was taken by Sweden, where, in a sequence of reforms between 1952 and 1962, the number of municipalities was drastically reduced from 2,500 to 248. This reform was partially rooted in the rationalist planning and state interventionist convictions of the period. Moreover, these territorial reforms were guided by the idea of creating "growth centres perceived as the crucial element for a balanced economic and occupational development ... The planners and Social Democrats won the day" (Kjellberg 1984, quoted in Norton 1994, 298 ff.). In the 1970s, Britain followed suit with "draconian reorganisation" (Norton 1994, 365) of its district and borough authorities (as the country's basic local government level). In

Table 6.2

Changes to counties between 1968 and 1978 (German Federal Republic)

Länder	Population	Population density (km²)	Total no. of counties in 1968	Total no. of counties in 1978	Reduction (%)	Average population (after reform)
Baden-Württemberg	10.4	294	63	35	44.7	na
Bayern	12	173	134	71	50.3	na
Hessen	6	287	39	20	48.7	na
Niedersachsen	7.8	166	60	37	38.3	na
Nordrhein-Westfalen	18	528	57	31	45.6	na
Rheinland-Pfalz	4	203	39	24	38.5	na
Schleswig-Holstein	2.7	176	17	11	35.3	na
German Federal Republic	**60.9**	**230**	**409**	**229**	**44.7**	**170,000**

Sources: Mattenklodt (1981, 156 ff.); Laux (1993, 140); author's own calculations.

1974, approximately 1,300 district and borough authorities were replaced by 369, bringing the average population to over 127,000 (Norton 1994, 40).

In contrast to the implementation of reforms in northern Europe, hardly any local territorial reforms were attempted or implemented in countries located in "southern Europe." For example, in France during the early 1970s, the national government made a cautious effort toward territorial reform of some of the smallest local governments (with some 35,000 municipalities having an average population of only 1,500). However, this effort foundered conspicuously (see Wollmann 2000a, 42).

Putting the territorial reforms of municipalities among the *Länder* in a European comparative perspective divided into the "northern European" pattern (embodied by the territorial reforms in Britain and Sweden) and the "southern European" pattern (epitomized by France), the approach to local government boundary reform pursued in Germany can, to a degree, be qualified as a middle-of-the-road course between the resolute and excessive pace of amalgamation typical of the northern European pattern and the abstention from amalgamation characteristic of the southern European pattern. Within the variance of the *Länder,* Nordrhein-Westfalen is the closest approximation to the northern European reform model, whereas Rheinland-Pfalz and Schleswig-Holstein (Figure 6.1), in their very restrained conduct of amalgamation, come closest to the southern European reform model.

A Tentative "Balance Sheet" of the Territorial Reforms of the 1960s and 1970s in the "Old" Federal Republic

To be sure, the territorial reforms during the 1960s and 1970s resulted in a fundamental redrawing of the German map of public administration (Seibel 2001, 80). Among the public sector reforms tackled during the 1960s and 1970s, the territorial reforms of local governments certainly brought about the most far-reaching and lasting effects on the politico-administrative structures, not least because of the crucial political and administrative role that local governments perform within Germany's intergovernmental system.

It is not easy, however, to create an empirically informed balance sheet that measures the success of the two main goals of territorial reform: to enhance administrative efficiency and to ensure democratic legitimacy of local government. Although quite a number of studies have been conducted, some of them with an (at least implicit) evaluation orientation (Thieme and Prillwitz 1981), the available information is far from conclusive. On the one hand, it is widely agreed that the administrative performance of public administration has been significantly improved, particularly for citizens in rural areas and small localities, whether in the enlarged unitary municipalities or through the joint authorities, which have been able to employ professional and specialized personnel. On the other hand, there has been a loss in local representation (with the number of elected local councillors dropping from 280,000 to 150,000; see Norton 1994, 255). Overall, the increase in service delivery and planning capacity has occurred, according to some accounts, at the expense of local autonomy (Gunlicks 1981).

Territorial Reforms of Local Government in East Germany since 1990

Local Level Administration in the German Democratic Republic's Socialist State

Building on Germany's traditional two-tier structure of local government consisting of counties *(Kreise)* and municipalities *(Gemeinden, Städte)*, including the differentiation between "municipalities within counties" *(kreisangehörige Gemeinden)* and "county cities" *(Stadtkreise)*, East Germany's Communist regime, in forging its socialist state tailored to the Stalinist blueprint of centralist party rule, assigned to the counties and municipalities the function of operating as the local offices subservient and subordinated to the centralist state (Wollmann 1996a, 151 ff.).

In this organizational scheme, counties were seen as a relevant level particularly in running the locally oriented state economy, while municipalities were accorded hardly more than a residual function. In a major reorganization of the socialist state in 1952, the territorial boundaries of the counties were redrawn, and their number was doubled (a total of 189 counties with an average population of 60,000), to make them more compatible with the centralist state model. At the same time, the large number of municipalities, approximately 7,600, was left unchanged, the territorial boundaries of which mostly dated to the nineteenth century and the majority of municipalities having fewer than 500 inhabitants (Wollmann 1997a, 282 ff.).

Factors Shaping East Germany's Territorial Reform Agenda after 1990

The political and administrative rebuilding of the local authorities was an important part of the process of German reunification. The importance stems from the fact that the local government system was the only institutional level that survived the political and institutional demise of the German Democratic Republic, which ceased to exist on 3 October 1990. After this date, the central government structures, a good deal of its once powerful regional administrative ("meso") layer, and most of its legal apparatus ceased to exist (Wollmann 1996b, 46 ff.). The local authorities, tailored to West Germany's democratic and multifunctional model of local government, started to operate as of May 1990. The East German *Länder* were formally reestablished only following 3 October 1990, with the new *Länder* parliaments being elected on 14 October 1990 and the new *Länder* governments and administrations subsequently being built up virtually "from scratch" (Wollmann 1997a, 2002).

The local authorities experienced a transformation from being local "cogs" in a centralist state machinery to being Germany's traditional autonomous and multifunctional model of local governance. Furthermore, given the unprecedented socioeconomic problems of East Germany's transformation that local authorities were the first to cope with, the actors involved widely agreed from the outset that the territorial format that East Germany inherited from the Communist era (with the small counties, averaging some 60,000 inhabitants, and the small, if not tiny, municipalities, averaging some 2,000 inhabitants, half of them with fewer than 500 inhabitants) was entirely inadequate for meeting this challenge. This view was particularly voiced by West German experts, who, coming as "administrative aides" *(Verwaltungshelfer)* from West German *Länder* and local authorities, carried with them the experiences and criteria relating to the territorial reforms that occurred in West German *Länder* during the late 1960s and early 1970s.

Not surprisingly, the rapidly unfolding political debate on the necessity of territorial reforms was noticeably propelled by the "West German model," and the criteria of territorial reforms were thus "exogenously" influenced. At the same time, however, the reform concepts and strategies that the East German actors articulated and pursued were shaped by specific East German concerns and, hence, bore "endogenous" traces.

Municipal Territorial Reforms

The decision of East German *Länder* governments and parliaments (with the notable exception of *Land Sachsen;* see Figure 6.1) to form areal jurisdictions of municipalities was informed by and a response to the political and emotional circumstances of East Germany's "peaceful revolution" in late 1989 and early 1990. Notwithstanding the great number of small localities, and in obvious defiance of expert advice (particularly referring to West German criteria and practice), the governments and parliaments of four East German *Länder* decided to do entirely without merging and amalgamating existing municipalities (which, during the municipal territorial reforms in the "old" Federal Republic, even the more cautiously proceeding *Länder* had not done in such "radical" abstention).

While leaving the existing municipalities territorially unchanged, the four *Länder* centred their strategy, as a kind of "soft" variant of territorial reforms, on the creation of joint authorities of which the municipalities were obliged to become members and that were to serve as administrative support units for them. While this strategy drew on West Germany's past reform experience with such joint authorities (see Table 6.1, column 7), the East German *Länder* made the municipalities resort to joint authorities at a rate of over 80 percent (and, in the cases of Brandenburg and Mecklenburg-Vorpommern [see Figure 6.1], nearly 100 percent), presumably as a reaction to and compensation for completely abstaining from amalgamation.

As the political debates revealed, complete restraint from abolishing municipalities by way of amalgamation was motivated by the political concern of the governments and parliaments in these *Länder* that it would be politically and morally intolerable to do away with even the smallest municipalities as the local political and democratic arenas. These municipalities had revived and reemerged as the crucial political achievement of the "democratic revolution" that, in many ways, was a victory of basic democratic movements and roundtables not least in small localities (Wollmann 1997a). Apart from the respect paid to the political legacy of East Germany's "political turn-around" *(Wende)*, the restraint was also nourished by political pragmatism, since it was well known from the West German experience (and communicated and confirmed by West German experts and advisors) that carrying out municipal territorial reforms, particularly in the form of amalgamation, was prone to arouse serious political conflicts that it seemed advisable to avoid.

The four East German *Länder* that introduced joint authorities also undertook the reform of counties, which went into effect in December 1993 (in Brandenburg) and June 1994 (in the other three *Länder*). Drawing on the pertinent institutional designs put in place in West German *Länder* during the territorial reform wave of the 1960s and 1970s, the joint authorities (under the different labels of *Amt, Verwaltungsgemeinschaft,* and *Verwaltungsgemeinde*) were meant to serve as the administrative support units and agencies for their member municipalities, which continued to operate as the political entities of local self-government. The joint authorities are run by boards whose members are appointed by the elected councils of the member municipalities. Their administrative staffs are directed by an administrative head (in the case of an *Amt* by the *Amtsdirektor*) appointed by and accountable to the board.

Land Sachsen's Early Course toward Amalgamation and Unitary Municipalities

Unlike the other four East German *Länder*, Sachsen's new government decided from the beginning to embark on a municipal territorial reform strategy that focused on the creation of unitary municipalities while pushing the formation of joint authorities for remaining smaller municipalities. The reason for Sachsen's reform strategy may be explained by the comparatively high degree of urbanization and industrialization of that

Land (expressed in a relatively high population density; see Table 6.3, column 2).

This strategy may also have been influenced by the fact that *Land Sachsen*, during the crucial reform period, cooperated closely with the (West German) *Länder Bayern* and *Baden-Württemberg* (Figure 6.1), which, as previously mentioned, had similar territorial reform strategies during the 1960s and 1970s. This strategy followed a middle-of-the-road course in pushing for the creation of new unitary municipalities and, at the same time, promoting the establishment of joint authorities. Evidently, West German advisors from these *Länder* were instrumental in persuading Sachsen's *Land* government to pursue a more determined course toward municipal territorial reforms from the outset (Wollmann 1997a, 293, with references). In a politically skillful mix of persuasion and financial incentives, the *Land* government succeeded, in the initial "voluntary" phase, in inducing as many as 75 percent of the municipalities to go along with its proposed reform concept. For the rest, the *Land* parliament decided by legislative fiat, which went into effect on 1 January 1999 (see Schnabel 2001, 394). As a result, the total number of municipalities was reduced from approximately 1,600 to 547 – that is, by two-thirds – with 60 percent of the municipalities linked to, and administratively served by, joint authorities (Table 6.3).

County Territorial Reforms

With regard to the counties, there was complete agreement from the beginning in all five new *Länder* that a territorial reform of the county boundaries, which had been left by the GDR's socialist state, was urgently needed. Enlarging the county territories, which had an average population of 60,000 compared with some 170,000 in the "old" Federal Republic as a result of the reforms in the 1960s and 1970s, was generally deemed indispensable for building up a county administrative structure capable of coping with the new demands of the "multipurpose" model of local (county) government and to the other problem associated with the transformation period (Wollmann 1997a, 289 ff., for details and references). In a rapid sequence of steps, working groups, with a heavy dose of West German expertise, were formed, and concepts and guidelines for territorial county reform were put forward by the *Länder* governments and swiftly put through by the *Länder* parliaments. Local conflict and protest flared up on the issue of which municipalities should be the seat of the new county's administration rather than on the direct issue of the appropriateness of merging counties. The territorial county reforms were politically debated and decided, in the last resort by legislative fiat of the *Länder* parliaments, in a remarkably brief period of time, particularly when compared with the protracted conflicts in the West German *Länder* during the late 1960s and

Table 6.3

Changes to the number of municipalities between 1990 and 1998 (East Germany)

Länder	Population	Population density (km²)	Total no. of municipalities in 1968	Total no. of municipalities in 1978	Reduction (%)	Average population (after reform)	% of municipalities having joint authorities
Brandenburg	2.5	88	1,739	1,739	0	1,500	96.8
Mecklenburg-Vorpommern	1.7	77	1,149	1,149	0	1,560	95.4
Sachsen	4.4	241	1,626	547	66	8,100	62
Sachsen-Anhalt	2.6	129	1,270	1,270	0	2,000	83.5
Thüringen	2.4	151	1,025	1,025	0	2,300	85.7
East Germany			**6,809**			**2,200**	

Sources: Wollmann (1997, 291); Laux (1999); Schnabel (2001, 394 ff.).

early 1970s. The territorial county reforms went into effect in December 1993 in Brandenburg and in June 1994 in the other four *Länder*.

In the restructuring of the counties, two patterns can be discerned (Table 6.4). *Land Brandenburg* and *Land Mecklenburg-Vorpommern* went furthest in reducing the number of counties (by almost two-thirds) and thus creating geographically large counties. As these two (comparatively sparsely populated) *Länder* decided to do without administrative districts (*Bezirksregierungen*, an administrative meso level between the *Land* government and the local government levels), the counties were seen also to play a meso role in addition to their typical county functions.

In the other three East German *Länder*, the number of counties was approximately halved. With a population between 100,000 and 130,000, the counties in the East German *Länder* remain, even after the territorial reform, significantly smaller than the counties in West Germany (with an average size of 170,000 inhabitants) (Table 6.4).

New Round of Municipal Territorial Reforms since the Late 1990s

In recent years, the East German *Länder*, which in the early 1990s decided against more deep-reaching territorial reform of their municipalities, have conspicuously changed their earlier strategy and have begun to push for a significant reduction of the number of existing small municipalities and an enlargement of the unitary municipalities by way of amalgamation. A number of factors explain this policy shift.

The East German *Länder* experienced, throughout the 1990s, precarious economic development, with the unemployment rate jumping as high as 18 percent (compared with 9 percent in the "old" Federal Republic) and with a continuing out-migration particularly of the younger age groups from rural areas to the East German urban centres and to West Germany. As rural areas experience a creeping process of depopulation, more and more small localities are becoming shams of local self-governments. (It has been reported, for instance, that in such small places it has become increasingly difficult to find candidates to have proper local council elections.) Thus, the erstwhile politically convincing argument that the multitude of small municipalities should be retained for the sake of "local democracy" has been losing legitimacy, just as the spell of the "democratic revolution" of late 1989 has been fading.

The concept of joint authorities has also come under growing criticism for a number of reasons. As a result of the great number and small size of the member municipalities, the joint authorities have been overburdened with minor technical matters that often prevent them from addressing the relevant problems within their jurisdictions. At the same time, problems of coordination and communication among the many member municipalities and their respective joint authorities have become increasingly

Table 6.4

Changes to counties between 1990 and 1998 (East Germany)

Länder	Population	Population density (km²)	Total no. of counties in 1990	Total no. of counties in 1998	Reduction (%)	Average population (after reform)
Brandenburg	2.5	88	38	14	65	143,000
Mecklenburg-Vorpommern	1.7	77	31	12	61.3	103,000
Sachsen	4.4	241	48	23	52.1	138,000
Sachsen-Anhalt	2.6	29	37	21	43.3	102,000
Thuringen	2.4	151	35	17	51.5	116,000
East Germany			**189**	**87**		

Sources: Mattenklodt (1981, 156 ff.); Laux (1993, 140); author's own calculations.

difficult. And political and personal frictions between the (part-time) mayors of the member municipalities and the director of the joint authority heading its professional staff have increased.

Criticism has also been voiced that installing the joint authorities as a new institutional layer has resulted in "institutional overcrowding" and "overinstitutionalization"; a "simpler" institutional design would be more suitable and sufficient. In the case of *Land Sachsen-Anhalt* (which, with 2.4 million inhabitants, is among the demographically smallest *Länder*), for instance, the joint authorities constitute a fifth institutional level within that organizational setting of the *Land,* in addition to the *Land* government, the administrative (meso) district, the county level, and the municipal level.

In the meantime, in all four East German *Länder,* the political debate and the legislative process will likely result in a significant reduction of the existing municipalities by way of amalgamation and the formation of unitary municipalities. In *Land Brandenburg,* for instance, the government put forward on 11 July 1990 concepts and guidelines pertaining to the future territorial design of the municipal level. The initial "voluntary phase" was meant to find, among as many municipalities as possible, acceptance of the proposed reform scheme. Recently, on 28 February 2001, the *Land* parliament passed a legislative act that practically finalizes the municipal territorial reform – against protests from the municipalities concerned and the municipal associations. Similarly, in the other East German *Länder,* the discussion and legislation on municipal territorial reforms have gained momentum. The new round of municipal territorial reform is scheduled to be completed at the latest by 2004 – that is, at the date of the next local council elections.

Functional Reforms

Falling in line with, and drawing on the pertinent concepts and experiences in the "old" Federal Republic, the territorial reforms of the local government levels of the East German *Länder* have, from the outset, been geared toward the idea that the pursuit of local level territorial reforms should be accompanied and followed by *functional reforms* in terms of transferring further public tasks from state agencies to local authorities. In fact, in East Germany's institutional transformation, the pursuit of functional reforms seems to be particularly relevant because, right after unification, in the initial phase of buildup of the *Länder* administration, a number of significant administrative functions and responsibilities (e.g., in environmental protection) were put in the hands of (single-purpose sectoral) administrative units of *Land* administration. In most West German *Länder,* these responsibilities have been transferred ("delegated"), by way of functional reforms, to the multipurpose competence of the local authorities.

On this background, in the East German reform debates, local level territorial reforms have been seen as important steps in preparing the ground to make the East German local authorities, as it were, administratively more fit to take on such additional delegated responsibilities and to further move toward the "normalcy" of the (West) German administrative world (see Wollmann 1997a, 294 ff.; and Wegrich et al. 1997, 43 ff., for further details on the functional reforms in the East German *Länder*). Germany's functional reforms and their influence on the debate concerning local government boundaries can be compared to the recent cases of municipal amalgamation in both Ontario and Quebec presented in Chapter 5.

Concluding Remarks: Territorial Reforms – A Vehicle toward a "Municipalization" of the Administrative Functions of the State?

Germany has experienced two waves of territorial reform of local government levels: in the "old" Federal Republic during the late 1960s and early 1970s and, after German unification, in East Germany during the 1990s. In internationally comparative terms, local level territorial reforms in Germany have, by and large (allowance made for significant variance between the *Länder*), pursued a middle-of-the-road strategy – between the relatively radical course of large-scale amalgamation ("northern European" approach), on the one pole, and the conversely radical option of refraining from redrawing the municipal boundaries ("southern European" approach), on the other.

Despite this middle-of-the-road approach to local level territorial reforms pursued by the German *Länder* (in the "old" Federal Republic as well as in East Germany), the impact on the country's entire administrative world was incisive if not fundamental. The reason lies in the key administrative role that the local authorities play in the entire intergovernmental setting of policy implementation, law application, and service delivery. As repeatedly highlighted in this chapter, this functional scope of local government (which, in international comparison, seems to be wider than in most other countries) has its roots in the territory-based, multifunctional, and general purpose model endemic to the German local government tradition.

While the discharge of public tasks and responsibilities at the local level through *general purpose* local government has thus been the rule in the German administrative tradition, the conduct by *special purpose* (sectoral) administrative units of state *(Land)* administration, operating at the local level outside local government, has been the exception. This functional prevalence of the territory-based, multifunctional, and general purpose model can be seen as a "path-dependent" characteristic of Germany's administrative system and probably shows in what Frido Wagener once called "the historical orientation (of German administration) towards territory" (quoted in Fürst 1996, 120).

While the territorial enlargement of local level government has, no doubt, contributed to strengthening the administrative capacity of the local authorities, it may have weakened the democratic legitimacy of local government and the political allegiance of the citizens and their (emotional) identification with the local world. In the German case, the number of elected councillors, for instance, has been significantly reduced as a result of amalgamation. Furthermore, local experience suggests that the emotional loss that local residents suffered when their locality lost its historically grown self-standing status and name is still significant even thirty years after this event. Yet there are counterindications. For instance, voter turnout (if one accepts this as an indicator of political participation and "identification") has remained remarkably high (also by international standards) over the years, ranging between 60 and 70 percent in local council elections. Moreover, since the early 1990s, the *Länder* governments have, in a remarkable sequence of congruent legislative acts, introduced direct democratic procedures into local politics, such as direct election of the mayors and (binding) local referendums (see Wollmann 2000b, 122 ff.). Hence, it can plausibly be argued that the political profile of local government, not least in the perception and political participation of the citizens, has, by and large, been not weakened but more recently even strengthened.

This (tentative) assessment may allow me to end this chapter with a fairly optimistic, albeit speculative, outlook. On Germany's (all but "path-dependent") trajectory of local government hinging on a territory-based, multifunctional model, territorial reforms have proven (and might increasingly prove in the future) to be an important precondition and vehicle for further functional reforms in terms of transferring public functions from (special purpose) state agencies to the (general purpose) local authorities. Such functional reforms might, in turn, usher in what has been called a progressive "municipalization" or "communalization" of the public (administrative) functions of the state (see Wollmann 1997b).

At the same time, advancement of citizen rights, including local referendums and the direct election of mayors, can be conducive to strengthening the political profile of a local government and the political accountability of its (political as well as administrative) actors before the citizens. So the contours of a democratically vigorous and functionally strong local government model gain insight. In the internationally comparative perspective, similar trends can be identified in the Scandinavian countries. Anglo-Saxon countries, however, seem to be removed – with local government being functionally beset and reduced by the expansion, encouraged by the central government, of single-purpose agencies and "quangos" while being politically enfeebled by the detachment of local citizens.

References

Fürst, Dietrich. 1996. "The Regional Districts in Search of a New Role." In Arthur Benz and Klaus Goetz, eds., *A New German Public Sector? Reform, Adaptation, and Stability*, 119-36. Aldershot: Dartmouth.
Gunlicks, Arthur. 1981. "The Reorganization of Local Government in the Federal Republic of Germany." In Arthur Gunlicks, ed., *Local Government in the German Federal State*, 62-89. Durham: Duke University Press.
Gunst, Dietrich. 1990. "Gebietsreform, Bürgerwille, und Demokratie." *Archiv für Kommunalwissenschaften* 29, 2: 189-209.
Marcou, Gérard, and Imre Verebelyi. 1993. *New Trends in Local-Government in Western and Eastern Europe*. Brussels: International Institute of Administrative Sciences.
Mattenklodt, Herbert-Fritz. 1981. "Territoriale Gliederung: Gemeoinden und Kreise vor uind nach der Gebietsreform." In Günter Püttner, ed., *Handbuch der kommunalen Wissenschaft und Praxis*, 154-82. Vol. 1. 2nd ed. Berlin: Springer.
Norton, A. 1994. *International Handbook of Local and Regional Government*. Aldershot: Edward Elgar.
Schnabel, Fritz. 2001. "Kommunale Gebietsreform im Freistaat Sachsen." In Eckhard Schröter, ed., *Empirische Policy und Verwaltungsforschung*, 392-98. Opladen: Leske and Budrich.
Seibel, Wolfgang. 2001. "Administrative Reforms." In Klaus König and Heinrich Siedentopf, eds., *Public Administration in Germany*, 73-89. Baden-Baden: Nomos.
Stern, Klaus. 1981. "Die Verfassungsgarantie der kommunalen Selbstverwaltung." In Günter Püttner, ed., *Handbuch der kommunalen Wissenschaft und Praxis*, 204-28. Vol. 1. 2nd ed. Berlin: Springer.
Stüer, Bernhard. 1978. "Verfassungsfragen der Gebietsreform." In *Die Öffentliche Verwaltung*, 78-92.
Thieme, W., and G. Prillwitz. 1981. *Durchführung und Ergebnisse der kommunalen Gebietsreform*. Baden-Baden: Nomos.
Wagener, Frido. 1980. "West Germany: A Survey." In D.C. Rowat, ed., *International Handbook on Local Government Organization*. Westport: Greenwood Press.
Wegrich, Kai, Wolfgang Jaedicke, Sabine Lorenz, und Hellmut Wollmann. 1997. *Kommunale Verwaltungspolitik in Ostdeutschland*. Basel: Birkhäuser.
Wollmann, Hellmut. 1996a. "The Transformation of Local Government in East Germany: Between Imposed and Innovative Institutionalization." In Arthur Benz and Klaus Goetz, eds., *A New German Public Sector?*, 137-63. Aldershot: Dartmouth.
—. 1996b. "Institutionenbildung in Ostdeutschland: Neubau, Umbau, und 'schöpferische' Zerstörung." In Max Kaase et al., eds., *Politisches System*, 47-153. Opladen: Leske and Budrich.
—. 1997a. "Transformation der ostdeutschen Kommunalstrukturen: Rezeption, Eigenentwicklung, Innovation." In Hellmut Wollmann et al., eds., *Transformation der politisch-administrativen Strukturen in Ostdeutschland*, 259-327. Opladen: Leske and Budrich.
—. 1997b. "'Echte Kommunalisierung' der Verwaltungsaufgaben: Innovatives Leitbild für eine umfassende Funktionalreform?" In *Landes und Kommunalverwaltung* 1: 105-21.
—. 2000a. "Local Government Systems: From Historic Divergence towards Convergence? Great Britain, France, and Germany as (Comparative) Cases in Point." In *Government and Policy* 18: 33-55.
—. 2000b. "The Development and Present State of Local Government in England and Germany: A Comparison." In Hellmut Wollmann and Eckhard Schröter, eds., *Comparing Public Sector Reform in Britain and Germany: Key Traditions and Trends of Modernization*, 107-31. Aldershot: Ashgate.
—. 2002. "Local Politics and Government in East Germany." In Harald Baldersheim, Michal Illner, and Hellmut Wollmann, eds., *Local Politics and Government in Former Socialist Countries*. Opladen: Leske and Budrich.

7
Changeless Boundaries Do Not Fix a Changing History: The Map of the Spanish Local Government
Abel Albet i Mas

> It's obvious that the real local concerns usually are not understood by far administrative bodies located in big cities where nothing recalls the fields, the forests and the beauty of the mountains ...
>
> But province, district and municipal borders are artificial, and they will also disappear but not before they break down many natural communities, disturbing in a thousand ways people's spontaneous movements.
>
> And if national boundaries depend on people's wishes and have to be modified according to their will, the same should be applied to the rest of the borders (conventionals as well) that artificially divide provinces and municipalities.
>
> It's a real contradiction to expect that a history that is in continuous transformation can be fixed through changeless borders.
>
> – Jean-Jacques Elisée Reclus, geographer and anarchist

Contemporary Development of Spain's Municipal Structure
Spain's contemporary municipal structure began with the liberal program of the Decree of 23 May 1812. In this decree, the municipality was recognized as a natural and individual body before the law, thus creating the framework for local councils to be established in localities. Before this legislation, Spain's local government organization was diverse. It was a product of the political, social, economic, and legal structures of the *ancien régime* and the legacy of medieval prerogatives. In this mixture, towns and villages without any kind of organization existed alongside cities with representation in the court, and constituted councils existed alongside noble dominions whose lords maintained the right to designate municipal leaders (Morell 1972, 52). The principle of equality had been imported from revolutionary France, and it had created more than 40,000 municipal bodies throughout the country, starting from the principle of equality of all citizens before the law. This setup led to the consideration in Spain that

any settlement of more than 1,000 inhabitants should constitute a local council. Smaller villages also received assistance to constitute a local council, including settlements with fewer than 100 inhabitants, when "other reasons of the public good" apparently made this advisable (Liesa 1972, 23).

This will to generalize the municipality, based on criteria of rationalization and homogenization, exemplifies the liberal tendency to abolish all kinds of privilege and to favour the formation of a market based on modern political-economic criteria. This municipalizing tendency was discontinued throughout the nineteenth and much of the twentieth centuries. Between 1812 and 1931, the basic legislation referring to the municipal organization of Spain was altered more than twenty times, with successive approvals and repeals of acts and the drawing up of another twenty that never got beyond the bill stage. This frequency of change reflects the political instability and alternating absolutist, liberal, and conservative governments that characterized Spain in this period, but it also demonstrates the importance given to the local government system.

The Military Directorate of General Primo de Rivera approved the Municipal Statute on 8 March 1924. Ideologically, this statute had few affinities with the dictatorship that implemented it; instead, it was based on a formula developed from the experiences of several aborted or inadequate previous projects. This technical and conceptually advanced (even progressive) statute recognized the municipality not exclusively as the product of a law but also as a fact of social coexistence previous to the state and even above the law itself. Given the evident lack of synchronization between the theories in the Municipal Statute and the political principles of the Military Directorate, few of its articles were ever put into practical application (Tusell and Chacón 1973).

According to the Republican Constitution passed in 1931, the central state and the autonomous regions, where constituted, shared the legislative power of the new regime. Owing to this opportunity, the Catalan Municipal Act was approved in August 1933, almost two years before the Basic Local Government Act of Spain was passed in July 1935. In the latter act, the full autonomy of municipalities was recognized, whether or not the mayor, who was chair of the council, maintained his position as representative of the state administration within the municipal boundaries.

However, during the Spanish Civil War (1936-39) and as a consequence of the Revolution of July 1936, many urban and rural municipalities organized themselves along communal lines. They based their restructuring on the socialist, communist, and anarchist principles put forward by the workers and peasant leaders who challenged many councils' administrations. Despite the exceptional circumstances dictated by the war, the experiment with alternative revolutionary governments can be considered successful.

On the other hand, the rebel faction of the republican army commanded by General Franco created "management committees" in areas under its control. These committees took the place of democratically constituted councils and consisted of new-order enthusiasts from the local public. After the war, various decrees and laws, which culminated in the Basic Organic Local Government Act of 1945 and the Revised Text of 1955, removed any form of democratic representation from local councils. Because it held state representation in the municipality, the authoritarian regime justified direct designation and the indefinite duration of terms of public office.

The Historical Development of Legislation for Municipal Change

The 1845 Municipal Corporations Law established the first measures to correct Spain's municipal map, albeit in an extremely timid form, with the proposal of eliminating all municipalities with fewer than thirty inhabitants. This minimum threshold increased to 50 inhabitants in an 1856 law and to 200 inhabitants in an 1866 law; in all cases, these measures were solely guidelines and were never compulsory. The Municipal Act of 1877 clarified the problems created by the rapid growth of Spain's large cities and presented the possibility of incorporating the localities and municipalities within ten kilometres of Madrid and within six kilometres of other cities containing more than 100,000 inhabitants.

Not until the Municipal Statute of 1924 had precise rules existed that clearly distinguished between the concepts of constitution, annexation, and alteration of municipalities. In all cases, the statute required the approval of the majority of the residents in the municipality and two-thirds of its councillors. In the case of separation, the statute provided that it could not be carried out in detriment to the independent wealth of the new municipalities. Any alteration required the exclusive agreement of the bodies involved and communication of this agreement to the civil governor of the province. This agreement illustrates the municipal sovereignty granted by this statute, notwithstanding that the central government could intervene in a matter of "general interest." General interest included incorporation of municipalities and cities of more than 100,000 inhabitants and forced annexation of municipalities with fewer than 2,000 inhabitants.

The Catalan Municipal Act of 1933 also distinguished various possibilities, such as annexation or separation, for altering municipal boundaries. The only corrective measure established by the Catalan Municipal Act was the compulsory association of municipalities in which the council secretary's salary was above 20 percent of the ordinary budget. Later the Spanish Municipal Act created a detailed typology of possible boundary modifications, noting the minimum requirements and procedures for each type.

Francoist legislation concerning the alteration of municipal boundaries, such as the Population and Territorial Boundaries Act of 1952, furthered the Basic Act and the Revised Text. Although this legislation was difficult to interpret, four possibilities for changing a municipality could be extracted from it: incorporation, amalgamation, separation, and annexation.

Again, in the case of expansion and confusion of urban centres, municipalities could start annexation procedures. In practice, this possibility was almost exclusively applied in the case of Madrid, clearly for political reasons associated with capital glorification. At the same time, obstacles were created for similar procedures in Barcelona. This type of dysfunction was, and still is, problematic in Barcelona (Nadal 1985). The annexation procedures could be initiated by local councils, by the central government, by the provincial councils, and by the state provincial governments. In all cases, the final decision belonged to the cabinet of ministers. Even in the best case, when all the reports required to formalize and justify the decisions were eventually completed, they often did not have the slightest degree of objectivity.

Evaluation of the Municipal Map's Legacy

Although the total number of municipalities in Spain decreased considerably between 1815 and 1860, this reduction resulted not from precise planning but from a logical adjustment by the recently installed municipal system. However, this revision did not have definite continuity. So, by the beginning of the twenty-first century, the municipal configuration of Spain remained relatively unchanged from that at the beginning of the nineteenth century.

Despite this lack of municipal change, the 1960s were characterized by a large number of municipal amalgamations and annexations resulting from the socioeconomic changes experienced by the whole country. Furthermore, these amalgamations and annexations were partly encouraged by the Partial Modification of the Basic Organic Local Government Act of 1945 passed in 1966, which provided subsidies and financial incentives directed at "groupings of municipalities" or bodies that had decided on amalgamation or annexation. This act was the exception in the middle of the legislative desert of the 1960s and 1970s on the subject. Using structural improvement as bait, the government ordered an immediate and systematic reduction in the overall number of municipalities. As a result, many small municipalities were pressured into "disappearing from the map."

In 1977, the government abandoned this policy of incentives, and, with it, disappeared the only inducement toward the integration of local authorities (even if it was inoperative and insufficiently used). Although 1,025 municipalities disappeared in Spain between 1966 and 1976 (Sosa and de Miguel 1987, 55), these legal incentives were the cause in only a few cases. Similarly, the success and the consequences of this legal channel must be evaluated based on the fact that many of the merged municipalities would later become independent again.

The municipal changes in Spain of the past forty years have resulted not from general policies or territorial planning but from the directive of the Ministry of Internal Affairs to systematically reduce the total number of municipalities. This directive was carried out by the various county councils and civil governments. The changes were sought only in municipalities where local initiative and support, private or public, proved significant enough to warrant action by the administration or, contrarily, where the population and local social forces did not have enough power to react to imposed annexations. In the latter case, many municipalities in Spain's mountains almost always merged in an arbitrary manner, and this procedure added to the serious dysfunctions.

Based on the above review, we can understand why a large number of municipalities disappeared during this period at the initiative of the provincial councils *(diputaciones)* of Soria, Segovia, Huesca, Guadalajara, Cuenca, and Burgos (INE 1981). In Catalonia, between the late 1960s and the early 1970s, the chair of the *Diputación* of Lleida undertook the systematic reduction of the number of Lleidan municipalities. At the time, leaders of Lleida's local administration considered the decrease from 320 municipalities in 1961 to 245 in 1971 "a great success and a great step towards modernity" (Liesa 1972, 3). The total change in the number of municipalities between 1900 and 2000 is noted in Table 7.1. Tables 7.2 and 7.3 compare the existing number of municipalities to the number of inhabitants and the total land area. Table 7.4 provides a numeric summary of the total number of local bodies for each autonomous community.

Despite the urgent need to resolve excessive fragmentation and the existence of many municipalities with scarce population and resources, the solution adopted by many municipalities was annexation. Their simple objective was to economize on administrative and management structures, and on infrastructure and services, but without seeking coherence between the new municipal units. Many municipalities had much of their historical inheritance eradicated with one stroke, thereby depriving the inhabitants of a channel of participation and direct management. On only a few occasions were the disappearing municipalities converted into "lesser local bodies."

Historical perspective has clearly demonstrated that such reform processes often seriously affected the character and individual identity of villages, valleys, and municipalities and even the coherence of counties. For example, in the High Pyrenees region, a large number of the annexations were based on faulty functional criteria. Neighbouring municipalities could be obliged to merge simply because they were contiguous, without any consideration of the possible affinities of their respective sources of economic resources, land relief, internal accessibility, traditions, and human relationships. In this way, some artificial, and even clearly absurd, new municipal bodies were formed (Mateu 1988, 34-40).

Table 7.1

Total number of municipalities in Spain, 1900-2000

Autonomous communities	1900	1910	1920	1930	1940	1950	1960	1970	1980	1990	2000
Andalusia	801	800	802	799	804	799	799	796	760	767	769
Aragon	947	947	946	944	942	935	935	820	725	729	730
Asturias	79	79	79	78	78	78	78	78	78	78	78
Balearic Islands	61	62	61	65	65	65	65	65	65	67	67
Basque Country	294	295	295	281	280	275	271	241	226	245	250
Canary Islands	90	90	91	90	89	88	87	87	87	87	87
Cantabria	102	102	102	102	102	102	102	102	102	102	102
Castilla y Leon	2,809	2,806	2,805	2,811	2,808	2,803	2,797	2,572	2,251	2,247	2,249
Castilla-La Mancha	1,071	1,071	1,072	1,088	1,087	1,086	1,085	1,004	912	915	919
Catalonia	1,075	1,073	1,070	1,062	1,064	1,059	1,059	976	936	942	946
Extremadura	384	383	383	388	386	385	385	381	380	380	383
Galicia	323	322	319	319	319	316	315	312	312	313	315
La Rioja	184	183	183	183	182	183	184	183	174	174	174
Madrid	195	195	195	196	196	184	183	183	176	178	179
Murcia	42	42	42	42	42	42	43	43	43	44	45
Navarra	269	269	269	267	266	265	265	265	264	265	273
Valencian Community	540	542	541	545	545	545	547	545	534	538	541
Ceuta and Melilla	2	2	2	2	2	2	2	2	2	2	2
Spain	9,268	9,263	9,257	9,262	9,257	9,212	9,202	8,655	8,027	8,073	8,109

Source: Census data.

Table 7.2

Number of municipalities according to population, Spain, 1999

Autonomous communities	(A)	(B)	(C)	(D)	(E)	(F)	(G)	(H)	(I)	(J)
Andalusia	769	2	88	95	338	184	51	9	2	9,500
Aragon	730	141	386	92	91	17	2	0	1	1,626
Asturias	78	0	4	12	32	22	6	2	0	13,901
Balearic Islands	67	0	2	8	27	21	8	1	0	12,266
Basque Country	250	4	66	42	75	45	15	3	0	8,402
Canary Islands	87	0	0	1	27	42	14	3	0	19,226
Cantabria	102	2	12	18	53	14	2	1	0	5,181
Castilla y Leon	2,247	419	1,241	301	238	34	10	4	0	1,107
Castilla-La Mancha	915	188	313	133	221	47	12	1	0	1,887
Catalonia	946	30	333	162	259	117	36	8	1	6,562
Extremadura	382	1	85	98	157	34	6	1	0	2,810
Galicia	315	0	1	12	178	105	16	3	0	8,668
La Rioja	174	49	83	16	19	6	0	1	0	1,524
Madrid	179	14	30	21	64	25	18	6	1	28,745
Murcia	45	0	0	2	7	24	10	2	0	25,136
Navarra	272	32	124	36	65	12	2	1	0	1,978
Valencian Community	541	23	128	83	170	95	38	3	1	7,517
Ceuta and Melilla	2	0	0	0	0	0	2	0	0	65,317
Spain	**8,101**	**905**	**2,896**	**1,132**	**2,021**	**844**	**248**	**49**	**6**	**4,963**

Notes: (A) Total number of municipalities.
(B) Municipalities to 100 inhabitants.
(C) Municipalities from 101 to 500 inhabitants.
(D) Municipalities from 501 to 1000 inhabitants.
(E) Municipalities from 1,001 to 5,000 inhabitants.
(F) Municipalities from 5,001 to 20,000 inhabitants.
(G) Municipalities from 20,001 to 100,000 inhabitants.
(H) Municipalities from 100,001 to 500,000 inhabitants.
(I) Municipalities with more than 500,000 inhabitants.
(J) Average population per municipality.

Source: Census data.

Table 7.3

Number of municipalities according to surface area, Spain, 2000

Autonomous communities	(A)	(B)	(C)	(D)	(E)	(F)	(G)	(H)
Andalusia	769	20	104	204	180	197	64	113.9
Aragon	730	19	130	282	169	114	16	65.4
Asturias	78	0	3	15	25	27	8	135.9
Balearic Islands	67	2	12	20	15	17	1	74.5
Basque Country	250	33	109	67	30	11	0	28.9
Canary Islands	87	0	7	36	14	27	3	86.1
Cantabria	102	1	21	45	28	7	0	52.2
Castilla y Leon	2,249	21	704	981	372	163	8	41.9
Castilla-La Mancha	919	10	133	328	221	184	43	86.5
Catalonia	946	47	374	334	140	50	1	33.9
Extremadura	383	8	35	114	105	98	23	108.7
Galicia	315	1	11	76	111	111	5	93.9
La Rioja	174	12	85	55	18	4	0	29.0
Madrid	179	1	32	96	39	10	1	48.8
Murcia	45	0	8	10	5	11	11	251.4
Navarra	273	20	97	95	47	10	4	38.1
Valencian Community	541	82	167	144	91	51	6	43
Ceuta and Melilla	2	0	2	0	0	0	0	15.8
Spain	**8,109**	**277**	**2,034**	**2,902**	**1,610**	**1,092**	**194**	**62.4**

Notes:
(A) Total number of municipalities.
(B) Municipalities to 5 km^2.
(C) Municipalities from 5.1 to 20 km^2.
(D) Municipalities from 20.1 to 50 km^2.
(E) Municipalities from 50.1 to 100 km^2.
(F) Municipalities from 100.1 to 300 km^2.
(G) Municipalities with more than 300 km^2.
(H) Average surface per municipality.

Source: Census data.

Table 7.4

Number of local bodies, Spain, 2000

Autonomous communities	(A)	(B)	(C)	(D)	(E)	(F)	(G)	(H)
Andalusia	769	8	80	0	0	0	35	892
Aragon	730	3	87	1	0	15	43	879
Asturias	78	–	13	0	0	1	37	129
Balearic Islands	67	3	7	0	0	0	1	78
Basque Country	250	3	36	7	0	1	338	635
Canary Islands	87	9	18	0	0	0	0	114
Cantabria	102	–	9	0	0	1	526	638
Castilla y Leon	2,249	9	200	1	0	32	2,229	4,720
Castilla-La Mancha	919	5	111	0	0	4	33	1,072
Catalonia	946	4	77	41	2	1	54	1,125
Extremadura	383	2	81	0	0	0	25	491
Galicia	315	4	37	0	0	0	9	365
La Rioja	174	–	19	0	0	6	4	203
Madrid	179	–	30	0	0	0	2	211
Murcia	45	–	8	0	0	0	0	53
Navarra	273	–	56	0	0	10	364	703
Valencian Community	541	3	56	0	0	0	8	608
Ceuta and Melilla	2	–	0	0	0	0	0	2
Spain	**8,109**	**53**	**925**	**50**	**2**	**71**	**3,708**	**12,918**

Notes: (A) Municipalities.
(B) Provincial (*diputación*) and insular bodies.
(C) Municipal associations (*mancomunidad*).
(D) County councils (*comarca*).
(E) Metropolitan areas.
(F) Other municipal associations.
(G) Minor local bodies (lower than municipalities).
(H) Total number of local bodies.

Source: Census data.

Due to the long abnormal situation suffered by the Catalan, Basque, and Galician languages and cultures during Francoism, local place names were also mistreated. In addition to many place names being converted to Spanish, the alteration of municipal boundaries sometimes meant the appearance of new names. On occasion, although they did not maintain a notable tradition, these names did pertain to the territories that they represented. However, in some places, important mistakes and even artificial constructions were found. Perhaps the most aberrant case appeared in Catalonia, where FORALLAC was the strange combination of syllables from the names of the three amalgamated municipalities (FOnteta, PeRAtallada, and VulpeLLAC).

The Current Legal Framework for Municipalities

Spain's political changes that began in 1976, which had their most spectacular moments in 1977 (legalization of political parties and the first general elections) and in 1978 (approval of the constitution and beginning of the process toward regional autonomy), did not affect local institutions until 1979, when municipal elections were held and democratic local councils were created for the first time since 1939.

The Spanish Constitution of 1978 recognizes the local level as one of the three spheres of power into which the country is organized. The other two are the central state and the autonomous regional communities. The constitution also establishes that local government regulation is shared between the central state and the respective regional autonomous governments instead of being under the exclusive jurisdiction of either. So superimposed on top of the state legislation, which takes priority, is the legislation that some autonomous communities may make. In this way, the central state reserves the right to determine the basis for the legal regime of local public administrations. The autonomous communities assume powers over municipal boundary alterations inside their territories and, in general, the functions over local corporations corresponding to the state administration.

In this sense, the Basic Regulatory Local Government Act passed on 2 April 1985 emerged as both the generic framework that inspired the rest of the state legislation on local issues and the vital reference point for particular sets of regulations developed by some autonomous communities. The act recognizes a range of "local entities": municipalities, provinces, islands, "lesser local bodies" (bodies inside a municipality), counties, metropolitan areas, and local communities (associations of municipalities). All are fully autonomous, with regulatory and executive power over finance and taxes, planning, compulsory purchase, executive action, and punishment.

Additionally, the municipality is recognized as the basic body for the state's territorial organization. It is defined by its territory, its population, and its organization. The Basic Regulatory Local Government Act reflects the rights and duties of residents as well as the organization, administration, and government of municipalities. The territorial aspects and those concerning population are treated in detail in the Royal Decree of 11 July 1986. Here the central state approved the regulating law for population and territorial boundaries of the local entities.

Catalonia (1987), Murcia (1988), Navarra (1990), Castile-la Mancha (1991), Andalusia (1993), La Rioja (1993), and Aragon (1999) are some of the autonomous communities that have passed legislation concerning local municipal administration. Asturias, the Balearic Islands, Cantabria, Castile and Leon, Extremadura, Galicia, and the Basque Country have some kind of law or decree referring to local communities and "lesser local bodies." Catalonia is one of the most exemplary and complete cases.

On 15 April 1987, Catalonia approved its own Municipal and Local Government Act, which established the maximum number of functions granted by its own Statute of Autonomy and the central state's Basic Law. Moreover, by a decree of 24 May 1988, the *Generalitat* of Catalonia (Catalan autonomous government) approved its own Regulation Law for Population and Territorial Boundaries of Local Entities using a specific form with greater precision than the central administration's regulations. The law regulated the essential features of the territories, names, symbols, and populations of the local Catalan entities.

In accordance with the principles of effectiveness, decentralization, anti-concentration, coordination, and participation, local entities must objectively serve their attached public interests. They exercise their functions with full autonomy, legal recognition, and responsibility. In this sense, the Basic Regulatory Local Government Act made all municipalities responsible for decisions concerning municipal boundaries, names, symbols, and census data as well as for a long list of "basic" functions depending on the number of inhabitants. They can also carry out certain other activities of a "complementary" nature.

From the outset, the clauses of the act foresaw that some municipalities would have to coordinate the delivery of some services, including those functions considered basic for all municipalities. Alternative channels for providing these services were established. These channels exempted those municipalities from that primary obligation. Among other reasons, this distribution of services could be granted for reasons such as lack of finances (services requiring more than 50 percent of the annual budget), particular arrangements of the territories and the settlements, or other technical reasons.

The act also recognizes that the lack of economic means, materials, and staff to manage the minimum compulsory services provides sufficient argument to annex the affected municipality to guarantee provision of essential services. Until now, annexation has not occurred based on these principles. Insufficiencies have been resolved through county councils and provincial governments. Both assist municipalities on technical or financial issues and in service coordination and management.

Current Legislation on Changes to Municipal Boundaries: The Legal Framework

The Basic Regulatory Local Government Act of 1985 and subsequent legislation have stemmed from the acceptance of the historical municipal system. The inherited inertia of this municipal system, considered altogether or case by case, is genuinely decisive. Although the possibilities for change occupy an extensive chapter in the current laws on local government, they are always suggested with restricted application, in particular cases, and without ever questioning the entire municipal structure. Any systematic reconsideration of the local government system would require a certain political will and a different – that is, more specific – legal background, not one with a Basic Act. It is also true that these subjects remain only vaguely noted: "it will be possible to establish measures that tend to encourage the annexation of municipalities" (chap. I, art. 13.3).

Therefore, the Basic Act expresses the generic aim of achieving the maximum number of municipal amalgamations in order to "improve the capacity to manage local public affairs" (art. 13.3), although the lack of practical incentives, necessarily of a financial kind, encouraging this process implies the de facto negation of these aims. However, rather paradoxically in recent years, the number of cases of municipal division has outnumbered municipal amalgamations despite the opposite intention of the central government. This development may be attributed to the lack of measures encouraging amalgamation and to the priority of municipal divisions for resolving problematic cases involving existing incoherent aggregations.

Possibilities for Changing Municipal Boundaries

Annexation and Amalgamation

Spanish legislation provides the following reasons for proceeding with the complete annexation of one or more municipalities: (1) the lack of financial means, materials, and/or staff to provide minimum compulsory services; (2) settlements that form an urban continuum; and (3) geographical, demographic, economic, or administrative situations that make it necessary. Under the second and third reasons, it is also possible to carry out partial annexations, or alterations that affect only part of the municipal area, but only if it is guaranteed that the municipality or municipalities can still provide the established minimum services. The procedures and requirements for amalgamations are the same as those described for cases of annexation. They apply only to neighbouring municipalities and involve the establishment of a new municipality replacing the former municipalities. The result is a completely new legal identity, administration, and name.

Segregation
Spanish legislation considers two possible types of municipal segregation: the first separates part of one or more municipalities to be joined to another municipality, and the second constitutes the removed part as an independent municipality. In the latter case, the Municipal Act requires a new municipality to affect territorially differentiated settlements, and the resulting municipalities should be able to carry out their municipal powers without a reduction in the quality of services. In any case, the Municipal Act requires an objectively evaluated justification of the improvement resulting from municipal changes.

Boundary Changes and Territorial Continuity
Although the legislation does not make specific references to the problems created by enclaves, the rationalization of territorial organization makes advisable a policy that tends toward the elimination of these "anomalies." It should start from the aggregation opportunities offered by the act itself (Sosa and de Miguel 1987, 86). This possible "normalization" of discontinuities, although always desirable, is not always easily achieved. In some cases, the issue can be resolved through compensatory agreements and pacts. In others, it requires delicate handling, and even special laws, if it affects different provinces or even different autonomous communities.

Name and Capital Changes
Current legislation maintains that the municipality's capital house the council's headquarters; any change requires two-thirds support of all councillors. A change in the municipality's name requires a similar agreement plus the final approval of the autonomous community's government. However, when faced with confusing names containing linguistic mistakes or not corresponding to local place names, the minister of internal affairs might propose a name change, although only with the agreement of specialized scientific institutions. Current legislation allows for a municipality's official name in Spanish, in another official language in each autonomous community, or simultaneously in both languages.

Legal Proceedings for Municipal Change
The Catalan Municipal Act recognizes that the process to change a municipal boundary can be initiated by the local councils involved, the county councils, the Ministry of Internal Affairs of the *Generalitat* of Catalonia, or

a petition of 50 percent of affected residents. The process must commence with a memorandum justifying the reasons for the change, receiving reports from all government bodies involved, including the Commission for Territorial Boundaries, and obtaining the opinion of the Legal Advisory Committee. Notably, the Catalan government is the final approval authority regarding boundary changes initiated by local councils or residents. Agreement must be unanimous or without objections from any other body involved.

The Boundary-Line Regulation Act recognizes that councils may promote the delimitation and marking of their boundaries. They have to communicate agreements to municipalities, owners of properties affected, and the Ministry of Internal Affairs of the *Generalitat* of Catalonia. The Commission for Territorial Boundaries, as a body for study, consultations, and proposals, is charged, on its own initiative, or at the request of the minister of internal affairs, to draw up proposals to correct problems relating to boundaries, enclaves, dysfunctions caused by infrastructures or urban continuums, and so on.

Policies for Municipal Change

Both the Basic Act and the Regulation Law for Population and Territorial Boundaries of Local Entities imply the need to establish policies to encourage municipal annexation and amalgamation, which still remain implicit. However, the Catalan Municipal Act in Articles 20 and 21 not only acts on this requirement but also proposes specific measures to stimulate voluntary annexation or amalgamation between municipalities. These economic stimuli provide financial and technical aid, preferential investment treatment, and other possible agreements and particular conditions established between municipalities in the framework of local government legislation.

The Boundary-Line Regulation Act appears to be more forceful than other legislation in that it lists specific possible reasons for proceeding with full municipal amalgamations, though application of some of the mentioned principles would be difficult or awkward. However, this legislation has been neglected since its approval because, if it were implemented, many municipalities would immediately see themselves open to questions because they are inhabited by fewer than 250 people. The act provides the opportunity to implement, on the part of the *Generalitat*, a process of compulsory annexation and/or amalgamation, though this process seems to be improbable.

The Current Legislation: Local Entities

Although the municipality is the best-known local entity, other local bodies have other levels of action. The Local Administration Department is responsible for creating and maintaining the Register of Local Entities.

This register contains lists of municipalities, counties, and provinces as well as lesser local bodies, local communities, metropolitan bodies, and other associations of municipalities. The proper management of some of these entities can provide a valid alternative to the necessary revision of the municipal map.

Lesser Local Bodies

Entities with a territorial scope smaller than the municipality ("decentralized municipal entities" according to the Catalan Municipal Act's terminology) may be constituted in settlements that make up a separate population structure within a municipality, but only if their constitution does not involve a reduced quality of general service, if they have enough resources to carry out their functions, or if there are necessitating geographical, historical, social, economic, or administrative circumstances. The initiative to constitute this body can be made either by a majority approval of residents or by the council itself.

Interestingly, the act recognizes the possibility that such a body might have a wide range of powers, possibly becoming the same as those of an independent municipality, if formed from the disappearance of an old municipality, either by addition or by merger. Also noteworthy is that the Municipal Act establishes that the approval of a lesser local entity involves defining its jurisdictional boundaries. This mandate implies that the body maintain a particular quality, identity, and well-defined and differentiated territorial nature, despite being integrated into the overall municipal entity and territory. The result is the preservation of an area's historical heritage, avoiding dilution in a wider organization or territory, plus the preservation of its administration and the identity of its inhabitants. In the case of municipal amalgamation, this preservation should overcome much citizen reticence.

Associations of Municipalities: Local Communities, Metropolitan Areas, and Counties

Local communities, metropolitan areas, and counties are, in fact, groups of municipalities created to make the provision of one or more services easier. They are a structural solution to certain problems of well-defined territorial areas but do not alter municipal institutions in question. Local communities *(mancomunidades)* are initiated by an agreement between the involved municipalities to perform common tasks or to manage services within their power for which collective management is more viable and rational. The legislation also allows the creation of metropolitan areas responsible for the planning, coordination, and management of municipal services requiring intermunicipal coordination, primarily because of the characteristics of the conurbation where they are performed. However, the act does not explicitly define when an association of municipalities can be considered "metropolitan."

Based on statutes established by some autonomous communities, the county is a legally recognized local entity formed by a group of adjoining municipalities. Take the case of Catalonia, where the county, not the province, is the traditional form of territorial organization and is responsible for providing public services of municipal or above municipal scope (Figures 7.1, 7.2, and 7.3). These areas can be converted into a decentralized level of the autonomous community government. In contrast to the other two municipal associations, county organization extends throughout the territory of the autonomous community, and no municipality can belong to only one county. Counties have their own form of government, consisting of a chair, an executive, and a council, and they can put legislative initiatives before the parliament. However, the importance of a county's power depends on the political will of the autonomous community's government.

Main Dysfunctions of the Current Municipal System

Faced with repeated lack of planning and minimal legislative provision, the failure to adapt the inherited municipal boundary coherently to the constantly changing reality of local life in Spain often created a series of dysfunctions that, on occasion, gave rise to serious problems.

Survival of Small Municipalities

Established criteria for classifying municipalities in terms of land area do not exist in Spain. There are considerable variations from the average land area of municipalities of approximately sixty-two square kilometres. Thus, it is necessary to differentiate between the large number of very small municipalities in Castille, the small municipalities in Catalonia, Aragon, and the Basque Country, and the very large municipalities in Murcia, Andalusia, and Extremadura, the final category corresponding to the final stage of the *Reconquista* (Gavira 1980, 35).

Classification by population size presents greater complexities than by land area because Spain has various definitions of what a "small" municipality constitutes: from those with fewer than 15,000 inhabitants to those with fewer than 1,000 inhabitants. Moreover, the different settlement patterns within municipalities must be considered. In the southern half of Spain, the population is heavily concentrated, and a municipality coincides with one population centre. Conversely, in Galicia and Asturias, the population is largely dispersed, so each municipality normally includes many villages and localities administratively organized into "parishes."

Enclaves and Arbitrary Municipal Boundaries

Enclaves are a territorial peculiarity that originated with the formation of municipalities themselves either during the Middle Ages or in the nineteenth century. Their purpose is attributed to historical, geographical, and economic issues, such as rights-of-way on paths, rivers, or pastures, old properties, seigneurial jurisdictions, and so on; on occasion, cartographic mistakes were the cause. There are hundreds of enclaves in Spain, many of which do not present special problems. Three enclaves are worthy of further discussion because of their territorial size, their involvement with municipalities, and their situation outside the provincial and autonomous community boundaries. There are documentary references dating back to

Figure 7.1

Municipal map of Catalonia, Spain, 2002

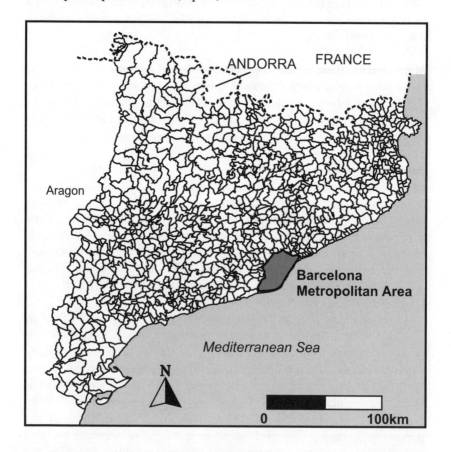

Note: One of the 946 pieces of this fragmented puzzle is the municipality of Llívia, a Spanish enclave in France.

the sixteenth century for the first two cases, Villaverde de Trucios (belonging to the autonomous community of Cantabria) and Condado de Treviño (belonging to Castile and Leon). Currently, their problem is especially relevant because their possible integration into the Basque Country, where they are enclaves, has notable political, cultural (the teaching of Basque), and, most significantly, economic implications, due to the special financial conditions enjoyed by the Basque Country.

The third case of Llívia, a Spanish enclave of 12.84 km^2 within France's boundaries, originated with the Treaty of the Pyrenees of 1659 that took away Catalonia's northern territory. The treaty mentioned that the "villages" of the northern slopes of the Pyrenees would be ceded to the kingdom

Figure 7.2

County *(comarca)* map of Catalonia, Spain, 2002

Note: The *comarca* is one of the traditional regional administrative levels of Catalonia; the forty-one county councils of the *comarques* have local government functions.

of France, so Llívia, because of its "town" status, avoided cession. Although this anomaly created serious problems over many years for its inhabitants, problems such as the removal of Europe's internal boundaries through the Treaty of Schengen, the establishment of the European Union has ended this isolation. However, the enclave formally remains.

Arbitrarily determined municipal boundaries present a similar problem. Akin to enclaves, these situations are simply anomalies of the historical process of boundary and frontier formations. They do not affect populated areas or areas that contain infrastructures and services. On the other hand, the established channels of municipal boundary changes (annexation or

Figure 7.3

Provincial boundaries of Catalonia, Spain, 2002

Note: Although initially imposed by the central Spanish government to establish its authority, nowadays the provincial *diputaciones* are local authorities that invest in municipalities and help to coordinate their policies.

division, partial or total) can resolve awkward situations because the legislation itself recognizes these situations as dysfunctions.

Recent Problems with Crossing Municipal Boundaries

The inherited municipal map maintains many, sometimes ancient, boundary disputes between neighbouring municipalities, whether they are over a few metres of land, the slope of a mountain, a beach, et cetera. These disputes usually originate in unclear delimitations and/or in areas with strong speculative interest.

Urban expansion in Spain since the 1950s, although not a new phenomenon, has shown itself to be an increasing tendency. Often growth spills over the limits of the respective municipal boundaries. If Madrid solved this problem by annexing neighbouring municipalities, however, the urban centre today is confused with almost all of its neighbours, to the extreme where pavements of the same street belong to different municipalities (Figure 7.4).

Figure 7.4

Barcelona's metropolitan area and its twenty-seven internal municipal boundaries, 2002

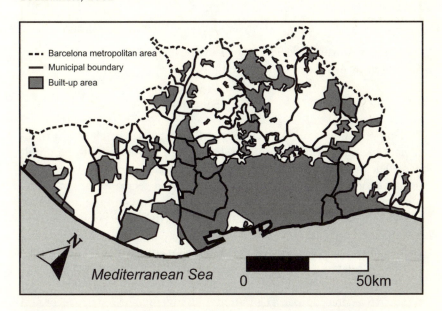

Note: At the end of the nineteenth century, five municipalities were amalgamated to Barcelona as well as parts of other municipalities. Since the 1960s, the constant sprawl has repeated the problem: Barcelona's built-up area includes several independent municipalities with no metropolitan authority.

El Portús, a border crossing between Spain and France, is another example of problems created when crossing boundaries. In this case, a settlement has developed along the international boundary for almost 500 metres running alongside the N-II Highway. The houses on the highway's eastern side are in Spain, called Els Límits, while the houses on the highway's western side are in France, called El Portús.

Increasing development of second homes or development in tourist areas has created similar problems. Almost always situated in rural areas, they create urban structures that demand public services and that alter the economy and character of the affected municipality. On many occasions, these developments cross municipal boundaries, making growth and development control extremely difficult.

Often a settlement's services or the infrastructure of a settlement is provided by a municipality, because of proximity, tradition, or improved communications. On some occasions, large infrastructure projects, mainly motorways, but also railways, dams, and airports, isolate parts of a municipality, thus encouraging a more involved relationship with neighbouring municipalities. The legislation recognizes all these situations as dysfunctions providing a reason for changing municipal boundaries. However, solutions can also be achieved by creating service communities or metropolitan areas in the case of conurbations.

Conclusions

> It is men who make monarchies and republics, but the municipality seems to come from God.
>
> – Alexis de Tocqueville

This important declaration by de Tocqueville appropriately reflects the traditional Spanish vision of municipalities, which still appears to be dominant. The municipality remains a basic structure for coexistence and social organization for a well-defined and differentiated geographical space having strong resident identification. Its ancestral origins and the undeniable ties existing between its characteristic elements (territory, population, and sociopolitical organization) give the municipality that almost divine aura of eternity, invulnerability, and self-legitimization mentioned by de Tocqueville.

Understandably, then, simple proposals to change the status of a municipality often incite significant citizen backlash, ranging from sentimental trauma to excited uproar. Legislation and government reports recognize this overwhelming importance of the municipality in Spanish society. Aragon's Local Administration Act, approved in April 1999, explicitly avoids "a remodelling of the municipal map, given the difficulty of representing it in the text and the delicacy of the subject because of the negative reaction generated in affected communities" (Chapter 5.1). Similarly, a report published in February 2001 by a multidisciplinary and multiparty group of experts commissioned by the parliament of Catalonia referred to revising the county map but noted the need to comply with the existing legislation and encourage the annexation and the creation of associations of municipalities. The negative reaction from local groups and citizens was intense, practically reaching the level of personal insults.

Thus, Spain's citizens view the municipality as the political entity most intimately linked with their identity and their voice in society. Alongside this view, the municipality continues to be perceived as strictly an administrative body that exists primarily to provide a series of increasingly complex services. The high cost of providing many of these services, and the economic and demographic decline of many rural municipalities, have had further negative impacts on service provision. These impacts include lack of resources, leaving residents uncovered by some services, welfare programs, and opportunities held to be the rights of all citizens no matter where they live but that in practice become comparative advantages for those living in large municipalities or in urban areas. Additionally, the dismantling of metropolitan bodies characterizing recent deregulation processes exemplifies the now absurd municipal limits within Spain's large conurbations. At the same time, these limits illustrate the difficulty in achieving best practices in tackling the many problems of these areas.

The systematic review of the regulations concerning municipal changes throughout nearly 200 years indicates that there is a double reality. On the one hand, there exists the excessive fragmentation and the problematic structure of the Spanish municipal map, and, on the other, there has never been any policy or legislation designed specifically to resolve the problems.

Consequentially, while facing the great difficulties of systematically revising the municipal structure, the Spanish local administration has focused on differentiating the specifically "political territory" (or area identified by citizens that allows democracy to be developed through direct participation as an expression of genuine representativeness) from the "ideal management territory" (to make public administration work at a local level, ensuring welfare and quality of life for the whole population). Both "political" and "ideal management" territories do not necessarily have to mark out different territories, but clearly it is not essential that they coincide with the municipality as it has been generally understood until now.

Therefore, the first step toward any reform remains a revision of the aspects (functions, powers, capabilities, finances) that should characterize a municipality. This step would involve establishing which of these aspects could be assigned to associations of municipalities, counties, provincial governments, autonomous regional community governments, or the central government. Once it is reinvested with full powers and full autonomy (legal, legislative, resources, etc.), recognized in its popular representative role, and liberated from its superfluous responsibilities of providing services, the municipality will be able to shed its traditional weaknesses.

References

Albet, A. 2000. "El mapa geopolític: la pervivència dels municipis i la divisió comarcal." *Revista de Girona* 200: 11-22.
Arias, F. 1980. "Los pequeños municipios en las áreas metropolitanas." *CEUMT* 23: 44-47.
Ballester, I. 1968. "Los enclaves municipales en España." *REVL* 3.
Barranco, R. 1993. *Creación y segregación de municipios*. Madrid: Marcial Pons.
Brugué, Q., R. Gomà, and J. Subirats. 2000. "Els governs de proximitat," in R. Gomà and J. Subirats, eds., *Govern i polítiques públiques a Catalunya: 1980-2000*, 211-63. Bellaterra: SPUAB.
Casasas, L. 1982-83. "Hacia unos nuevos principios de ordenación territorial de base municipal en Cataluña." *Revista de Geografía* 16-17: 73-86.
Castelao, J. 1994. *El término municipal: Extensión y alteraciones*. Madrid: Abella-El Consulor.
Castells, J.M. 1983. "Nueva problemática de las alteraciones territoriales municipales." *RAP* 3, 100-2.
Fariña, J. 1977. *Agonía y muerte del municipio rural*. Madrid: Imp. Sáez.
Ferret, J. 1986. "Uniformitat i varietat en la regulació del municipi." *Autonomies* 4: 61-79.
Font, T. 1985. "Perspectives d'organització supramunicipal." *Autonomies* 1: 49-70.
Garcia, G. 1972. *El Concejo Navarro y los pequeños municipios*. Pamplona: Aranzadi.
Garcia, J. 1983. *El origen del municipio constitucional*. Madrid: IEAL.
Gavira, C. 1980. "Municipios pequeños y pequeños municipios: Las bases geográficas y demográficas del poder local en España." *CEUMT* 23: 34-44.
INE. 1981. *Relación de municipios desaparecidos desde principios de siglo*. Madrid: Instituto Nacional de Estadística.
Liesa, C. 1972. *Reestructuración de términos municipales*. Barcelona: Bayer.
Martin, R. 1987. *Entes locales complejos*. Madrid: Trivium.
Mateu, X. 1988. *La administración local y los servicios municipales*. La Seu d'Urgell: MAB 6-Alt Pirineu.
Mir, J. 1999. "El marc jurídic," in O. Nello, ed., *20 anys d'ajuntaments democràtics*, 17-51. Barcelona: Federació de Municipis de Catalunya.
Morell, L. 1972. *Estructuras locales y ordenación del espacio*. Madrid: IEAL.
Nadal, F. 1985. *Política territorial y anexiones de municipios urbanos en España (siglos XIX-XX)*. Barcelona: Pub. Universitat de Barcelona.
Perdigó, J. 1987. *El municipio y su territorio: Alteración de términos municipales*. Madrid: Banco de Crédito Local.
Pujol, R., ed. 1998. *L'administració local a Catalunya: Proposta de model d'organització territorial*. Barcelona: Diputación de Barcelona.
Roca, M., ed. 2000. *Informe sobre la revisió del model d'organització territorial de Catalunya*. Barcelona:. Generalitat de Catalunya.
Rueda, I., J.M. Camarasa, and X. Mateu. 1987. *Diagnòstic del mapa municipal de Catalunya*. Barcelona: Generalitat de Cataluña.
Ruiz, R. 1976. *Llívia: Enclave español en Francia*. Madrid: Servicio Geográfico del Ejército.
Sosa, F., and P. de Miguel. 1987. *Creación, supresión, y alteración de términos municipales*. Madrid: IEAL.

Torres, F. 1985. *Las entidades locales menores en el derecho administrativo español*. Madrid: IEAL.
Tort, J. 1993. *Les entitats municipals descentralitzades a Catalunya*. Barcelona: Generalitat de Catalunya.
Tusell, J., and D. Chacón. 1973. *La reforma de la administración local en España (1900-1936)*. Madrid: Instituto de Estudios Administrativos.

8
Changing Local Government Boundaries in Israel: The Paradox of Extreme Centralism versus Inability to Reform

Eran Razin

Procedures for municipal boundary change in Israel are still largely based on British colonial legislation from the 1930s and reflect the hierarchical-centralized nature of the colonial regime. The State of Israel was established in 1948, but the centralized legislation conformed to prevailing ideologies and policies of governments in the early postindependence years. A strong central government that left only limited autonomy to local governments was the broadly accepted norm, in line with the struggles and challenges faced by the young Jewish state (Elazar and Kalchheim 1988). The strong socialist roots of the early Israeli governments were also supportive of tendencies of centralization. However, since the 1970s, trends of political decentralization have become stronger in Israel. Increased fragmentation and polarization in Israeli society have weakened the central government, frequently leading to paralysis in the decision-making and policy formulation capacities of the legislature and the government. Increased court intervention in societal conflicts has become a particularly notable aspect of growing pluralism in the Israeli political scene (Barzilai 1999).

A remarkable feature of the Israeli case is that, despite the marked change in the political environment, no major reform has taken place in Israel's local government map or in its municipal boundary change procedures. The numerous incremental municipal boundary changes that took place lacked broad vision or clear policy guidelines concerning the desired future structure of local government in Israel. Comprehensive reforms were occasionally proposed but were never seriously followed, neither in the early years characterized by centralization, nor in the later years of decentralization. Moreover, procedures for municipal boundary change have hardly been reformed at all, despite the marked shift in the political environment and the growing mismatch between the legal basis of procedures that assumes strong centralization and the actual practices that reflect increasing decentralization and fragmentation of power.

This chapter first describes the Israeli procedures for municipal boundary changes and compares them with those in other democracies. This is followed by an evaluation of the effects of the changing political, ideological, and economic environment on these procedures. The increasing court intervention instead of conscious reforms or policy shifts initiated by the government or the legislature is then brought up. Finally, the causes of failures to reform the local government map and the procedures for municipal boundary changes are discussed.

Local Government in Israel and the Potential for Municipal Boundary Conflicts

Israel's local government system is composed of four basic types of local authorities:

- municipalities (cities that generally include more than 20,000 inhabitants);
- local councils (smaller urban settlements);
- regional councils (federations of villages, each having its own local committee); and
- local industrial councils.

The number of local authorities has continuously increased since the establishment of the state (Table 8.1), reflecting the marked increase in the state population (from 1.5 million in 1951 to 6.5 million in 2001), leading to granting municipal independence to new settlements and to growing settlements that were previously included within the jurisdictional areas of regional councils or that lacked municipal status.

Municipal mergers and abolition of existing local authorities were rare, but the average population of a local authority grew due to the rapid population growth in Israel. The largest municipalities in 2000 were

Table 8.1

Number of local authorities in Israel, 1951-2001

Year	Municipalities	Local councils	Regional councils	Local industrial councils	Total
1951	20	64	42	0	126
1961	25	104	50	0	179
1971	29	117	48	0	194
1981	37	125	54	0	216
1991	47	140	54	2	243
2001	69	141	54	2	266

Source: Central Bureau of Statistics and Ministry of Interior.

Jerusalem (657,000 inhabitants), Tel Aviv (354,400), Haifa (270,500), and Rishon LeZiyyon (202,200), the first three being the core cities of Israel's three prime metropolitan areas and the fourth being the largest suburb of Tel Aviv (Figure 8.1). Nevertheless, nearly 60 percent of Israel's local authorities in 2000 had fewer than 10,000 inhabitants, and about 10 percent had fewer than 2,500 inhabitants. Predominant among small local authorities were Arab villages and Jewish settlements that were not included in the regional councils, because in the past the latter tended to be exclusive federations of rural-cooperative settlements (Newman 1995).

The regional councils control most of Israel's rural space, and only a small portion of land has remained unincorporated (termed "no municipal status" in Figure 8.1). Thus, most urban local authorities in Israel are surrounded by land of regional councils and of other urban local authorities. This attribute of Israel's local government map leads to an intensification of municipal boundary conflicts, because nearly any expansion of an urban local authority involves transfer of land from one local authority to another rather than annexation of an unincorporated area (Razin and Hasson 1994).

Most land in outer areas of the Tel Aviv metropolitan area – Israel's main urban concentration, comprising about 43 percent of its population – is controlled by regional councils (Figure 8.2). Thus, substantial urbanization pressures in metropolitan fringe areas are most likely to lead to municipal boundary conflicts in which expanding urban municipalities and local councils claim land from rural regional councils that hold the needed land reserves. The regional councils could either oppose these claims, sometimes backed by an environmental lobby that supports preservation of agricultural land and open space, or put a price tag on the requested land, representing the loss of potential betterment and development levies or future property taxes. The crisis in agriculture and the high cost of servicing rural areas are the main justifications given by regional councils for viewing land needed by adjacent cities and towns as an economic asset. The increasing tendency of regional councils and rural settlements within these councils to promote the development of out-of-town retail centres and industrial parks, as well as ex-urban neighbourhoods, within their jurisdictional areas also complicates the nature of urban-rural municipal boundary disputes. Conflicts of a different type involve growing ex-urban settlements that seek to leave the regional councils and become independent local councils.

The Lachish region, south of the Tel Aviv metropolitan area, presents a typical example of a nonmetropolitan region where cities and towns are surrounded by regional councils rather than being the centres of local governments that include both the town and its rural vicinity (Figure 8.3). Expansion initiatives of Qiryat Gat and Qiryat Mal'akhi – for the establishment of new residential neighbourhoods, for the development of

Figure 8.1

Local government boundaries, Israel, 2001

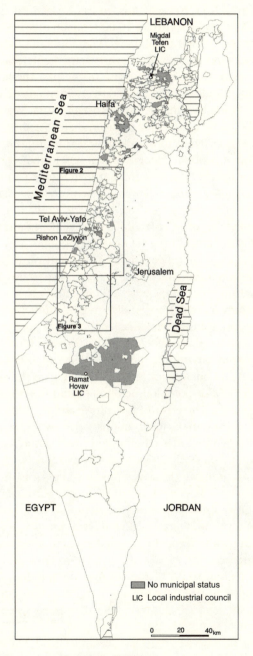

Source: Geography Department, The Hebrew University.

158 Eran Razin

Figure 8.2

Local government boundaries in the Tel Aviv metropolitan area, 2001

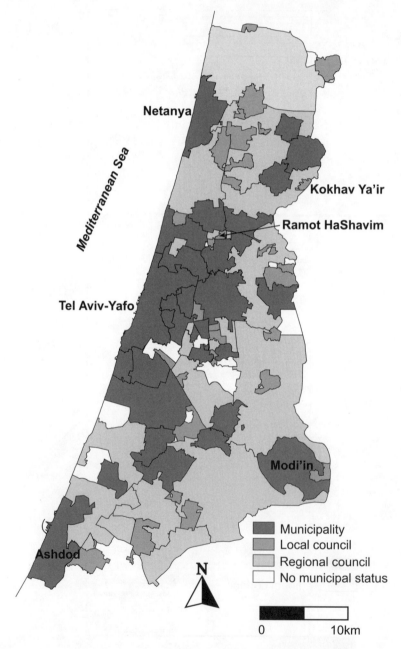

Source: Geography Department, The Hebrew University.

industrial parks, or even aimed at the annexation of existing industrial zones in the regional councils – thus involved bitter conflicts. Such conflicts between the two towns and their surrounding regional councils have persisted for decades.

The Formal Procedures: The Absolute Power of the Minister of Interior

The roots of legislation that concerns modification of jurisdictional areas of municipalities in Israel can be found in the Municipal Ordinance of 1934. This legal basis has largely remained intact after the establishment of the state in 1948, except for the transfer of responsibilities from the British high commissioner to Israel's minister of interior. Article 3 in the Municipal Ordinance refers to the procedures for the establishment of

Figure 8.3

Urban and rural local authorities in the Lachish region, 2001

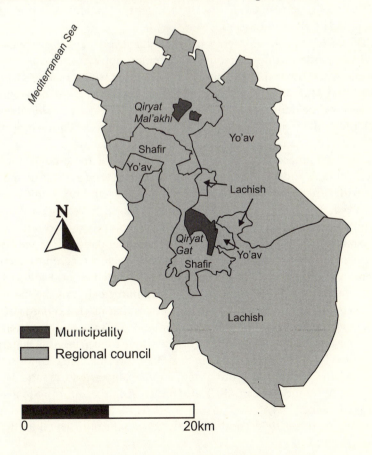

a municipality. The minister of interior has the authority to appoint a commission of inquiry, of which at least one of its members is not a state employee, in order to examine a proposal to establish a municipality (usually upgrading the status of an existing local council). After studying the report of the commission, the minister is free to accept the recommendations, modify them, or act contrary to them. A similar procedure, defined in Article 11, applies to the abolition of a municipality.

Article 8 of the Municipal Ordinance deals with changing the jurisdictional area of an existing municipality. Such changes are the prerogative of the minister of interior. If the minister finds merit in changing the boundaries of a municipality, either due to the desire of the majority of its residents or because of any other reason, he or she is required to appoint a commission of inquiry (a boundary commission) to examine the proposal. After studying the commission's recommendations, the minister makes the final decision. The minister can accept the recommendations and implement them or implement only some of the recommendations. The minister can also reject the recommendations and either stick to the existing boundaries or implement boundary changes that are different from those proposed by the commission.

Thus, the minister of interior has the full authority to delineate municipal boundaries, while the requirement for an inquiry commission is only intended to ensure that the minister is informed before making the decision. The Municipal Ordinance mentions enterprises and development projects of the municipality as possible criteria for evaluation but does not determine the criteria that should be taken into account in the evaluation of boundary change proposals and the minister's decision.

The legal procedures are even more minimal for the establishment of local councils and changes in their boundaries, as long as these boundaries are with other local councils or regional councils and no municipality is involved. The Local Councils Ordinance – also in force since the British mandate years – does not even require the appointment of a commission. The minister is only obliged to receive a recommendation from the district commissioner – an employee of the ministry – before reaching a decision. New local authorities in Israel are usually established as local councils and occasionally as regional councils but not as municipalities – the status of a municipality is granted only to local councils that reach a certain size and urban character. Thus, the minister of interior in Israel has absolute powers to establish new local authorities, without even receiving the report of an advisory commission of inquiry. Only the amalgamation of several existing local authorities into a new municipality would require a commission of inquiry. The minister also has an absolute authority to abolish local councils.

Article 3 in the 1958 Local Councils (Regional Councils) Order defines special rules for regional councils, intended to ensure that local committees of the individual villages in the regional councils are informed of proposed changes. The article requires the minister to notify the regional council of an intention to change its boundaries. The regional council then has three days to inform all local committees within its jurisdictional area of this intention. The local committees have seven days to submit to the regional council their comments on the proposed boundary change. The regional council then has to submit to the minister its position and the positions of individual local committees within twenty-one days of the initial notification by the minister. The minister is then empowered to decide according to his or her judgment.

Orders, such as the one that concerns regional councils, are issued by the minister of interior, largely providing details for the implementation of main legislation: laws approved by the Knesset (Israel's legislature) and ordinances that remained in place since the British mandate period. It is easier to change orders than to change main legislation. Indeed, a modification was introduced by the ministry in 1997: the minister was exempted from the special procedure for regional councils in the case of a proposed boundary change between a regional council and a municipality, examined by a boundary commission.

Three major traits can be defined on the basis of the above description of the legal basis.

- Extreme centralization: the minister of interior (previously the British high commissioner) has absolute legal powers to determine Israel's local government map.
- Minimal details: procedures are simple, and the legal basis does not touch on issues such as relevant criteria, composition of boundary commissions, time framework, et cetera. The judiciary has not been granted any role in the procedures, neither as a formal level of appeal nor as an arbitrator. Thus, court intervention is limited to rulings of the High Court of Justice, based on general principles of justice rather than on specific legislation.
- Remarkable stability: the legal basis has hardly been modified, despite establishment of the state and substantial social, political, and spatial transformations that have occurred over more than half a century since the state was established.

Recent Legal Modifications

In spite of the remarkable stability of the legal basis for the procedures, emphasized above, three legal modifications did take place in the past fifteen years, the first one in 1988 and the other two in 2000. These modifications, while modest, do reflect shifts in the political environment.

The first modification gave the minister of interior the authority to establish a local industrial council, with the consent of the minister of industry and trade and of the minister of finance. This legislation was passed in the Knesset due to pressures by industrial corporations and by the Ministry of Industry and Trade and despite opposition from the Ministry of Interior. It was intended to solve particular problems of two interurban industrial parks – Ramat Hovav and Migdal Tefen – but could serve industrial corporations as a way to avoid payment of high local taxes that subsidize other functions of the local authorities.

The second modification was the inclusion of a minimal size for the establishment of a new local authority in the Municipal and Local Council Ordinances. While in line with the formal policy of the Ministry of Interior, the real force behind this modification was the Ministry of Finance. It first managed to insert a minimal size of 3,000 inhabitants in the ordinances, increased to 5,000 in the year 2000. The Knesset has included the above modifications in the legislation package that accompanies approval of the annual government budget. Intended to save costs, since small local authorities are particularly dependent on government grants, the modification practically limits the freedom and flexibility of the minister of interior, although it is in line with the expressed policies of the ministry.

The third modification endows the minister of interior with the authority to approve agreements for the transfer of local property tax and betterment levy revenues from one local authority to another. Such transfers are meant to compensate local authorities that surrender land to other local authorities by tax revenues collected in the transferred land by the local authorities that have gained the land. These transferred revenues cannot include property taxes from residential areas, because servicing residential areas costs far more than local tax revenues collected in these areas. This modification apparently provides the minister of interior with additional powers, but in fact it acknowledges local initiatives that lead to such agreements and represent, to some extent, decentralization and transfer of powers to the local authorities.

These few modifications of the legal basis for municipal boundary changes hint at a trend to limit the absolute powers of the minister of interior. However, the modifications are small and largely represent attempts by other government ministries to intervene in the process rather than pluralism and greater power awarded to local parties, pressure groups, or professional evaluations.

The Legal Basis in a Comparative Perspective:
A Case of Extreme Centralization

Municipal boundary change procedures in democratic countries can be divided into two major types (Razin and Lindsey 2004). In the first type, the state retains the authority to decide on boundary changes and can initiate such changes. In the second type, initiative and decision are at the hands of local parties or arbitration bodies not subordinate to the state, so that the role of the state is limited to determining the framework and legal basis for municipal boundary change. Alternatives of this second type, practised mainly in the United States, include popular determination, in which changes are subject to the consent of the sides involved; municipal determination, in which cities hold the power to annex, subject to specific regulations; and judicial determination and quasi-legislative determination, in which authority is largely given to the court or to a quasi-legislative commission.

Alternatives in which the state retains the authority to change municipal boundaries also vary widely. The minister in charge of local government affairs, the government at large, the legislature, or the regional levels of government can hold this authority. The first option, in which authority is granted to a single person (usually the minister of interior or the minister of local government), has the most centralized nature.

The extent of centralization is determined not only by the identities of decision makers within the central state but also by the nature of the procedure undertaken before a decision is reached. An internal bureaucratic assessment conducted by employees of the relevant ministry is the most centralized procedure, in which the involved sides and external interest groups are least able to influence outcomes. Other procedures could have a more pluralistic-professional nature. They could require a transparent professional-objective assessment prior to the decision and include in the most extreme case a nonbinding referendum prior to the decision (Razin and Lindsey 2004).

The Israeli procedures, as defined by law, are thus the most centralized of a wide range of alternatives applied in democratic countries. The minister of interior is the sole decision maker, and decisions are subject to very minimal regulations that concern the steps to be taken prior to a decision. During the British mandate time, the British high commissioner formally held these absolute powers, but in practice local government in the Jewish sector evolved largely through local initiatives, and the decisions of the colonial government were frequently merely confirmation of steps already undertaken by the local population. Similarly, resistance of Arab localities toward the imposition of modern forms of local government was also accepted by the colonial government. It was only after establishment of the State of Israel that these powers were more fully utilized by the central state to delineate the local government map, based on ideologies and policies of the central government. Nevertheless, whereas the legal foundations have remained unchanged, the ability to retain the centralized form of decision making has eroded rapidly since the 1980s.

The Fragmentation of Power: Society and Government

Trends of political decentralization have prevailed in Israel since the 1970s, associated with the departure of the state-founding generation of leaders from the political arena. Prolonged economic stagnation has constrained the central government budget, and the shift from national-collectivist values to individualism and materialism has eroded the authority of the central government and the coherence of its actions. Increasing polarization of Israeli society along ethnoreligious lines has also contributed to the decentralization process. These lines of social fragmentation have included tensions between Jews of European origin and those of Middle Eastern and North African origins, between secular and ultra-orthodox Jews, between new immigrants and the more veteran population, and between Jews and the Arab-Palestinian citizens of Israel.

This emerging pluralist political scene has led to growing political pressures on the decision-making process in the Ministry of Interior. The minister has become more constrained by these political pressures because the government has frequently depended on shaky coalitions that have included representatives of many of the ethnoreligious sectors mentioned above. Despite the absolute powers granted to the minister by law, he or she cannot disregard groups such as Arabs, rural regional councils, and other sectors with significant power in the legislature. Mayors can also apply pressure effectively on the minister of interior, particularly if the minister is a member of a party that holds some sort of primaries to elect its candidates for the Israeli legislature. These mayors have been able to mobilize local votes among party members. When the minister belongs to a Jewish ultra-religious party, an appeal of stakeholders to its spiritual leaders can also constrain the minister.

Decentralization has not led the Israeli government to cease to act as a stakeholder in municipal boundary changes. However, rather than acting as a single stakeholder, the government and its affiliated agencies have increasingly acted as several, often competing, stakeholders. Government ministers in Israel represent different political parties, and their nominations are approved by the parliament; thus, conflicting interests are frequent, and the ability of the government to form a single coherent policy is constrained. Many of the stakeholders in municipal boundary changes in Israel are therefore central government agencies, whose representatives frequently take opposing positions in their testimonies in boundary commission meetings. These public stakeholders include the Ministry of Interior, the Ministry of Construction and Housing, the Ministry of Transportation, the Ministry of the Environment, Israel's Land Administration, the Ministry of Defence, and so on. Interests of these central government agencies can be based on agendas of elected politicians, on concerns of the particular sector under their responsibility, or on bureaucratic concerns of organizations to preserve and concentrate power in their hands. Even representatives of different units within the same ministry sometimes express opposing views.

An increasingly visible phenomenon in recent years has been the growing intervention of the Ministry of Finance in redelineating Israel's local government map. This intervention is unveiled in both "negative" and "positive" ways.

Intervention of the negative type includes delaying the operation of municipal boundary commissions by forbidding them from commencing their work without budgetary approval. Thus, appointing boundary commissions as a first step toward municipal boundary change has practically become, since the late 1990s, subject to the approval of the Ministry of Finance. The required budget for the operation of a commission can be very small, but frequently, perhaps usually, a sufficient earmarked budget is unavailable. In this way, the Ministry of Finance can control timing and priorities in the operation of commissions, some of them being delayed for many months due to lack of budgetary approval. In some cases, prolonged delays can reduce the motivation of the minister of interior to act, and in other cases a new minister with a different agenda can replace the one who opted to make the boundary change.

A positive mode of intervention by the Ministry of Finance has utilized the legislation package passed concurrently with the government's annual budget. As mentioned before, the Ministry of Finance attempts to promote through this tool the policy to reduce the number of local authorities in Israel in order to save costs, particularly high government grants per capita allocated to small municipalities. The Ministry of Interior is formally committed to this goal as well, and this policy has been reaffirmed in its approval of the 1998 recommendations of the Commission for the Amalgamation of Local Authorities (Ministry of Interior 1998b). However, in practice, the Ministry of Interior has been more attuned to local political opposition to such moves than the Ministry of Finance. Thus, the latter opts to limit the establishment of new municipalities through the legislation that determines a minimal size for the establishment of a new local authority. The Ministry of Finance has even proposed to abolish small local authorities, of fewer than 3,000 inhabitants, through the 2002 budget-associated legislation rather than through the ordinary procedure that involves the appointment of a boundary commission by the minister of interior.

This growing involvement of the Ministry of Finance in modifying the local government map can be viewed as another facet in the fragmentation of political power in Israel. However, it can also be viewed as a step in the concentration of powers in the hands of the Ministry of Finance, at the expense of the sectoral ministries. This step can be regarded as a response of the Ministry of Finance to the increasingly chaotic political arena, in which the government and the legislature are unable to conduct a rational process of decision making that takes into account long-term considerations.

Implications for Court Intervention

The courts, particularly the High Court of Justice, have increasingly become the arenas for societal conflicts in Israel (Razin and Hazan 2001). Judicial activism has been justified by the weakness of the system of checks and balances in the Israeli political system (Zamir 1993). The Israeli government, according to this argument, has extensive powers that are subject to minimal monitoring – hence the need for frequent court intervention in its decisions. However, court activism can also be viewed as a symptom of government weakness rather than excessive power. While holding extensive powers legally, the government is increasingly unable to implement coherent policies and to decide on societal conflicts; thus, sensitive policies that divide Israeli society are challenged in appeals to the High Court of Justice.

The influence of this court on setting new norms for municipal boundary change procedures became particularly evident in the 1990s (Razin and Hazan 2001). It has become accepted that an employee of the Ministry of Interior should not normally serve as a chair of a boundary commission. This restriction is meant to ensure that those submitting their recommendations to the minister will not be under the direct authority of the minister. Government employees should not generally form a majority in the commissions, and the composition of commissions should be balanced. Thus, local government officials, academic experts, and civil servants, usually not subordinate to the minister of interior, are appointed to head most commissions. Commission members have included indirect representatives of sectors involved in the boundary change (urban municipalities, rural regional councils, etc.). The Ministry of Interior has been represented by one or two members, usually affiliated with the land use planning department. However, the composition of boundary commissions has not been defined by law or by a clear legal precedent. Another norm that has evolved gradually is to appoint a boundary commission for any proposed change, even if no city (municipality) is involved, only local councils and regional councils. However, rules that concern commissions of the latter type are more flexible.

Court rulings in the 1990s called for professional, transparent, and balanced assessments of proposals for municipal boundary change. According to various rulings, the boundary commission should ensure that its appointment is advertised sufficiently and should provide the involved parties and interest groups with an adequate opportunity to present their cases before formulating its recommendations. Members of the boundary commission should refrain from expressing their views before hearing all parties involved. The commission should examine all proposed changes, as defined by the minister of interior, and reasonably justify its recommendations, including discussion of arguments raised by the parties involved. If a party appeals to the High Court of Justice, then the minister should be able to reasonably explain his or her decision in court.

There are limits, however, to the power of the High Court. It usually focuses on the assessment of procedures and refrains from intervening in policy issues. Moreover, small procedural faults are frequently insufficient to provoke radical court intervention. Thus, in the vast majority of appeals, the decisions and practices of the Ministry of Interior have been upheld (Razin and Hazan 2001). In these cases, court appeals only managed to delay decision, sometimes by several years. However, after losing in court, it was usually too late to launch a public campaign or seek compromise, and, if the minister remained consistent in his or her position, the appealing party was likely to lose it all. Precedents set by court rulings can also be interpreted in different ways, and the influence of the High Court in establishing norms not specified in written procedures or laws is not necessarily stable over time.

The Formulation of a Written Procedure

During the late 1990s, pressures to modify municipal boundary change procedures evolved in three major directions. The first direction consisted of attempts to move to what is perceived as an "American" local democracy model that requires the consent of all sides involved for each boundary change. In particular, lawyers representing small middle-class suburbs or ex-urban municipalities expressed such views. They argued that merging one local authority with another against its will is antidemocratic and violates personal rights that have been secured in the Basic Law: Personal Dignity and Freedom. However, legislative proposals in this direction did not gain momentum, and rulings of the High Court, while reflecting a desire for increased public participation in the decision-making process, did not accept the "American" local democracy lines of argument. In one case, the tiny local council of Ramot Hashavim (1,000 inhabitants) failed in 1999 in an appeal to the High Court that objected to the appointment of a boundary commission to examine its annexation by a larger local authority. The court did intervene in the appointments to the boundary commission, but it did not object to the principle of merging one local authority with another against the will of its residents. In another case, the court turned down in 2001 an appeal of the ex-urban local council of Kochav Yair that objected to the annexation of a slightly less affluent ex-urban settlement onto its jurisdictional areas. Thus, major barriers to the amalgamation of small municipalities are considered political, and court intervention can only somewhat delay implementation if the Ministry of Interior has the will to take steps despite local resistance.

A second, more influential, direction in reforming municipal boundary change procedures was based on the perception that the procedures were a major bottleneck that retarded development. Such pressures were led in particular by government ministries and agencies engaged with development: the Ministry of Construction and Housing, Israel's Land Administration, and the Prime Minister's Office. Similar complaints were also expressed by urban local authorities that either lacked sufficient land for development or faced stiff competition from commercial and residential projects initiated on land of the rural regional councils.

Pressures of this type have led to discussions on how to make procedures more efficient and quick. A legal reform to simplify procedures has occasionally been proposed. However, one can be skeptical about the outcome of such a reform because legal requirements are already minimal at present. Attempts to cancel the requirement for a boundary commission or to transfer authorities from the minister of interior to more development-oriented ministries would not touch the major sources of inefficient procedures: fragmentation of society, weakness of government, and administrative flaws in the functioning of the government that would not be eliminated by changing legal frameworks. Moreover, court intervention has become a major source of delays, and such intervention can even increase if procedures are to become less transparent and fair.

A third direction of pressures to revise procedures thus focused on the need to define written procedures for the functioning of boundary commissions and for other steps in the process of changing municipal boundaries. The High Court recommended the preparation of written procedures in several of its rulings. Other advocates of such a step have been motivated either by a desire to secure norms of proper administration and fairness or by a perception that such a formal document would eliminate bottlenecks of administrative inefficiency.

In 1996, the government appointed an interministerial commission to propose reform in boundary change procedures. The commission principally recommended defining formal written procedures that would apply to all forms of local government (Ministry of Interior 1998a). They would include a precise definition of the information to be specified in each request for a boundary change, the composition of boundary commissions, the time framework for the operation of commissions, and their method of functioning. The need for national policy guidelines was also debated, but it was unclear whether it would be possible to form a consensus on such guidelines, even among government ministries.

The impact of the commission's report was modest. Development pressures eased with the economic recession of the late 1990s, and the functioning of commissions even slowed down as fewer resources were allotted to the procedures. The Ministry of Finance assumed a particularly active role in delaying procedures by demanding budgetary approval prior to the commencement of a commission's work. Steps were made to subcontract out the technical aspects of the procedures: coordination of commissions and preparation of statutory jurisdictional area maps to be signed by the minister. However, as of 2002, no substantial changes were made.

Nevertheless, a formal written procedure for changing municipal jurisdictional areas was published by the Ministry of Interior (2001). For years, the ministry had refrained from preparing such a document, which could reduce flexibility and make procedures more prone to court appeals, based on lack of adherence to technical aspects of a written procedure. Rapid turnover of ministers and pressures of court rulings could have been the major factors in the acceptance of such a document by the ministry.

The approved procedure deals first with requests of local authorities to change their jurisdictional areas. Such requests should include proper documentation and justification and should be accompanied by a decision of the council of the local authority to submit the request. The request should also include a report on attempts to negotiate the proposed boundary change with the relevant adjacent local authorities. The written procedure also refers to the hearings and meetings of the boundary commission, which should be public, except in rare cases when witnesses want to be heard confidentially. The report should be submitted within six months from signing the contract between the ministry and the commission members. Considerable details concern the preparation of maps following the decision of the minister to modify boundaries. It is too early to conclude whether this written procedure will have any impact on the procedures in practice and on court battles over municipal boundary changes.

Conclusions: Why Is It So Difficult to Redelineate the Local Government Map?

The legislation that determines municipal boundary change procedures in Israel is characterized by extreme centralization that awards nearly absolute powers to the minister of interior. This legal basis that defines simple procedures with minimal details has shown remarkable stability for over half a century. A few recent modifications can be viewed as modest steps that constrain the power of the minister, but they largely represent attempts by other ministries to intervene in the procedures rather than a real process of decentralization.

The fragmentation of Israeli society and the increasingly fragmented action of the central government in recent decades have practically constrained actions of the minister of interior and have led to more open procedures, influenced substantially by the positions of the involved sides and interest groups. Increasing intervention of the High Court of Justice has also led to more transparent and pluralist procedures, although the court has been limited in its ability to influence policies and consolidate reforms of decentralization. The various pressures to reform the procedures in recent years, either in the direction of popular determination or in the direction of speeding up the process and reversing the declining effectiveness of central government action, have only led so far to the formulation of a written procedure. However, this relatively minor step cannot be expected to trigger a radical shift, neither toward popular determination nor toward enabling the government to implement substantial reforms in the local government map.

The exceptional inability to implement comprehensive reforms in the local government map and to revise boundary change procedures, despite the extremely centralized legal basis and the substantial decentralization that took place and apparently called for the adjustment of this legal basis, does require explanation.

I propose four major explanations for this conservatism and failure to reform territorial aspects of Israel's local government system.

- Local government reorganization was not on the public agenda until the early 1970s because of the remarkable centralization that characterized the Israeli political system and the emphasis given to central government institutions in the early decades of building a new Jewish state for the first time in 2,000 years. It can also be argued that municipal fragmentation served the central government by ensuring its practical control over functions performed by local authorities.
- The close links between local and national politics in Israel have hampered reforms. Reforms are easier to implement in countries such as Canada, where local politics have not been an arena in which national parties directly play. In Israel, with its multiparty coalition government structure, reforms and even controversial incremental municipal boundary changes are particularly risky because they can lead to conflicts within the central government – and not only between the party in power and its opposition.
- Lack of ethnoreligious homogeneity also hampers the implementation of territorial reforms, particularly when they are interpreted as influencing interethnic relations rather than only administrative structures for the provision of services. Amalgamation of Arab local authorities and transfer of land from Jewish to Arab local authorities and vice versa are extremely difficult for this reason.
- Political decentralization and social fragmentation since the 1970s have

made reforms even more difficult to implement. The fragmentation of ruling coalitions and central government action, in which different ministers and Knesset coalition members aim to advance different agendas, has created formidable obstacles for the implementation of broad rational reforms.

The above factors constitute high barriers to most attempts to modify municipal boundaries in Israel. However, rapid population growth and severe land shortages in local authorities surrounded by regional councils make incremental changes absolutely necessary, and freezing present municipal boundaries is not an option at all in the Israeli case. Growing competition over rateable land uses and the ethnoreligious identities of many local authorities also ensure that municipal boundary conflicts will continue to be numerous and intense in Israel.

References
Barzilai, G. 1999. "Courts as Hegemonic Institutions: The Israeli Supreme Court in a Comparative Perspective." *Israel Affairs* 5, 2-3: 15-33.
Elazar, D., and C. Kalchheim, eds. 1988. *Local Government in Israel*. Lanham, MD: University Press of America.
Ministry of Interior. 1998a. *The Inter-Ministerial Commission for Reforming Municipal Boundary Change Procedures, Report* (Hebrew). Jerusalem.
–. 1998b. *The Commission for the Amalgamation of Local Authorities, Final Report* (Hebrew). Jerusalem.
–. 2001. *Circular of the General Director (no. 2001/2)* (Hebrew). Jerusalem.
Newman, D. 1995. "Creating Homogenous Space: The Evolution of Israel's Regional Councils." In S.I. Troen and N. Lucas, eds., *Israel: The First Decade of Independence*, 495-519. Albany: State University of New York Press.
Razin, E., and S. Hasson. 1994. "Urban-Rural Boundary Conflicts: The Reshaping of Israel's Rural Map." *Journal of Rural Studies* 10: 47-59.
Razin, E., and A. Hazan. 2001. "Redrawing Israel's Local Government Map: Political Decisions, Court Rulings, or Popular Determination." *Political Geography* 20: 513-33.
Razin, E., and G. Lindsey. 2004. "Municipal Boundary Change Procedures: Local Democracy versus Central Control." In D. Wastl-Walter and M. Barlow, eds., *New Challenges in Local and Regional Administration*. Aldershot: Ashgate.
Zamir, Y. 1993. "Judicial Activism: The Decision to Decide" (Hebrew). *Law Review* 17: 647-58.

9
Confusing Responses to Regional Conflicts: Restructuring Local Administrative Boundaries in Korea
Dong-Ho Shin

Korea's phenomenal industrial growth and subsequent rapid urbanization in the past several decades have created many spillover effects from major cities to their peripheries. These spillovers have, in turn, resulted in various regional conflicts. In response, municipal governments have altered their boundaries through city expansion and city creation. Annexation and incorporation have been the primary means used for altering these jurisdictional boundaries for continually expanding metropolitan cities by the Korean government. Cities such as Pusan, Taegu, and Inchun (see Figure 9.1) have been separated from their surrounding provinces and designated as the "Metropolitan Cities" of Kyungnam, Kyungbuk, and Kyungki, respectively, creating new provincial-level governments. Many rural towns have also been incorporated into new municipal cities, such as Kyungju and Ahnyang, a movement referred to as "urban-rural separation" in Korea.

Designating large cities as metropolitan cities and separating smaller cities from their hosting counties have been the general trends during the process of urban expansion and decentralization since the 1960s. This process has also involved larger urban centres' annexation of neighbouring areas, resulting in frequent alternations in Korea's local government structure. These reforms and jurisdictional changes, however, have been inconsistent, ad hoc, and without clear definition and theoretical foundation. These problems have apparently complicated the coordination of competing interests between cities and their neighbouring areas. Such problems have been further compounded by increasing public demands and individualistic institutional behaviour under Korea's process of decentralization and democratization that has occurred since the early 1980s.

This chapter provides details of the reforms to Korea's local governance structure, primarily the main actors, principles, legal foundations, and political processes. The next section briefly describes the Korean administrative structure and its historical background. The following section highlights two case studies that focus on the conflicts arising from metropolitan

Figure 9.1

Regional context of Korea and Korean provincial boundaries

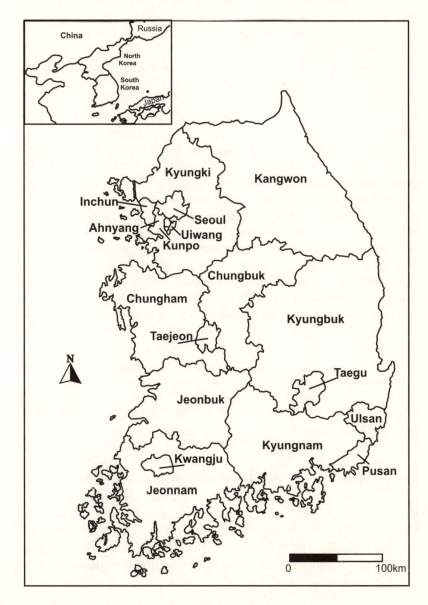

city expansion and city incorporation. The chapter then describes similar conflicts arising from the series of national-scale reforms that occurred in Korea in the mid-1990s. The next section discusses the criteria, process, actors, and outcomes of Korea's local administrative reform. The concluding section summarizes the processes and outcomes of Korean local governance reforms, attempting to provide some valuable lessons for other countries requiring similar reforms as well as for future local government changes in Korea.

Korean Local Government Systems and Administrative Boundaries: Korean Government System

Korea's government is a unitary system, organized hierarchically along three levels: central, provincial, and municipal governments (Figure 9.2). Each level is headed by an elected member of the national assembly or local councils. The central government consists of the presidential office and the ministries. The Ministry of Public Administration and Home Affairs (MPAHA) and the Ministry of Construction and Transportation (MCT) are the prime ministries concerned with local governance and urban expansion. The provincial-level governments are grouped according to three categories: the Special Metropolitan City of Seoul, the Metropolitan Cities (of which there are six: Pusan, Inchun, Taegu, Taejon, Kyangju, and Ulsan), and the provinces.

There are nine provinces considered to be remnant territories after most of their urbanized areas were removed to form metropolitan cities. The current provincial jurisdictions were laid out 100 years ago, and there have been no major changes except for the independence achieved by the metropolitan cities from the provinces. In fact, four out of the seven current metropolitan cities were provincial capitals in the past. The municipal

Figure 9.2

Administrative hierarchy of Korean local government system

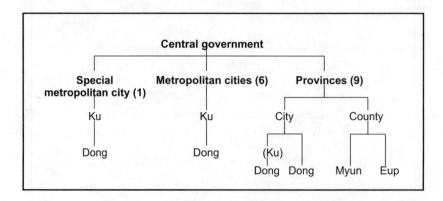

administration below these provinces concerns the cities and counties, and both are governed by political representatives, who include mayors and council members. These counties and municipal-level cities are divided into smaller administrative units, called *Myun* or *Eup* in Korean. These are administrative units without any political functions (Hong and Cho 1998, 11-13; Kim, Kum, and Kwon 1998, 39-40).

The seven metropolitan cities, including Seoul, have a status equivalent to that of the provinces and are governance units with more than one million inhabitants. In the case of Seoul, the city acquired its "special" status by being separated from the Province of Kyungki and being placed under the Office of Prime Minister in 1963. The city could have provincial status; however, it is "metropolitan" since its status is the same as that of provinces, operated under the MPAHA. It is special in the sense that the governor of the city, since it is the nation's capital, has the same status as ministers of the central government, in contrast to the provincial governors and the mayors of other metropolitan cities, who rank one step lower than the ministers of the central government. Under these metropolitan cities, including Seoul, are districts *(Kus)*, which have a municipal status. Like the other municipalities, these districts are governed by elected mayors and council members. The Korean administrative unit below this district of metropolitan city is *Dong* in Korean, an administrative unit with the same status as *Myun* and *Eup* in counties.

The local governance system, with elected governors, mayors, and councils, is relatively new, stabilized in the first half of the 1990s. Until then, only the president was elected by public vote, while provincial governors and municipal mayors were appointed by the president, and there were no representative bodies of provincial and municipal governments. Now it is essential to understand the organization of the relations between the governing bodies, beginning with some historical background.

Historical Background of the Current Administrative Boundaries

The current Korean provincial system was inherited directly from the administrative boundaries of the late Chosen Dynasty (1896). These provincial boundaries were a legacy of the more than 1,500-year-old nations of Shilla, Paekchae, and Kokuryo, which divided the Korean peninsula into northern, southeastern, and southwestern regions (Kim, Kum, and Kwon 1998, 44-48). Prior to Korea's modernization, which began in the 1940s, mountains and rivers divided these regions, making communication difficult. The Korean population is still identifiable by different regional backgrounds, and people still identify themselves with these unique regional characteristics. This regional identification is particularly with the southeastern and southwestern regions, which often compete both in national politics and at the individual level.

The late-nineteenth-century provincial boundaries remained relatively unchanged until the end of Japanese colonial rule in 1945, when the country was divided into South and North Korea. This division, however, only slightly influenced the boundaries of the nine provinces that constitute South Korea's territory, with the exception of the independence of the metropolitan cities.

These cities were separated from their host provinces on the assumption that urbanized areas could be better serviced and managed separately from less urbanized areas. The Korean Local Autonomy Law has supported this idea by maintaining that an administrative unit with more than one million people is entitled to become a metropolitan city, while a township with more than 50,000 inhabitants may become a municipality. Bureaucrats of those affected administrative units generally favoured such a process of "upgrade" or "promotion." Politicians also favoured this upgrade because of the benefits from the organizational and budgetary expansions, in addition to the promotion of their status in the national and local political arenas. Additionally, when residents expected increases in their local taxes, they tended to prefer promotion of their administrative units. Opposition from the host province, however, was very strong since it would lose a crucial component of its provincial territory. Separation of their provincial capitals caused significant reductions in economic, financial, and political power for most of the provinces.

Few municipal boundary changes were made before the 1960s. After that decade, many areas were classified as cities resulting from significant urban expansion. While there were twenty-four cities at the municipal level in 1960, municipal alterations had increased this number to seventy-four by 2001. Existing townships were promoted to cities, and new municipal boundaries were drawn between these new cities and their host counties. Municipal boundaries were frequently altered by the creation and expansion of metropolitan cities.

These frequent alterations to municipal and provincial boundaries have apparently caused problems for managing urban and regional growth in recent years (Kim, Kum, and Kwon 1998, 44-48). Enhanced individualistic behaviour of almost all of the local governments has increased these problems. A consensus emerged among Korea's national political and planning circles that the local governing system had to be reformulated. Korea's highly fragmented local government system led to the idea of amalgamating cities with their host counties or with other cities. Essentially, this approach represented a shift back to the old system of local government. In 1994, the Ministry of Home Affairs announced a massive plan for governance reform. Since this plan was announced, eighty cities and counties have been amalgamated into forty integrated cities.

Case Studies
This section will highlight some case studies that illustrate the details of the creation and expansion of the metropolitan and municipal cities and the subsequent reforms to correct the problems arising for local governance.

Kyungki Province and Ahnyang Region

Kyungki Province
The Metropolitan Cities of Seoul and Inchun previously belonged to Kyungki Province and now comprise the Capital Region. This area was the political and economic centre of the Chosun Dynasty (1392-1910). Seoul became a metropolitan city in 1946, independent from the province, and went through three subsequent territorial expansions, while Inchun was designated a metropolitan city in the 1980s. The remaining territory comprises Kyungki Province. This province is economically the most active among Korea's provinces. It has only 5.4 percent of the South Korean population but accounted for 20.2 percent of the gross domestic product (GDP) in 1999, up from 11.5 percent in 1985. The Capital Region's population grew from three million in the early 1960s to twenty million in 2000. This population growth was created mainly by the spillover effects of Seoul's growth at the early stage of Korean industrialization. Kyungki Province, surrounding the Capital Region's most populated cities of Seoul and Inchun, has received much of this growth.

Kyungki Province consisted of twenty-five cities and six counties in 2001, compared with 1954, one year after the end of the Korean War (1950-53), when there were only two cities and nineteen counties. During the past several decades, the number of cities has increased, while that of counties has decreased because of Korea's "urban-rural separation" policies. During this process, many fragmented counties have been designated as cities, while others have lost territory to newly separated cities.

Since the late 1960s, the Korean government started to implement growth control policies for Seoul. One such policy involved the creation of satellite cities surrounding Seoul. The government offered incentives and set barriers of entry for Seoul to divert migrants and economic activities to these satellite cities. The population and economic growth of Kyungki Province discussed above was a result of such growth control policies.

Kyungki Province's population and economic growth also occurred in the areas surrounding the planned satellite cities. Growth spread to the surrounding areas, especially in Seoul's southern border areas. Counties such as Siheung and Koyang received considerable portions of the incoming population and economic activity. The traditional town centres of these counties, now with more than 50,000 inhabitants, qualified for city status.

The centre was separated from its host county to become a city with municipal status that would report directly to the province. As many traditional town centres pursued independent status during the rapid urban growth of the 1970s and 1980s, the host county's territory became fragmented. Thus, the number of cities within the current jurisdiction of Kyungki Province increased from only three in the early 1960s to twenty-five in 2001. This fragmentation was exemplified by the cities of Ahnyang, Kunpo, and Uiwang, all of which were separated from Siheung County.

On the one hand, this movement toward separate municipal status for urban areas was positive since these areas could be more effectively governed based on their urban interests. On the other hand, such a movement also caused problems because traditional communities and their community spirits embedded in people's lifestyles were removed. However, a more pressing problem created by this fragmentation regarded the coordination and cooperation required for interjurisdictional decision making. This problem will be illustrated with an example of a triangular region consisting of the cities of Ahnyang, Kunpo, and Uiwang (Koo and Shin 2000).

Ahnyang Region
Korea's triangular region to the southwest of Seoul consists of the three cities of Ahnyang, Kunpo, and Uiwang (see Figure 9.1). Ahnyang was designated a satellite city in 1973 when it reached a population of 58,000. The city was the centre of Siheung County, located about thirty kilometres from central Seoul on an important transportation corridor linking Seoul with southern Korea and its main regional centres of Taejon, Pusan, and Kwangju. By 2001, Ahnyang's population had grown to 588,000, a tenfold increase in less than three decades. Many industries chose to locate in Ahnyang since they were prohibited from locating in Seoul because of either government plans or high land costs.

However, there are considerable differences between the cities of the Ahnyang Region. Uiwang has a very rural setting, especially since much of its territory is within Seoul's designated Greenbelts Area, which has strict controls. In contrast, Ahnyang and Kunpo are highly urbanized and congested, with little available land for future growth. Both cities' growth has benefited from Seoul's growth control policies. Together the three cities of the Ahnyang Region possess a relatively small land area of 150 km^2, which, compared with only 36 km^2 for the average Korean city, is much lower than the average Korean county's territory.

The different jurisdictions within this relatively small land area have created many problems in the management of urban services, such as public transportation, water supply, and sewage treatment. For instance, the effective management of water quality in river systems and air quality requires coordination and cooperation. Ahnyang and Kunpo require additional space for future growth, while rural Uiwang requires an economy and urban services. Thus, cooperation and coordination are essential within the Ahnyang Region. An urban-planning system responsible for the region was established by a mandatory plan in 1995. However, cooperation among these cities has been extremely difficult because of the separate decision-making systems, with individualistic administrative and political behaviour: each city now has its own elected mayors and council members, generally creating a system of competing parochial interests often with elected politicians pursuing their own interests.

During the 1980s, there was a growing trend to separate small town centres from their rural counties by giving them city status. The cities of Kunpo and Uiwang were separated from Silheung County. The cities of Ahnyang, Kunpo, and Uiwang were excluded from the mid-1990s reform that promoted amalgamation since they had not maintained their rural peripheries and therefore did not meet the legislated standards of Korea's central government.

Since 1995, Ahnyang's political leaders, in the largest city of the region, have attempted to form a metropolitan city by uniting the three cities. However, these attempts have failed mainly because of opposition from Kunpo and Uiwang. Particularly, their elected representatives have strongly opposed the idea, perceiving it as a scheme to reduce their political representation in the region.

Kyungnam Province and Pusan

Kyungnam Province is located in the southeastern end of the Korean peninsula (see Figure 9.1). Similar to other provinces, Kyungnam was designated a province in 1896. Its provincial capital was Jinju, an educational and cultural centre located in the western part of the province. The provincial capital was moved to Pusan in 1925 since Pusan was developing more rapidly as a gateway to other countries, primarily Japan. After Korea's independence in 1945 and the establishment of the national government in 1948, Kyungnam was established as a provincial government with three cities under its jurisdiction in 1949. The number of cities in Kyungnam Province increased to ten by 1989, while the number of counties did not change.

However, only ten cities and eleven counties remained in Kyungnam Province after Korea's amalgamation thrust in the mid-1990s. In 1996, the former county of Yangsan was incorporated into the city of Yangsan, and in 1997 the former city of Ulsan was promoted to a metropolitan city, giving Ulsan a separate government with provincial status. This separation reduced Kyungnam Province's territory by 9.1 percent – added to the loss of 6.5 percent from Pusan's separation – and its GRP by 47 percent. The separation occurred despite opposition and rising antagonism from Kyungnam

Province and its residents. The following section describes this rising antagonism, focusing on a period of formulating an extended metropolitan plan between the two provincial governments.

Kyungnam and Pusan share a southeastern regional identity, yet a relationship of rivalry and competition exists between them, reflective of different local interests. In earlier stages of Pusan's growth, the Pusan government attempted to solve the perennial problem of land shortage by expanding its territory (Shin 2000). Even after its separation from Kyungnam, three successful attempts were made to incorporate land within its boundaries, increasing Pusan's total land area from 373 to 749 km^2 despite Kyungnam Province's strenuous opposition.

Pusan's first attempt to enlarge its territory occurred in 1978, when parts of Kimhae County were incorporated. A second attempt followed in 1989, when further portions of Kimhae were incorporated. The third attempt to expand Pusan's territory was initiated in 1994 and completed during the period of *The Plan for the Extended Metropolitan Pusan* (PEMP; MoCT 1995) process in 1996. Led by Pusan's national assemblymen, this "land grab" became one of the most contentious regional disputes in Korea. The annexation was successful despite strong opposition from Kyungnam Province. The area transferred was a portion of Yangsan totalling about 115 km^2. Although the area was not especially valuable for urban development, this conflict contributed to the erosion of the cooperative spirit of Kyungnam officials.

Further efforts to annex Kyungnam lands, without any changes to the administrative boundaries, were made through the formal interregional planning process of the PEMP (Shin 2000). Initiated by Pusan in 1994, which had sought some form of macroregional planning for some time, the PEMP was strongly supported by Korea's central government. Pusan's Chamber of Commerce and Industry initiated the first round of this macroregional planning with two reports released in 1988 and 1992 (CCIP 1988, 1992). A third report was produced by the Institute of Pusan Development Systems, a private consulting firm owned by a powerful local politician (IPDS 1992). This third report made specific recommendations for Pusan's future, comparable in quality to the CCIP reports. Although none of the studies was acted on at the time, material from all three surfaced again in the PEMP.

Kyungnam's provincial government concurred that Pusan's problems needed to be resolved. To promote a healthy metropolitan economy, the province sought to form a balance among the heavily concentrated economic powers in the capital region of Seoul. However, the concerned parties strongly disagreed about which issues and whose interests were priorities. Urban transit line extensions, new road construction, industrial development, housing and resort complex development, and waste dump locations were all highly contentious issues. The entire planning process can be regarded as a battle between metropolitan Pusan and Kyungnam Province about who should bear the financial, environmental, and social costs.

Massive Administrative Boundary Changes in 1994 and 1995
The above case studies (see also Kim, Kum, and Kwon 1998, 40-43) illustrate that Korea's local government reforms until the early 1990s created a fragmented local government system. Such problems were expected to be aggravated from the early 1990s because of decentralization to the local government (Hong and Cho 1997, 18). Local councils with elected representatives had been established since 1991, and municipal elections were scheduled for August 1995. Complexities from local government fragmentation were exacerbated by increasing activities of local council members and rising public demands on the government during the period of rapid transition from an authoritarian to a more liberal society in Korea.

By the mid-1990s, Korean politicians, bureaucrats, and planners realized that certain problems associated with fragmentation had to be resolved through municipal amalgamations. There was also consensus that these municipal amalgamations would be more complicated after the municipal elections. Therefore, the Ministry of Home Affairs announced a plan for local governance reform in early 1994 (Hong and Cho 1997, 18-21). The announcement detailed the proposed amalgamation process and the list of affected municipalities.

The reform process consisted mainly of two steps: the selection step and the institutional and legal integration step. The main activities included in the selection step were public hearings, municipal referendums, and local councils' recommendations. The selection step itself contained three stages. The first stage involved screening the affected municipalities, identified in the list of the potential amalgamation candidates prepared by the Ministry of Home Affairs. The second stage involved mainly metropolitan cities' territorial expansions, such as in Pusan, and further divisions of large districts within metropolitan cities. The third stage involved the creation of agreements between those municipalities that failed to develop an agreement in the first attempt. To finalize the whole process before the municipal elections, the central government established deadlines for each stage: the first stage was to be completed by August 1994, the second stage by December 1994, and the third stage by May 1995 (Hong and Cho 1997, 18-25).

The goal of these reforms was to amalgamate as many municipalities as possible in a democratic manner. To achieve this goal, the government actively advertised expected benefits of the reform through various media, received public input from municipal referendums, and sought input from local councils. The government emphasized a "bottom-up approach," which contrasted with its past authoritarian approach and policies. The details of the final decision were not established in advance but were decided after the fact rather spontaneously. There were no clear indications about what to do, for example, if there were inconsistencies between municipal referendum results and local councils' decisions.

The ministry's list of amalgamation candidates included forty-seven cities and forty-three counties. These municipalities were selected based on criteria – thoroughly described later in this chapter – such as the spatial scope of daily life, a shared regional identity of the local population, governance efficiency, and the existence of balanced growth between an urban core and its surrounding hinterlands. The reform sought a return to the old system in which each county hosted one town centre – but as a city rather than a county. Each of the ninety candidates fit into one of the three restructuring categories: the integration of two or three cities, the integration of a city within a county, or the incorporation of a county into a city. This reform of "urban-rural integration" contrasts with the earlier reforms of "urban-rural separation" since it sought to create consolidated municipalities containing an urban core and its surrounding rural hinterlands. Thus, some cities without such hinterlands, such as Ahnyang, Kunpo, and Uiwang, were excluded as amalgamation candidates.

The second step of the reform process entailed the institutional and legal integration of those municipalities selected in the first step. The central government's plan for this integration consisted of formulating the appropriate laws, creating national assembly decisions, and integrating the affected municipalities' organizations and properties. Responsibility for the first two tasks was given to the national government and national assembly. For the third task, the central government established guidelines and created a task force that consisted of twenty people, including representatives from the municipal bureaucracy and civic organizations, but the provincial governments were responsible for its implementation.

The central government coordinated the reform process by allowing each province to set dates for municipal referendums and local councils' decisions, both within a fairly limited time frame. Based on principles and rationales developed by the Korea Local Administration Research Institute (KRILA), a semigovernment policy institute, national government representatives, national politicians, and academics actively debated the amalgamation issue; in part, to publicize the agenda. Local level counterparts also actively debated the issues in order to delineate local implications of the proposed reform. Local politicians, in particular, did not miss the opportunity to make themselves known to the public, since the debates were highly controversial and well covered by various local and national news media.

The first round of the screening process began in March 1994 and continued for three months. While heated debates continued, the municipal referendums occurred in the ninety amalgamation candidates, under the provincial government's guidance, only two months after the official announcement of the reform policies. In the affected municipalities, each household's representative was asked for his or her opinion and level of support for amalgamation, either through agreement or disagreement. While most municipalities conducted this referendum through community meetings, the municipalities in Kyungnam and Chunnam Provinces voted through a mail survey. In thirty-three cities and thirty-two counties, more than 50 percent of voters agreed with amalgamation, thus allowing thirty-three integrated cities. Notably, 82.6 percent of the total number of authorized households voted, while 85 percent of the urban voters and 67 percent of the rural voters agreed to reform proposals.

The second round of the referendum was executed several months after the end of the first round. This round focused on the territorial expansion of metropolitan cities and municipal subdivision. However, it also included some municipalities that failed to generate an agreement on their earlier reform proposals. In particular, the city of Dongkwangyang in the province of Junnam was urged to repeat its referendum since the first attempt had failed because of a disagreement with Kwangyang County, its partner county. The nearby city of Yoesoo also conducted a second referendum but with a different reform proposal, which included one additional municipality, the city of Yoechun. Eventually, the Kwangyang-Dongkwangyang referendum succeeded, while the Yoesoo area's referendum failed again (Hong and Cho 1997, 21-25).

Following the two rounds of municipal referendums, municipal and provincial councils made their recommendations for reform. Council members were asked to express their opinions about each of the sixty-five municipalities screened by local referendums. Municipal councils made positive recommendations for fifty-seven of these municipalities, while provincial councils' recommendations parallelled the results of the municipal referendums. This process was completed by the end of June 1994.

Concurrent to the local process of reform, the national assembly prepared for the legal basis for amalgamation. Since such a reform was uncommon in Korean history in terms of its scale and characteristics, a new law had to be developed. The Ministry of Home Affairs drafted the bills of these urban-rural integrated cities, bills that were approved in national assembly meetings in August 1994 and December 1994. Given this legal base, thirty-five new urban-rural integrated cities came into existence in January 1995 to replace seventy existing municipalities.

Even after the initial completion of local governance reform, with its several complicated steps, the Korean central government's efforts persisted. Based on lessons gained from the previous municipal referendums, the government attempted a third round of referendums. Supported by local initiatives in some cases, the central government sought agreements from municipalities that had failed earlier but that still had potential if the reform proposal were altered. Through this third round of municipal referendums, an additional five urban-rural integrated cities were added to the total. Ultimately, forty integrated cities, containing forty-one former cities and thirty-nine former counties, were established through Korea's local government reform in the mid-1990s.

Discussion

Based on the above case studies, this section describes the criteria used in selecting amalgamation candidates, the process of reform implementing, the main reform actors, and the reform outcomes.

Criteria

As indicated previously, the Korean local governance reform of the mid-1990s implied in general a return to the old system, involving a county with an urban centre. Therefore, the reform's focus was on municipalities that had experienced fragmentation during the period of urban expansion. The central government, however, wanted to have some criteria to justify its reform initiative and screening scheme, hiding its previous policy mistakes – that is, the division of municipalities. KRILA had developed the four criteria used in the reform process: efficiency, scope of daily life, common local identity, and balanced growth (Hong and Cho 1997, 10-15).

The criterion of efficiency involved reducing the costs of local government management. This criterion was introduced because Korea's fragmented local government landscape generated redundancies in local governance. A large number of small municipalities required extra budgets to support additional politicians, government officials, and office space. Additional operating costs and expenditures were created by the expansion of the organizational and physical structures of Korea's fragmented local government. These expenditures were perceived as redundant under the trend of reducing government size since the mid-1980s.

The criterion of scope of daily life reflected the spatial range of the average person's daily activities, such as commuting and shopping. Generally, the core cities remained as both the geographical and functional centres of the counties. Even after many of the county centres were separated to form new cities, county residents relied on the former county centre for their employment, education, government, and shopping opportunities and services. This criterion, therefore, was employed to target counties and cities linked both geographically and functionally, with strong economic, employment, and civic ties.

The criterion of common local identity represented the identity shared between residents of a city and its neighbouring municipality (or municipalities). In the Korean context, residents of a county and a city that shared the same territory for their daily activities often shared a common local identity. This is especially true in Korea when the territorial size of a county is very small and when any place within the county can be accessed by an hour's drive from the county's centre. However, as local government fragmentation occurred after the separation of cities, counties and cities tended to lose their shared local identities and their cooperative spirits, and this loss negatively affected intermunicipal coordination and cooperation, as documented in the Ahnyang and Pusan case studies above.

The Process

Arguably, the central government's goals for Korea's local government reform in the mid-1990s were reasonably well achieved within a given time frame. The reform occurred so suddenly, however, that it left local residents without adequate time to fully understand its implications. The central government ultimately failed in achieving its desire for a democratic process. Instead, it forcefully urged local residents and councils to reach an agreement on amalgamation, particularly regarding municipalities that had conducted several rounds of municipal referendums, such as the Yoesoo area (Hong and Cho 1997, 18-25). Clearly, the central government preferred amalgamation, as evidenced by its intervention in the process by persuading local councils and residents through various means.

Additionally, there were several occasions when the central government unfairly interpreted referendum results. In the case of the Yoesoo region, the majority of voting households did not approve the reform in the first round of municipal referendums. The central government, however, considered only valid votes, which raised the approval level to 53 percent, to further its purpose of creating more amalgamated cities (Hong and Cho 1997, 23). Although the design of the process was fair, especially given the short time frame, ad hoc and spontaneous decision making was common at the local level. In fact, there were several referendums with considerable disagreement between the parties. For example, even if one municipal council had agreed to amalgamate, its counterpart might have disagreed. In such situations, the central government tended to intervene and exercise its authority, making a final decision often with a strong preference toward amalgamation. This intervention was one of the reasons for the large number of amalgamations.

Main Actors

Local governments maintained little political autonomy in Korea's authoritarian governing system before the decentralization policies of the 1980s and 1990s. Previous local administrative units, without elected representatives, were simply instruments for executing central government policies. However, the central government has been forced since the early 1980s to devolve its powers to local government and the public because of increasing grassroots demands for decentralization and democracy. Consequentially, fundamental changes in the local government systems occurred in the late 1980s and 1990s. Elections for provincial governors and municipal mayors have been held every four years since 1991, the first local elections since abolishment of the system in 1962.

Korea's local government reforms seriously considered public input. Municipal referendums were introduced as an essential step in screening municipal candidates for amalgamation. Clearly, the central government wanted conformity with public opinions and attitudes, although it was not completely neutral in interpreting and complying with the results of municipal referendums. The central government attempted to increase support for amalgamation through repeated referendums with revised reform proposals.

However, the national government was also a major contributing factor during the process of amalgamation and reform. The central government established the reform process. Although it rarely intervened directly in the screening process, it designed the procedures and guidelines governing the whole process. The Ministry of Home Affairs was supported by KRILA in providing the theoretical and logical bases for the reform. Funded primarily by the ministry, KRILA was easily influenced by its requests. KRILA often published extensive reports under its own name or through the ministry for documentation purposes.

Although Korean politicians and academics were also important factors concerning governance issues, they did not have a significant effect on the local government reform process. National politicians simply approved the new legislation regarding the establishment of integrated cities drafted by national bureaucrats. Local politicians tended to follow public attitudes and opinions rather than initiating them. There was not a single case in which a local council went against the results of a municipal referendum. Similarly, the provincial councils' recommendations generally parallelled the results of municipal referendums.

Outcomes

After the reform process, Korea's fragmented local government system has now been streamlined, correcting for the problems created in earlier reforms since the 1960s. Now the territorial and population sizes of municipalities and the balance between urban and rural characters within the integrated cities are believed to be reasonable. Therefore, the mid-1990s reform of Korea's local government system is believed to have been a success.

However, it is questionable whether the reform was necessary even though the current system is better than the previously fragmented system. Had the reforms from the 1960s through the 1980s not occurred, reforms that involved the widespread separation of urban centres from host counties, the 1990s local government reforms would have been unnecessary. The latter reforms might have been avoided had some urbanizing counties simply been incorporated into urban municipalities. Instead, the Korean local reform policies opted for three stages: integration, separation, and integration again. Korea could have saved the political energy and prevented the controversy that arose from the reform processes of the mid-1990s by avoiding the redundancies and fragmentation in the local governing system created through urban-rural separation.

Conclusions

This chapter introduced the mid-1990s process of local government restructuring in Korea. The chapter described the local government system and its historical background related to the current administrative boundaries. To discuss lessons from the Korean experience, the chapter distinguished the "urban-rural separation" policies prevalent in Korea from the 1960s through the 1980s and the "urban-rural integration" policies of the mid-1990s. Finally, the chapter delineated the main criteria used in selecting municipal amalgamation candidates, the main actors in the decision-making process, and the final outcomes of the reforms.

This progression revealed that Korea currently possesses a less fragmented and more streamlined system as a result of these reforms. The political process of these reforms has been perceived as effective, reasonably democratic, and fair but as needing some improvement. A large number of municipalities were rapidly amalgamated through several stages in the decision-making process. The process mobilized various sectors of the society and used diverse means of decision making, such as municipal referendums and recommendations from local councils and the national assembly. In terms of designing the process and encouraging public input, the Korean experience could be used as an international model of reforming municipal boundaries. However, the necessity of such a complicated reform process is questionable had the Korean government not separated urban centres from their host counties prior to the 1990s.

Ultimately, it is too early to determine whether the central government's reform goals have been achieved: goals of balancing growth, promoting cooperation between urban and rural areas, recovering local identities, and reducing administrative redundancies. Several reports question the achievement of these goals. For instance, Jun-Hyun Hong and Jin-Rae Cho (1997, 53-67) argue that the reforms have not corrected the administrative redundancies that existed in the former government system related to the organizational structure and the number of government officials. Arguably, these reforms have provided a platform for ameliorating fragmentation in Korea's local government structure but have not fully achieved the central government's goals.

References

Chamber of Commerce and Industry of Pusan (CCIP). 1988. *A Study on Directions of Development for Pusan Metropolitan Region* (Korean). Pusan: Chamber of Commerce and Industry of Pusan.

–. 1992. *A Study on the Characteristics of Pusan Metropolitan Region* (Korean). Pusan: Chamber of Commerce and Industry of Pusan.

Hong, Jun-Hyun, and Jin-Rae Cho. 1997. *An Evaluation of Local Government Restructuring by City-County Consolidation* (Korean). Seoul: Korea Institute of Public Administration.

–. 1998. *Local Government Restructuring and Boundary Adjustment in Korea* (Korean). Seoul: Korea Local Administration Research Institute.

Institute of Pusan Development Systems (IPDS). 1992. *An Exercise of Five-Year Development Planning for Pusan-Kyungnam Region*. Pusan: Institute of Pusan Development Systems.

Kim, Byung-Kuk, Chang-Ho Kum, and Oh-Chul Kwon. 1998. *An Alternative Approach to Local Autonomous Systems: Focused on Administrative Tiers and Areas* (Korean). Seoul: Korea Local Administration Research Institute.

Koo, Bon-Young, and Dong-Ho Shin. 2000. "Conflicts between Neighbouring Cities in the Korean Capital Region: The Cases of Ahnyang, Gunpo, and Uiwang." Paper prepared for the Second Conference of the International Critical Geography Group, Taegu, Korea, 9-13 August.

Ministry of Construction and Transportation (MoCT). 1995. *The Plan for the Extended Metropolitan Pusan* (Korean). Pusan: Ministry of Construction and Transportation.

Shin, Dong-Ho. 2000. "Governing Inter-Regional Conflict: The Planning Approach to Managing Spill-Overs of Extended Metropolitan Pusan, Korea." *Environment and Planning A* 32, 3: 507-18.

10
Reorganizing Urban Space in Postreform China
Jianfa Shen

China has undergone rapid economic development and urbanization since 1978. During this postreform period, annexation and a new "system of city governing county" has given urban China many new cities as well as expanding city boundaries. Numerous studies have examined urban growth, urban systems, and the urbanization process in China (Ma and Fan 1994; Shen 1995, 2000, 2002; Shen and Spence 1996; Guldin 1997; Fan 1999; Lin 2001; Shen, Wong, and Feng 2002). However, these studies have mostly neglected the procedures, governance, and consequences of city designation and boundary change. The exceptions include Ma and Cui (1987), who considered the impact of the changing administrative areas of cities based on the scope and size of the urban population; Zhou and Hu (1992), who conducted a study of the impact of the system of city governing county on the economic development in counties; and Liu and Wang (2000), who thoroughly examined the Chinese city system and its evolution.

City governments are critical components of a hierarchical administrative system operating under the strong control of China's central government. Reorganization of the urban territory and urban governments has been considerable in postreform China, although open disputations are rare. The majority of the urban reorganizations are consistent with the needs of economic development and social change. Rural area residents are generally happy that their community/municipality is designated as a city or is annexed by a city because they perceive such a change from rural status to urban status as an improvement. Nevertheless, various problems and conflicts do exist between two cities or between the central city and the counties under its administration. Such situations raise important questions of urban-regional governance. These situations also drive further urban space reorganization for efficiency. As urbanization continues, the organization and reorganization of the urban space in China is an important project (Shen 2000).

China's recent experience with this organization and reorganization is the focus of this chapter. It examines the procedures and reforms of city designation and boundary adjustment in postreform China. The next two sections will discuss the procedures, regulations, and major forms of city designation and boundary change in China. The following two sections will examine the reforms, progress, and conflicts of city designation and boundary change. The final section will conclude the chapter.

Procedures and Regulations for City Designation and Boundary Change

In 1909, the Qing Dynasty government announced the earliest state regulation on the designation of autonomous cities in China, the Regulation on Autonomous Cities, Towns, and Townships (Liu and Wang 2000). The autonomous cities and towns were subject to the monitoring of the powerful provincial, prefecture, or county governments. In 1930, the government of the Republic of China introduced the Law on the Designation of Cities, revised in 1943. In 1947, China had twelve cities under the administration of the state executive council and fifty-seven cities under the administration of provincial governments.

The central government administered 132 cities, including twelve municipalities, when the People's Republic of China was founded in 1949. In 1954, the first National People's Congress passed the Constitution of the People's Republic of China, which, along with other relevant legislation concerning the organization of local governments, established the political power structure for Chinese cities. A People's Congress for a city was the organization delegated with the state power. The People's Committee, the form of the city government, was both the executive arm of the People's Congress and the state's local administrative arm and thus responsible to both levels. Such a power structure ensured that the central government had control over the various levels of local governments and initiating changes.

The central government influenced city designation and boundary change both before and after the 1978 economic reform. During the 1950s and 1960s, China's regulations concerning city designation were repeatedly changed. In 1955, the People's Republic State Council announced the first regulation concerning city and town designation. This regulation stipulated that settlements with populations over 100,000, and other important settlements with populations under 100,000, could be designated as cities. The introduction of a household registration system in 1958 was a significant accomplishment since it differentiated nonagricultural and agricultural populations. The system was introduced to control the increasing rural to urban migration and the rapid urban growth. Between 1958 and 1982, only urban nonagricultural population was counted as urban population. This restriction was significant because only the nonagricultural population was granted food tokens and access to the housing, jobs, and education facilities in cities. This control over the transfer of designation to nonagricultural population status was practised up to the 1990s (Shen 1995; Shen, Wong, and Feng 2002). Between 1949 and 1978, the designation of cities was also tightly controlled, and the total number of cities increased from only 132 to 193.

With rapid economic growth in the postreform period, urban development has been recognized as an important factor in China's development. Changes and new institutional arrangements have been introduced in city designation and expansion. The revised constitution passed by the fifth National People's Congress in 1982 established the current procedure for city designation and boundary change. This constitution stipulates the following.

- The country shall consist of provinces, autonomous regions, and municipalities. These are the provincial-level administrative units, and municipalities are cities at the provincial level.
- A province or an autonomous region may consist of autonomous states, counties, autonomous counties, banners, autonomous banners, and cities. Autonomous states are prefecture-level administrative units. Cities can be designated at the prefecture level or county level. The remaining other units are county-level administrative units.
- Municipalities and large cities may consist of districts and counties.
- The designation of a province, autonomous region, or municipality needs to be approved by the National People's Congress, the body with the highest political power in China.
- The boundaries of provincial-level units and the designation and boundaries of an autonomous state, county, autonomous county, or city need to be approved by the State Council, the body with the highest administrative power in the country.

China's current state administrative system consists of six levels: (1) the State Council; (2) the provincial-level units; (3) the prefecture-level units; (4) the county-level units; (5) the town-/township-/street-level units; and (6) the villages'/residents' committees. Formal government establishments exist down to the town/township level. The street level unit is a government agency typically found in urban settlements, while the villages'/residents' committees are grassroots organizations under government guidance. Urban residents' committees are organized within a street or town, while villagers' committees are organized within a town or township. The components of the administrative system detailed above are critical in a city's designation and boundary changes, because they are often implemented as a whole unit at the town/township level or county level. For example, a whole county might be designated as a city or a county, or a county-level city may be annexed as an urban district of a prefecture-level city.

Cities may be designated at the provincial level (e.g., municipalities of Shanghai, Beijing, Tianjin, and Chongqing), the prefecture level, or the county level (Figure 10.1). A large city may have several urban districts designated as county-level units. In 1985, the State Council announced the Regulation on the Management of Administrative Divisions, which further formalized the procedures for the designation and boundary changes of administrative units. The Bureau of Administrative Division and Place Names of the Ministry of Civil Affairs is primarily responsible for the management of administrative divisions and their boundaries. The regulation maintained that the State Council must approve important city boundary changes, while the provincial governments may be empowered by the State Council to approve partial city boundary changes. Before any boundary is changed, the Ministry of Civil Affairs is requested to consult various government departments on ethnic population, personnel, finance, foreign affairs, urban and rural construction, and place names. The following sections discuss the various forms of city designation and city boundary adjustment in China.

Forms of City Designation and Boundary Change

There have been two major forms of city designation in China. The first form of "separating a city from a rural county" was commonly used before 1978, when the separation of urban from rural areas was emphasized (Figure 10.2). Under this form of city designation, a central town, usually the seat of county government or an important town with economic functions, and its surrounding area would be separated from the original county. As a result, the original county would be divided into two administrative units: a county possessing the majority of the original county's area and a city with only the central town's area. The new county would usually adopt the name of the original county. In many cases, the new city was fully surrounded by the new county, which had been deprived of its central town. For example, Shishi City was originally part of Jinjiang County and was designated as a city in 1987 (Anonymous 1993). The new Shishi City had an area of 160 km^2, a population of 250,000, and administrated one street and three towns. The new Jinjiang County had an area of 649 km^2, a population of 900,000, and administrated fifteen towns. Jinjiang County was designated as another county-level city in 1992 (Gu, Qiu, and Ye 1999).

The second form of city designation, the "redesignation of an entire county as a city" (Figure 10.2), has been widely used in China's postreform period and has accounted for approximately 70 percent of China's current cities. Through this form of city designation, a whole county is redesignated as a city if it meets the established criteria for city designation. For example, Conghua County, under the administration of Guangzhou City, was designated as a county-level city in 1994 (DCA and MPH 2000). It had an area of 2,009 km^2 and a population of 470,000 in 1998; in the same year, though, the city had a nonagricultural population of only 130,000. This setup was different from the conventional concept of a city with a central built-up area. A county-level city often consists of several towns and townships. In the case of Conghua City, it consists of fifteen towns and 1,865 rural settlements throughout its territory.

In China, there have been three major forms of city boundary changes: (1) "the system of city governing county," (2) "the annexation of a part of or the whole city/county as an urban district," and (3) "the merger of two cities." The first form of city-governed counties is an important method of city area expansion (Figure 10.2). This form was initially practised in the 1950s. In 1950, Luda City administered Lushun City (county level), Jin County, and Benxi County. By the late 1950s, one-eighth of China's counties were affected by this form of boundary change, in which the counties were placed under the jurisdiction of 243 cities. With the postreform

Figure 10.1

Chinese provincial and municipal governments

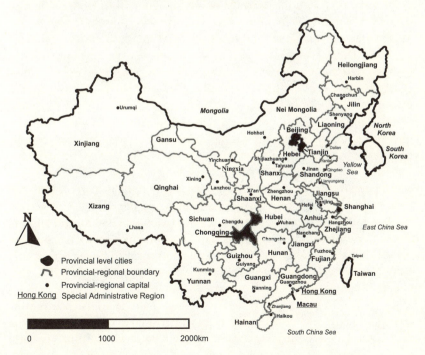

Figure 10.2
Schematic diagram of various boundary changes in China

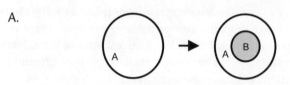
a. Separating a city (B) from a rural county (A)

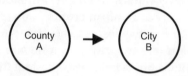
b. Redesignation of a whole county (A) as a city (B)

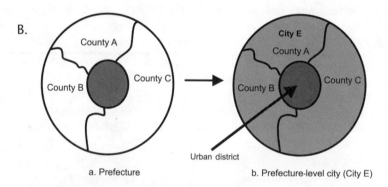

a. Prefecture   b. Prefecture-level city (City E)

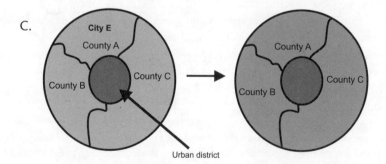

A. Two forms of city designation in China
B. Urban expansion through system of city governing county
C. Annexation of whole county/city as urban districts of a city (city E)

economic recovery and development in China, this form was again attempted in Jiangsu Province in 1982 and was subsequently introduced nationally after 1983. Typically, the central city in a prefecture is designated a prefecture-level city, all counties in the prefecture are placed under its administration, and the prefecture is abolished. In the postreform period, a county under a city's administration might later qualify for county-level city status. Thus, "a system of city governing city" has also emerged.

The second and third forms of boundary changes involve the expansion of a city's urban districts, generally within the city governing county system. Under the system of city governing county, a city consists of urban districts, counties, and county-level cities. Although urban districts and counties or county-level cities are both under the administration of a central city, the central city has only weak control over its counties or county-level cities because these latter governments have stronger political power than the governments of urban districts. As the urban proper of the central city, urban districts are under full control of the central city. Thus, expansion of a city's urban districts is more significant than the expansion of a city's boundary through the system of city governing county.

The second form of boundary change entails annexation of the whole or a part of a city or county (Figure 10.2). For example, prior to 2000, Guangzhou City had eight urban districts and administrated four county-level cities. Between 1992 and 1994, the latter were upgraded from county status. In 1998, these four county-level cities had an area of 6,022 km^2 and a population of 2.7 million. In May 2000, Guangzhou City, with the support of the provincial government and the approval of the State Council, annexed Huadu and Panyu as two new urban districts. It did so to gain control of the new international airport being constructed in Huadu City and the port facilities in Panyu City. After annexation, the total area of Guangzhou's urban districts increased by 2,275 km^2, its total population increased by 1.5 million, and its density decreased from 3,326 to 1,067 persons per square kilometre.

The third form of city boundary change entailing city mergers generally involved one prefecture-level city and one county-level city, both with strong economic powers. Merging two cities involves the reorganization of government functions in the two cities. For example, in Jiangsu Province in 2001, the county-level city, Wuxian, was merged with the prefecture-level city, Suzhou. Similarly, the county-level city Xishan was merged with the prefecture-level city Wuxi. Each city's situation was transformed from that of county surrounding city to that of city surrounding city, after the designation of the county also as a city. Urban development and construction in the region were undermined by the conflicting interests of two city governments. The merging of such twin cities appears to be an appropriate response to the acute problem of urban and regional governance.

Reforms and Progress of City Designation and Boundary Change

In postreform China, several counties have been designated as cities, and the city governing county system has been widely implemented throughout the country. Several large cities have also expanded their urban districts by annexing a part of or the whole county or county-level city. Economic considerations are the main reasons for such rapid city designation and boundary change. Continuous economic development in postreform China, with an annual gross domestic product growth rate between 7 and 10 percent, has induced the need for rapid urbanization. Urbanization has been considered a positive process, conducive to economic development. Cities are regarded as sources of wealth creation and perceived as economic centres that enhance the integration of urban and rural economies (Shen 2000).

China's central government has initiated several measures to accelerate the process of city designation. In 1983, the State Council approved a report on the *Institutional Reform of Prefectures and Cities* prepared by the Ministry of Civil Affairs. Some criteria in the report were then used internally for assessing cases of city designation and city governing county. These criteria of city designation were revised in 1986 and 1993, respectively (Liu and Wang 2000).

Before 1983, for city designation, a settlement required a nonagricultural population of 100,000. The 1983 report lowered this requirement. Such changes facilitated the widespread designation of cities in Chinese history. According to the 1983 report, a county with a population of fewer than 500,000 could be designated as a city if the seat of the county government had over 80,000 residents and its manufacturing output was over 200 million yuan. Also, a county with a population of more than 500,000 could be designated as a city if the nonagricultural population in the seat of county government accounted for over 20 percent of the county's total population and its manufacturing output was over 200 million yuan. Discretion was used for areas with special conditions.

The 1986 criteria had three main revisions to the 1983 report: they included a new section for upgrading a town to a city, they detailed required conditions for the introduction of a system of city governing county, and they raised the minimum thresholds for city designation of a county, since too many places had qualified for city status under the 1983 criteria. A town could be designated as a city if it had a nonagricultural population of over 60,000 and GDP of over 200 million yuan. Medium-sized cities with nonagricultural populations over 250,000 and a GDP over one billion yuan could administrate other counties. A county with a population of fewer than 500,000 could be designated as a city if the seat of county government had a nonagricultural population of over 100,000, had a proportion of nonagricultural population of over 60 percent, and had a manufacturing output of over 400 million yuan. A county with a total population of over 500,000 could be designated as a city if the seat of the county government had a nonagricultural population of over 120,000 and a manufacturing output of over 400 million yuan. Again discretion was used for cases with special conditions.

In 1993, China's State Council approved more sophisticated criteria for the designation of county-level cities and prefecture-level cities. This approval represented the first explicit stipulation of designation criteria for prefecture-level cities. The criteria stipulated that the main urban settlement, the seat of the city government, must have a nonagricultural population of over 200,000 and a strong economy for prefecture-level city designation. Criteria for the designation of a county as a city varied, depending on population density. The minimum nonagricultural population in the seat of city government was set at 80,000 for areas with a population density of fewer than 100 persons per square kilometre, 100,000 for areas with between 100 and 400 persons per square kilometre, and 120,000 for areas with over 400 persons per square kilometre.

In the postreform period, the total number of county-level and prefecture-level cities has dramatically increased, from 193 in 1978 to 668 in 1997 (Table 10.1). Of the 484 new cities designated in this period, only 65 were established through the form of separating a city from a rural county, while 419 were established by designating a whole county as a city (Liu and Wang 2000, 139). Nine cities had been merged or abolished, so the net increase was really only 475 cities in this period. This increase was particularly rapid between 1982 and 1997, when the designation criteria were revised in 1983, 1986, and 1993. The most significant increases occurred with county-level cities, which grew from 245 in 1982 to 517 in 1992. The rate of growth slowed down when more detailed and restrictive criteria were introduced in 1993. Indeed, the number of total cities was reduced from 668 in 1997 to 663 in 2000 due to the merging of the cities mentioned before. However, in 1997, the State Council had to freeze all applications for the city designation of a county as more counties qualified for city status. It is estimated that in the future most counties may disappear if the current practice of city designation of a county persists. Thus, the position of cities in the administrative system of China is urgently in need of reconsideration. One possibility is to designate cities within a county. On the other hand, the adoption of the system of city governing county after 1982, and the upgrading of some county-level cities to prefecture-level cities increased the number of prefecture-level cities from 112 in 1982 to 244 in 2000.

As previously mentioned, the rationale in introducing the system of city governing county was to strengthen a city's leading role in a regional economy and to integrate the urban and rural economies. The city governing county system was first tried in 1982 in Jiangsu and Liaoning, two

Table 10.1

Number of cities and the share of city population and city nonagricultural population in total population in China, 1949-2000

Year	Municipalities	Vice-provincial city	Prefecture-level city	County-level city	All cities	Share of city population (%)	Share of city non-agricultural population (%)
1949	12	-	53	67	132	7.3	5.1
1950	13	-	63	68	144	N/A	N/A
1951	13	-	67	76	156	N/A	N/A
1955	3	-	82	79	164	N/A	N/A
1958	2	-	68	114	184	14.0	9.2
1960	2	-	87	110	199	N/A	N/A
1961	2	-	79	127	208	15.4	10.5
1963	2	-	78	97	177	13.1	9.4
1965	2	-	76	90	168	12.2	9.2
1970	3	-	79	95	177	11.2	8.0
1975	3	-	96	86	185	11.4	8.0
1978	3	-	98	92	193	12.1	8.3
1980	3	-	107	113	223	13.6	9.2
1982	3	-	112	130	245	N/A	N/A
1985	3	-	162	159	324	20.1	11.2
1990	3	-	185	279	467	29.3	13.2
1992	3	-	189	325	517	32.5	14.0
1995	3	16	194	427	640	41.3	16.5
1997	4	15	207	442	668	42.7	17.6
1998	4	15	212	437	668	42.6	18.0
1999	4	15	221	427	667	N/A	N/A
2000	4	15	244	400	663	N/A	N/A

Sources: Urban Socioeconomic Survey Team (1999, 4-5, 23); State Statistical Bureau (2000); Wang (2001, 227).

highly developed coastal provinces. By 1994, the system had been implemented in all of China's provinces except Hainan on mainland China. A total of 741 counties, thirty-one autonomous counties, nine banners, and two special districts were put under the administration of 192 cities, accounting for 93.8 percent of the total number of municipalities and prefecture-level cities. On behalf of provincial governments, prefecture-level cities also administered 240 county-level cities. In Hainan Province, all counties or county-level cities fall under the administration of the provincial government. In Hebei, Liaoning, Jiangsu, Zhejiang, Fujian, and Guangdong, all counties and county-level cities come under the administration of prefecture-level cities (Ministry of Civil Affairs 2000).

Besides the changes in the prefecture-level and county-level cities, a new provincial-level municipality, Chongqing, was established in 1997. Chongqing is yet another example of the economic considerations in the designation of new cities. The new municipality was established to cope with the construction, migration, and development related to the "Three Gorges Project," which commenced in 1994 and is anticipated to be operational by 2009. The project involves an investment of over 200 billion yuan and the resettlement of over one million migrants (Changjiang Hydrological Commission 1997). In 1998, Chongqing had an area of 82,300 km^2 and a total population of over thirty million. The urban proper of the municipality had an area of 12,479 km^2, a total population of 8.4 million, and a nonagricultural population of 3.5 million in 1998 (Urban Socioeconomic Survey Team 1999). The municipality had thirteen urban districts, four county-level cities, eighteen counties, and five autonomous counties under its administration. In many senses, the municipality looked more like a province than a city (RIPN and AADPN 1999).

In the postreform period, pro-provincial cities were also introduced in China. A pro-provincial city's status is higher than that of a prefecture-level city but lower than a municipality's. A city is designated as pro-provincial to promote its autonomy for economic development purposes. In 1983, some of the large cities and some provincial capitals received a privileged position – that is, listing of their economic programs in the national plan. In 1994, there were sixteen such cities, including Chongqing, Shenzhen, Dalian, Qingdao, Ningbo, and Xiamen, in addition to some provincial capitals with strong economic and political status. A formal pro-provincial status was granted to these cities in 1994. In 1997, when Chongqing was designated as a municipality, the total number was reduced to fifteen (Table 10.1). The fifteen pro-provincial cities and four municipalities were the primary economic and urban centres in China. They remained under the administration of provincial governments, but they had the same power as a provincial government in developing and implementing economic plans and in economic administration. Thus, in

China's postreform period, an administrative system was established with four different levels of cities: municipality, pro-provincial city, prefecture-level city, and county-level city.

Problems and Conflicts of City Designation and Boundary Change
Under a hierarchical administrative system, China's central government has substantial power in the process of city designation and boundary change. Its influence is derived from three main points. First, the National People's Congress or the State Council is empowered by China's constitution to approve city designation and boundary change. Second, the State Council has the power to establish and revise criteria and guidelines for city designation and boundary change. Third, the power of the central government has been implemented through the hierarchical administrative system as local governments are made responsible to both the People's Congress of their territory and the governments at the higher level. Thus, local governments are not completely autonomous in China.

Nevertheless, local governments at the provincial, prefecture, and county levels play an active role in the overall process of city designation and boundary change. Local governments often initiate and experiment with new forms of city designation and boundary change. For example, if a county seeks designation as a city, it must prepare relevant documents to make an application. Thus, there are bottom-up initiatives and feedback from the local levels of government in addition to the solely top-down directions and guidelines from the central level of government. Once successful, the central government would endorse these grassroots forms of city designation and boundary change and introduce them to other areas. For example, the system of city governing county was first tried in Jiangsu Province in 1982 and then was introduced in other regions of China.

Overall, city designation and boundary change are matters of both local and central governments. Public participation concerning city designation and boundary change is rare, although in 1961 the State Council stipulated that, for changes in administrative divisions, the city must consult the public. In most cases, designating a county as a city, putting a county or a county-level city under the administration of a prefecture-level city, and designating a part of or the whole county-level city as an urban district are all in the interests of the local government and its residents. Local governments are the most affected stakeholders concerning city designation and boundary change, but they must follow the decisions of higher levels of governments according to the hierarchical administration system. Open disputations are rare in this regard, and most issues get solved behind doors. Nevertheless, some conflicts do exist, and they must be handled properly.

The separating a city from a rural county form of boundary change, the main form of designating a new city prior to 1978, often resulted in problems associated with a rural county losing its main urban centre. This separation had a negative impact on urbanization in the rural county. Without a strong economic and urban centre, urbanization and development in the rural county were delayed. After 1978, the redesignation of a whole county as a city form of boundary change avoided this problem. This form had a positive impact on the region's urban development and urban-rural integration. Traditionally, the products produced by a region could be marketed as the products of a more prosperous, urban city instead of those of a more rural county. Some new county-level cities were able to attract foreign investment that may not have come in with county status.

However, three problems have occurred with the redesignation as county-level cities. First, under this form, some counties that are economically strong, with only a small urban centre, have also been designated as cities. For example, in 1997, there were twenty-eight county-level cities with nonagricultural populations of fewer than 50,000. Twelve of these cities had a share of nonagricultural population of less than 20 percent. Such cities operated more as a county than a city. This setup resulted in confusion between the urban concept and the urban population statistics (Zhou and Shi 1995).

Second, the emphasis on industrialization and urbanization, after county-level cities are established, has resulted in the loss of much arable land. Additionally, industrial and economic development zones have surrounded and encircled large amounts of arable land (Cartier 2001; Marton 2000), thus limiting their future agricultural potential.

Third, a rural county with an urban centre that previously held city status may also have been designated as a county-level city. Thus, a new phenomenon of a new city surrounding an old city has occurred. Generally, the old city has a small area, and its further development is constrained by its city boundary, while the new city is interested in developing its own urban centre in its territory. Where the new city's urban centre lies adjacent to the old city's urban centre, problems emerge in coordinating the urban infrastructure now under the jurisdiction of two local governments. The cases of Foshan City and Nanhai City in Guangdong Province exemplify these problems. Nanhai City was originally a rural county with an urban centre designated as Foshan City many years ago. In 1992, Nanhai was also designated as a city, which completely surrounded Foshan. By 2000, Nanhai had become economically stronger than Foshan, more than doubling its GDP with 33.9 billion yuan, compared with Foshan's 15.9 billion yuan (Statistical Bureau of Guangdong 2001). In some other cases, a new county-level city would try to relocate its seat of government from the old city to a town in its own territory. Doing so would ultimately reduce the agglomeration effects of urban facilities.

The city governing county system has been designed to enhance the integration of the central cities and their surrounding hinterlands. However, determining which counties and county-level cities are to be administrated by a central city is often a result of negotiations between the central city and the provincial government, or solely by the provincial government, instead of by negotiations between the local governments. In some cases, from the very beginning, intense conflict has occurred between the governments of the central city and the county-level units.

Two major problems of the city governing county system have been identified. The first problem is that the central city is interested in the overall planning and administration (centralization) of the whole city. However, due to limited resources, the government of a central city might focus on urban issues and neglect the interests of county-level units. For example, a central city might give priority to urban interests in bidding for large construction projects, foreign investment, and the right to direct foreign trade. In some extreme cases, a central city can use its administrative power to import agricultural products at low prices from the counties, thus exploiting the counties economically. Thus, the city governing county system has been regarded as a system of "city eating county" instead of "city helping county" (Liu and Wang 2000, 1-2).

Initially, county-level units favoured administrative centralization in the central city and anticipated an equitable allocation of investment and resources. When these expectations did not materialize in many instances, some county-level units changed to favour decentralization to achieve their own development independently. A survey in 1990 on the city governing county system revealed that 88 percent of counties responded that competition existed between counties and the central cities for raw materials supply, investment, and projects. Factories were also duplicated. A third of the counties complained that the central cities put the most profitable enterprises, which had previously been under the jurisdiction of county-level units, under their direct jurisdiction (Zhou and Hu 1992).

The second problem resulted when city-governed counties generally replaced prefectures. Prefecture-level city designation has major implications for state organization. A prefecture is only a representative agency for the provincial government. But a prefecture-level city has its own fully-fledged government, adding a middle layer between the county-level and the provincial-level governments. Counties and county-level cities are subject to the decisions of prefecture-level cities, the provincial government, and the State Council. The government's overall efficiency is reduced since a province often administrates only eight pro-provincial or prefecture-level cities. In turn, these cities each administrate about six county-level cities or counties.

Conclusions

China's postreform period since 1978 represents the most significant period of urban expansion in the country's long history. The urban space has been repeatedly expanded, organized, and reorganized through the designation of new cities and the constant adjustment of city boundaries. Several factors have made these urban expansion and boundary changes necessary: the rapid urbanization process, state administrative reform toward decentralization, the need to achieve scale and agglomeration economies, and the need for efficient urban and regional governance. This chapter has examined the procedures, reforms, progress, and problems of these city designations and boundary adjustments in postreform China.

The city is an important political unit in China. There are currently four types of cities: municipalities, pro-provincial-level cities, prefecture-level cities, and county-level cities. China's constitution maintains that a city government is both the executive arm of the People's Congress in the city and the local administrative arm of the state. The city government is responsible to the state administrative organization. Thus, local governments are not completely autonomous. Although the state has devolved much of its power to local governments in the postreform period, the central government remains highly influential in China's hierarchical administrative system. The designation of a municipality still requires approval by the National People's Congress, and the designation of and any major changes to a city require approval of the State Council, which establishes and revises criteria and guidelines. The provincial governments are empowered by the State Council to approve a city's partial boundary changes.

While not fully autonomous, local governments play an active role in the process of city designation and boundary change. First, local governments often initiate new forms of city designation and boundary change. There are bottom-up initiatives and feedbacks from local to central governments. Second, local governments initiate the process to designate a new city or change the boundary of a city. But public participation is rare. In most cases, city designation and boundary change are in the interests of the local government and the local people. Local governments are also required to follow the decisions of higher-level governments. Open disputations are rare in this regard. Nevertheless, some conflicts do exist.

Two major forms of city designation are separating a city from a rural county and redesignating a whole county as a city. For the integration of urban and rural areas, the second form of city designation has been widely used in the postreform period. The criteria for city designation were revised in 1983, 1986, and 1993 to regulate the process of city designation.

The number of total cities increased from 193 in 1978 to 668 in 1997. Over 70 percent of the current cities in China are designated in this form. But such cities often consist of several urban settlements and many rural settlements and are thus different from the conventional concept of a city with a central built-up area. This type of city designation has also caused problems in measuring China's urban population and the level of urbanization.

Three major forms of city boundary change are the system of city governing county, the annexation of a part of or the whole city/county as an urban district, and the merger of two cities. The system of city governing county has been introduced to enhance the integration of a city and the counties in its hinterland. Prefecture-level cities have largely replaced prefectures in the government structure, and this addition of a prefecture-level city government between a provincial government and a county government has made the state system less efficient. A county under the administration of a city may later qualify for city status and be designated as a county-level city. Thus, a system of city governing city also emerged.

Introduction of the system of city governing county has had a positive impact on the urban development and the urban-rural integration in a region. But due to limited resources, the government of a central city focuses on the urban proper, while the interests of the county-level units are compromised. The system of city governing county is regarded by some as a system of "city eating county" instead of "city helping county."

In some cases of city governing city, there have been even more intense conflicts between the central city and the county-level city. Both cities may have strong economic power, but the central city may be physically bounded by a county-level city and have limited land for industrial and urban expansion. Two cities then compete in urban land and real estate development that can bring generous land revenues for the government. There are also problems in coordinating the urban infrastructure that now falls under the jurisdiction of two city governments. The solution to such problems is to merge two cities together. Such merging has already taken place in Jiangsu Province. The number of total cities in China was reduced from 668 in 1997 to 663 in 2000.

China's recent experience with city designation and boundary adjustment illustrates the challenges faced by a developing country in coping with rapid urbanization and urban expansion. In China, the state has used decentralization and institutional reform to reorganize the ever-expanding urban space toward a market economy. The state has been only partially successful in its attempts where acute conflicts of interest among various cities and counties still exist. A more transparent and open mechanism with more public participation is required to solve such conflicts and future city boundary adjustments. This change will accommodate further urban space expansion, reorganization, and reform.

References

Anonymous. 1993. *The Atlas of Fujian Province*. Fuzhou: Map Publishing House of Fujian Province.
Cartier, Carolyn. 2001. "'Zone Fever,' the Arable Land Debate, and Real Estate Speculation: China's Evolving Land Use Regime and Its Geographical Contradictions." *Journal of Contemporary China* 10, 28: 445-69.
Changjiang Hydrological Commission. 1997. *A Study on the Migration Related to Three Gorges Project*. Wuhai: Hubei Science and Technology Publishing House.
DCA and MPH (Department of Civil Affairs of Guangdong Province and Map Publishing House of Guangdong), eds. 2000. *Atlas of the Administrative Divisions of Guangdong Province*. Guangzhou: Map Publishing House of Guangdong.
Fan, C.C. 1999. "The Vertical and Horizontal Expansions of China's City System." *Urban Geography* 20, 6: 493-515.
Gu, C., Y. Qiu, and S. Ye. 1999. "The Designation and Development of New Cities in Mainland China." In Y.M. Yeung, D. Lu, and J. Shen, eds., *Urban, Rural, and Regional Development*, 223-46. Hong Kong: Hong Kong Institute of Asia-Pacific Studies.
Guldin, G.E., ed. 1997. *Farewell to Peasant China*. Armonk, NY: M.E. Sharpe.
Lin, G.C.S. 2001. "Metropolitan Development in a Transitional Socialist Economy: Spatial Restructuring in the Pearl River Delta, China." *Urban Studies* 38, 3: 383-406.
Liu, J., and Y. Wang. 2000. *Systems and Innovation: On the Development and Reform of the City System in China*. Nanjing: South-East University Press.
Ma, L.J.C., and G. Cui. 1987. "Administrative Changes and Urban Population in China." *Annals, Association of American Geographers* 77, 3: 373-95.
Ma, L.J.C., and M. Fan. 1994. "Urbanization from Below: The Growth of Towns in Jiangsu, China." *Urban Studies* 31, 10: 1625-45.
Marton, A.M. 2000. *China's Spatial Economic Development: Restless Landscapes in the Lower Yangzi Delta*. London: Routledge.
Ministry of Civil Affairs. 2000. *Summary of Administrative Divisions in the People's Republic of China 2000*. Beijing: China Map Publishing House.
RIPN and AADPN (Research Institute of Place Names of the Ministry of Civil Affairs and the Association of Administrative Divisions and Place Names). 1999. *Handbook of Administrative Divisions and Place Names of China 1999*. Beijing: China Social Publishing House.
Shen, J. 1995. "Rural Development and Rural to Urban Migration in China 1978-1990." *Geoforum* 26: 395-409.
–. 2000. "Chinese Urbanization and Urban Policy." In C.M. Lau and J. Shen, eds., *China Review 2000*, 455-80. Hong Kong: Chinese University Press.
–. 2002. "Urban and Regional Development in Post-Reform China: The Case of Zhujiang Delta." *Progress in Planning* 57, 2: 91-140.
Shen, J., and N.A. Spence. 1996. "Modelling Urban-Rural Population Growth in China." *Environment and Planning A* 28: 1417-44.
Shen, Jianfa, Wong Kwan-yiu, and Feng Zhiqiang. 2002. "State Sponsored and Spontaneous Urbanization in the Pearl River Delta of South China, 1980-1998." *Urban Geography* 23, 7: 674-94.
State Statistical Bureau. 2000. *China Urban Statistics Yearbook 2000*. Beijing: China Statistics Press.
Statistical Bureau of Guangdong. 2001. *Guangdong Statistical Yearbook 2001*. Beijing: China Statistics Press.
Urban Socioeconomic Survey Team. 1999. *Cities of New China over Fifty Years*. Beijing: State Statistical Bureau and Xinhua Publishing House.
Wang, Y., ed. 2001. *A Study on the Development Planning of Urbanization for the "Tenth Five-Year" Plan*. Beijing: China Planning Publishing House.
Zhou, Y., and D. Hu. 1992. "Questionnaire Survey on the Impact of 'Municipality Governing County System' to the Counties' Economy." *Economic Geography* 12, 1: 8-14.
Zhou, Y., and Y. Shi. 1995. "Toward Establishing the Concept of Physical Urban Area in China." *Acta Geographica Sinica* 50, 4: 289-301.

11
Local Government Reorganization in South Africa
Robert Cameron

Reorganization of local government boundaries has taken place in many developed and developing countries in recent years. South Africa is no exception to this global trend. What does make this country somewhat different is that it has had two major local government boundary reorganizations in the space of a few years. The 1994-95 reorganization was part of the interim constitutional phase that built in certain transitional safeguards for minorities at all levels of government (Cameron 1996; Cloete 1995). The final constitutional phase involved the move toward a majoritarian form of democracy with limited safeguards for minorities (Cameron 2001). A further boundary reorganization occurred during this final phase.

This chapter is a critical analysis of the local government reorganization of this final phase. The author was a member of the Municipal Demarcation Board that in 1999-2000 demarcated local government boundaries for the December 2000 local government elections.

Overview of South African Local Government
In 1910, South Africa became a union consisting of a central government, provincial governments, and local governments. Until the early 1990s, South African local government was characterized by segregation and apartheid. Separate local government structures were set up for whites, blacks, coloureds, and Asians. However, only urban white local government could be described as having a proper functioning system of local government with legitimately elected leaders and a viable tax base. There was no system of democratic local government in rural areas, even for whites (Cameron 1995).

The makers of South Africa's Constitution in the 1992-93 negotiations decided to divide the local government democratization into three phases. The pre-interim phase (1994-96) was basically a holding phase with nominated councils until the first local government elections. The interim phase (1996-2000) introduced a quasi-federal system in the country with a central government, nine provincial governments (up from four), and local governments (Figure 11.1). The new local government system was characterized by a number of power-sharing constitutional measures. It also entailed the rationalization of local government structures to 843, the amalgamation of many (but not all) black areas with surrounding white cities and towns, the creation of metropolitan government in the larger cities, and the introduction of democratic, two-tier local government in most rural areas in the country (Cloete 1995; Cameron 1996).

The Final Constitution came into partial effect in February 1997 and became fully effective after the 2000 local government elections. South African local government has always been relatively centralized, even for white local governments during the apartheid era. This centralization was largely due to the political need to enforce apartheid at the local level, although there were controls over local government finance as well. These controls were exercised largely by the provincial governments (Bekker and Humphries 1985; Cameron 1995). Although the interim phase deracialized

Figure 11.1

Provinces and metropolitan areas, South Africa

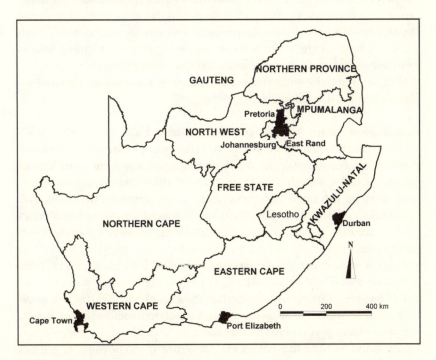

Source: Municipal Demarcation Board (2003).

local government, the hierarchical system of intergovernmental relations persisted.

The Final Constitution introduced the notion of cooperative governance whereby the three spheres of government – namely national, provincial, and local – were deemed to be "distinctive, interdependent, and interrelated." Theoretically, the Final Constitution has uplifted local government from a subordinate level of government to a significant sphere in its own right. Local government was also given important new development functions, including the promotion of social and economic development. The Constitution made provision for three different categories of local government. Category A municipalities are metropolitan, single-tier authorities, while Category B and C municipalities are lower- and upper-tier models, respectively, of the nonmetropolitan local government system (Cameron 2001).

Local Government: Municipal Demarcation Board

The Local Government: Municipal Demarcation Act of 1998 created a single Municipal Demarcation Board in South Africa. The demarcation of local government boundaries for the previous elections held in 1994-95 was performed by nine different provincial demarcation boards. One of the problems of the previous round of demarcation was unevenness in the boards' reports. Some provincial boards were technically competent, while the reports of some of the other boards were not of a particularly high standard. Some of the problems of nonviability of certain municipalities were due to poorly designed boundaries (Cameron 1999a).

Notable problems with the local government system in the interim phase included the following.

- Local governments were largely defined according to subjective needs and preferences rather than on the basis of any national norms and standards. For example, in certain provinces, there were some Transitional Local Councils (TLCs) with fewer than 100 registered voters, whereas in the same provinces some urban communities with over 15,000 voters had no primary local government. In the case of District Councils, they ranged from some 19,584 voters to over 1.5 million voters in size.
- There were major disparities in council sizes. In the cases of TLCs, the average number of registered voters per councillor ranged from 10 to 7,192 voters. Particularly in the KwaZulu-Natal and North-West provinces, approximately 50 percent of all registered voters did not have a primary local government to vote for.
- Approximately one-third of all TLCs and rural councils were quite small and had fewer than 2,000 voters.

Furthermore, problems emerged around situations in which communities were split by provincial boundaries (Sutcliffe 1999). Attempted gerrymandering of local boundaries for narrow partisan gain was also a major problem in many provinces. In the interim phase, demarcation boards had advisory powers only. Some provincial ministers for local government attempted to demarcate local government boundaries that would have advantaged their respective parties' electoral chances rather than supported provincial demarcation boards' proposals for more rational boundaries that would, at least theoretically, have facilitated service delivery and promoted development (Cameron 1999a).

A study of the demarcation process in the interim phase in the three major cities in South Africa, Johannesburg, Cape Town, and Durban (see Figure 11.1), showed that the respective provincial minister of local government had attempted to gerrymander metropolitan boundaries in all three cities. The three provinces were in fact controlled by three different political parties, the African National Congress (ANC), the National Party (NP), and the Inkatha Freedom Party (IFP), respectively, which indicated that gerrymandering was widespread among political parties. Government concern about gerrymandering was a major reason for the creation of an independent board with final decision-making powers.

The Final Constitution required that municipal boundaries should be demarcated by an independent board. The principles of independence are embodied in the Municipal Demarcation Board Act 27 of 1998. Provision is made for a board, which is a juristic person, is independent, and must be impartial and perform its functions without fear, favour, or prejudice.

The appointment procedure conformed to the independence requirements. Applicants with relevant local government experience were shortlisted by a selection panel headed by the deputy president of the Constitutional Court, Justice Pius Langa. Public interviews were held with these shortlisted candidates, and the selection panel submitted a list of fourteen names to the president. The president made eleven appointments from the fourteen given to him. There was one representative from each province, along with a chair and a vice chair. All the appointees were part-time except for the chair, Dr. Mike Sutcliffe, who was a full-time member.

Functions

The Municipal Demarcation Board became the final decision-making body when it came to the demarcation of local boundaries. All municipal boundaries had to be demarcated before the December 2000 municipal elections. It is rare in international terms for politicians to grant decision-making powers of this sort to appointed boards, so this board was novel in many respects (Cameron 1999b).

Provision was made for an appeal mechanism enabling stakeholders aggrieved by the determination of boundaries to appeal the decision. The board had to consider any objections and confirm, alter, or withdraw its determination.

The board's other functions included

- delimiting the wards and local government;
- working with other government departments to align functional boundaries such as health, police, transport, magistration, and education with municipal boundaries; and
- giving advice to the national minister of provincial and local government and the nine provincial ministers of local government on more general reorganizational issues provided for in the Local Government: Municipal Structures Act 117 of 1998 (Municipal Demarcation Board 1999a).

Demarcation Criteria

Demarcation criteria should reflect the purposes or objectives of local government. They are a way of encapsulating policy norms. In South Africa, the guiding framework is the Constitution, and the criteria in Sections 24 and 25 of the Municipal Demarcation Act attempt to embody many of these constitutional principles. Section 24 deals with demarcation objectives. It states that, when a board determines a municipal boundary, its objective must be to establish an area that would:

a   enable the municipality for that area to fulfil its constitutional obligations, including: the provision of democratic and accountable government for the local communities; the provision of services to the communities in an equitable and sustainable manner; the provision of social and economic development; and
b   the provision of a safe and healthy environment.
c   enable effective local governance;
d   enable integrated development; and
e   have a tax base as inclusive as possible of users of municipal services in the municipality.

These demarcation objectives are mainly found in Section 152 of the Constitution, which lays down the objects of local government. There is a strong emphasis on the need to promote socioeconomic rights, an important element that the board needs to take into account when demarcating boundaries.

Section 25 lists the factors that have to be taken into account when determining municipal boundaries:

a   the interdependence of people, communities and economics as indicated by: existing and expected patterns of human settlement and migration; employment; commuting and dominant transport movements; spending; the use of amenities, recreational facilities and infrastructure; and commercial and industrial linkages.
b   the need for cohesive, integrated and unfragmented areas, including metropolitan areas;
c   the financial viability and administrative capacity of the municipality to perform municipal functions efficiently and effectively;
d   the need to share and redistribute financial and administrative resources;
e   provincial and municipal boundaries;
f   areas of traditional rural communities;
g   existing and proposed functional boundaries, including magisterial districts, health, transport, police and census enumerator boundaries;
h   existing and expected land use, social, economic and transport planning;
i   the need for co-ordinated municipal, provincial and national programmes and services, including the needs for the administration of justice and health care;
j   topographical, environmental and physical characteristics of the area;
k   the administrative consequences of its boundary demarcation on: (i) municipal creditworthiness; (ii) existing municipalities, their council members and staff; and (iii) any other relevant matter; and
l   the need to rationalise the total number of municipalities within different categories and of different types to achieve the objectives of effective and sustainable service delivery, financial viability and macro-economic stability.

There was no weighting of criteria, and the board had discretion on how to interpret them.

Metropolitan Government Boundaries

Prior to 1994, no form of metropolitan government existed in the country. In 1994, a two-tier system of metropolitan government was established in the country. The ruling ANC had long favoured single-tier metropolitan authorities, and for the final phase, shorn of the constitutional measures of the interim phase, it was able to push through such structures (commonly called megacities).

The White Paper on Local Government (Department of Provincial Affairs and Constitutional Development 1998) provided three main reasons for the creation of metropolitan government: (1) metropolitan government creates a basis for equitable and just metropolitan governance; (2)

metropolitan government provides strategic land use planning and co-ordinated public investment in physical and social infrastructure; and (3) metropolitan government is able to develop a city-wide framework for economic and social development that can enhance the economic competitiveness and well-being of cities.

The ANC argued that a single-tier body was best suited to implement these goals. It was believed that a two-tier system led to fragmented metropolitan governance. Legislation was accordingly passed to replace the two-tier system with a single-tier authority (Cameron 2000; Wooldridge 2002).

The task of demarcation was initially to determine the boundaries of metropolitan authorities. The board had to take into account the following provisions of the Local Government Municipal Structures Act when determining the boundaries.

An area that must have Category A municipalities is a conurbation featuring:

a areas of high population density; an intensive movement of people, goods, and services; extensive development; and multiple business districts and industrial areas
b a centre of economic activity with a complex and diverse economy
c a single area for which integrated development is desirable
d strong interdependent social and economic linkages between its constituent units.

It was originally the responsibility of the minister of provincial affairs and constitutional development to determine whether an area should be a Category A metropolitan authority. The opposition-controlled Western Cape and KwaZulu-Natal provinces argued that the Structures Act encroached unconstitutionally on the powers of local government and of provinces and took the matter to the Constitutional Court, the final arbitrator of intergovernmental relations. The major objection of these two provinces was the imposition of unitary-tier structures in metropolitan areas. However, both the province and the national ministers were losers in the case. The court ruled that the application of criteria for metropolitan areas formed part of the boundary determination, which is vested through the Constitution in the Demarcation Board. This meant that the declaration of metropolitan areas by the minister is invalid (Constitutional Court of South Africa 1999; Cameron 2000).

The act was accordingly amended, and the board was given the powers to determine whether an area must have a Category A municipality and thereafter to determine boundaries. The research process coordinated by the board involved an evaluation of the existing TLCs and Transitional

Metropolitan Councils (TMCs). Three research reports were compiled. These research findings indicated inter alia that some nonmetropolitan cities such as Port Elizabeth showed greater metropolitan characteristics than some existing metropolitan governments such as Khayalami and Lekua/Vaal. Based on this, the board developed a strategic framework for assessing criteria discussed below.

The board came to the conclusion that nodal points for metropolitan areas could be classified into four distinct groups:

- Nodal points which should definitely be considered as metropolitan areas – Greater Johannesburg, Cape Town, and Durban – fulfilled the requirements of being classified as category A municipalities (Figure 11.1).
- Nodal points which should probably be considered are metropolitan areas such as Greater East Rand and Pretoria (Figure 11.1).
- Nodal points which could possibly be considered as metropolitan areas are, for example, Greater Port Elizabeth.
- Nodal points which should be regarded as aspirant Metropolitan areas are, for example, Greater Vereeniging, Bloemfontein, East London, Pietermaritzburg and Richards Bay (Municipal Demarcation Board 1999a, 11).

After extensive consultation, Johannesburg, Durban, Cape Town, Pretoria, and East Rand were proclaimed as metropolitan authorities. Port Elizabeth was originally not a metropolitan authority, but after a further round of investigation it was belatedly made a metro. Khayalami and Lekua/Vaal metros were deproclaimed.

Boundaries of District Municipalities

During the interim phase, District Councils were created in nonmetropolitan areas (they were called Regional Councils in KwaZulu Natal). Within District Council areas were TLCs and then, depending on which form of rural local government provinces adopted, transitional representative councils, transitional rural councils, or remaining areas (i.e., no primary local government). District Councils did not have any authority over the functioning of TLCs, the nonmetropolitan cities and towns.

In terms of the Final Constitution, District Councils became District Municipalities and became the upper tier of a more defined two-tier system with certain strategic powers over the functioning of not only rural local government but also now nonmetropolitan cities and towns (Cameron 2001; Pycroft 2002).

The board developed a framework detailing the number and possible locations of District Municipalities. The board suggested four principles that should underpin the determination of nodal points for districts:

- wherever possible a coherent economic base should be identified around which the district would coalesce;
- the districts should not be too large: in settled areas a radius of 50-100 kilometres was utilized;
- while the population of Districts should not be too large, for economies of scale it was felt districts should have a base population of at least 100,000 persons; and that
- wherever possible, there should be some coherence to the economic and social base of districts (Municipal Demarcation Board 1999a, 6-7).

Category B Municipalities
Unlike the Interim Constitution, which made provision for separate metropolitan, urban, and rural local governments, the Final Constitution made reference only to Category A, B, and C municipalities. The Constitution did not specify that a Category B municipality should be urban in character. *The White Paper on Local Government* in fact encouraged a departure from the concepts of separate urban and rural local governments (Ministry of Provincial Affairs and Constitutional Development 1998). The white paper argued that many boundaries had irrationally divided settlements. It stated that future boundaries had to correspond to settlement patterns so that municipalities could promote integrated social and economic development of settlements.

As discussed, new legislation made provision for a district municipality with defined upper-level strategic responsibilities and lower-tier authorities called local municipalities. This system replaced the means of primary local government structures that existed in the interim phase. The following settlement pattern types were identified by the board.

- *Large urban centres* – formal cities and towns characterized by a significant population with moderately high population densities of over 100,000. These places had important regional significance.
- *Intermediate towns* – while these towns varied greatly, they tended to have a subregional significance and were characterized by small to medium populations.
- *Small towns* – these were towns with a population of fewer than 2,000, with limited or no subregional impact, and with dependence on high-order towns for economic and social services.
- *Villages* – these settlements resulted from apartheid policies primarily located in the former homeland areas. The size, density, and socioeconomic complexity vary greatly. Such areas have predominantly been excluded from urban-based local government structures. Included in the area are deep rural areas of dispersed homelands.

A diverse typology of settlements had to be accommodated within Category B structures. The board developed a typology of existing settlement patterns (Table 11.1).

The principles for rationalization of Category B municipalities included the following.

- *Geographical contiguity and coherence*: Because municipal government is so closely tied to local identity and accessibility to local representatives, rationalization should generally follow "nearest neighbour" principles – that is, there should be geographically coherent, consolidated Category B municipalities and not "leapfrog" amalgamation of areas.
- *Capacity development*: Another objective of rationalization was to develop a critical mass of municipal capacity (staff, assets, finances) especially where undercapacitated municipalities existed.
- *Resource sharing:* Wherever possible, existing municipalities and/or other areas should be combined with a view to realizing fiscally sustainable units, with weaker areas being paired with stronger areas so as to achieve a sharing of existing or potential resources.
- *Manageable size:* A statistical-derived indicator of 3,500 km^2 and 80,000 persons was suggested as the probable norm for Category B municipalities. However, deviations from the norm were inevitable given the uneven geographical distribution of population and economic activity throughout the country. The board's empirical research suggested that populations of fewer than 20,000 are generally undesirable for Category B municipalities given the objectives of realizing economies of scale in municipalities. On the other hand, given the need for geographical

Table 11.1

Summary of South African local governments by population, area, and density

Type of local government	Population	Percent	Area	Percent	Density
Metropolitan councils	11,400,000	28.1	10,685	0.8	1,067.5
Urban Category B	5,350,000	13.2	5,364	0,4	901.7
Urban/rural	14,630,000	36.0	65,035	5.2	226.9
Exclusive rural	9,100,000	22.5	750,992	59.4	11.1
Desert/semi-arid	82,000	0.2	430,517	34.1	0.2
Total	40,562,000		1,262,593		

Source: Municipal Demarcation Board (1999d, 1-3).

coherence and local identity, areas greater than 10,000 km² were also desirable.
- *Functionality*: Amalgamation of places with internal linkages was an important consideration when determining Category B boundaries. To some extent, interdependence was a function of geographical proximity. The alignment of transportation routes and physical features can alter patterns of functional interdependence. If some places are aligned along an integrated transport network, and others are divided by an impassable mountain range, simple distance between places can mean quite different things in each case.

Many Category B cities and large towns shared several of the features of metropolitan areas but lacked the overall size and multinodal character of the metros. The demarcation of the areas followed the same principles as the demarcation of the metros – that is, the demarcation of a boundary that makes some provision for some future growth and attempts to redress the effects of apartheid-era displacement.

Urban Category B municipalities included Bloemfontein/Botshabelo, East London, Kimberley, Nelspruit, Welkom, Witbank, and Pietermaritzburg. There were also broad principles for towns/villages/rural areas: amalgamation of small towns and settlements in remaining areas, and integration of agricultural and rural hinterlands (Municipal Demarcation Board 1999d, 3-5).

Cross-Boundary Municipalities

The Constitution was amended to make provision for an act of parliament authorizing the establishment of cross-boundary municipalities that was duly promulgated. The reason was that the provincial boundaries for the nine provincial governments put in place in 1994 in some cases divided settlements.

After conducting its research, the board noted that there were a number of areas in South Africa where fairly large tracts of land, including a number of different communities, straddled provincial boundaries. The board made recommendations to provincial and national governments on possible cross-boundary municipalities such as Kuruman-Mothibistad, Umzimkulu-Mount Currie, Bushbuckridge-Kruger National Park, and East Rand Metropolitan area – Mpumalanga (Municipal Demarcation Board 1999b, 11-13). However, while there was principled agreement among provinces for most of the board's cross-boundary recommendations, getting consensus on operational issues such as which province would administer and financially support such cross-boundary areas initially proved difficult.

Principled agreement was eventually reached between provinces for the proposed cross-boundary areas, with the exception of KwaZulu-Natal province, where the majority party, the IPF, indicated that it was opposed to the linking of Umzimkulu with Mount Currie in the Eastern Cape. The board had to redemarcate these areas as part of their existing provinces. Much work was still required around the operationalization of these agreements after the elections in the proclaimed cross-boundary areas.

Traditional Leaders

The influence of traditional leaders was one of the major factors that had to be taken into account when demarcating boundaries. Traditional communities were the major bedrock of support for the IFP, which controlled the KwaZulu-Natal province (albeit in an uneasy alliance with the ANC). The role of traditional leaders (chiefs) in the new democratic South Africa was one of the thorny issues that South Africa's Constitution makers had to deal with in 1992-94. Indeed, the question of the status of traditional leaders had almost scuppered the entire negotiations with the IFP, which agreed only at the eleventh hour to participate in the national elections.

At the local government level, traditional leaders had a number of functions, including certain legislative executive and administrative powers, many of which were local government functions in other parts of the country (Ministry of Provincial Affairs and Constitutional Development 1998). The IFP-controlled KwaZulu-Natal province dealt with this problem in 1996 by not proclaiming primary local governments in traditional areas.

The Final Constitution, however, made provision for wall-to-wall local government, which meant that the whole country had to be governed by either an A municipality or a combination of B and C municipalities. As a concession to traditional leaders, the "areas of traditional rural communities" comprised one factor that had to be taken into account when demarcating boundaries. Table 11.2 shows the provinces that had tribal authorities recognized by the Department of Provincial Affairs and Constitutional Development.

Table 11.2

Tribal authorities by province, South Africa

Provinces	Tribal authorities
KwaZulu-Natal	285
Northern Province	228
Eastern Cape	176
North-West	70
Mpumalanga	49
Free State	15

There was also negotiation about the registration of further traditional leaders. The board's approach to traditional leaders was that, wherever possible, it would not divide the geographical areas of traditional leaders as long as these areas were single pieces of land and there was unity between the traditional sector and the people living in the traditional authority. Some traditional communities, however, were fragmented. There was also no complete record of all recognized traditional authority areas. Of the country's 232 Category B municipalities, 114 have traditional leaders within their jurisdictions (Municipal Demarcation Board 2000a).

District Management Areas
In terms of the Municipal Structures Act, the minister of local government, on recommendations of the Municipal Demarcation Board and after consulting the provincial minister for local government in the province concerned, may declare part of an area that must have municipalities of both Category C and Category B as a district management area (DMA) if the establishment of a Category B municipality in that part of the area will not be conducive to fulfillment of the objectives set out in Section 24 of the Demarcation Act.

The Constitutional Court and its metropolitan hearing ruled that the establishment of DMAs impacted on the boundaries of municipalities and was accordingly a function to be performed by the board (Constitutional Court of South Africa 1999). The board decided that DMAs should be state-owned national and provincial parks and protected areas, deserts, and regions in which a low population density over an extended area would make fulfilling the objectives of local government difficult. DMAs were only considered under these circumstances. They were not intended to be used to resolve the issues of financial viability, administrative capacity, and areas of high social and economic need (Municipal Demarcation Board 1999c).

Despite this policy statement, many groups, including traditional leaders, farmers, and small towns, indicated that they did not want to fall under Category B municipalities and preferred to be DMAs. There are DMAs in seventeen of the country's forty-six district municipalities.

Stakeholders and Role Players
Meetings were held with a number of stakeholders outlining the process of the demarcation and presenting draft boundaries. Important stakeholders consulted included the National Parliamentary Portfolio Committee on Constitutional Affairs, the minister and officials of the Department of Provincial and Local Government (previously Constitutional Development), provincial ministers of local government, the South African Local Government Association (SALGA) and its provincial affiliates, houses of

traditional leaders, national departments, political parties in the legislatures, key private sector agencies, and key nongovernmental organizations (Municipal Demarcation Board 2000b, 19-21). In addition, although it was not a statutory requirement, the board held a number of public meetings for its Category B hearings.

Final Boundaries

The board's final determination of Category B boundaries is illustrated in Table 11.3. The number of municipalities in the country was rationalized from 843 to 284. Given that there was no primary tier of government in KwaZulu-Natal and North-West provinces, the scale of rationalization was greater than these numbers indicate. Theoretically, there could have been around 1,100 municipalities in the country (Figure 11.2).

The Board's Approach

The board believed that the best means of determining the interdependence of people, communities, and economies was through commuting patterns. Such commuting is probably the best single measure of the relationship between human settlements on the one hand and employment, spending, and amenity-usage patterns on the other. In South Africa, there had been an artificially enforced separation between places of work and shopping and places of residence for poorer people. Apartheid had forced people into spatially separate communities, and black areas were often located some distance from commercial and industrial areas.

The board was of the view that a metropolitan or local council should encompass at least 50 percent of all people who live, work, and shop within that area. The board tested whether its boundaries encompass interdependent communities by analyzing data from household surveys for 1995 and 1996. These surveys were conducted by Statistics South Africa and were probably the best national and annual record of social trends.

Table 11.3

Number of local governments by category in South Africa, 2000

Category	Number	Description
A	6	Johannesburg, Cape Town, Durban, East Rand, Pretoria, Port Elizabeth
B	232	8 were cross-boundary local municipalities
C	46	7 were cross-boundary district municipalities
Total	284	
DMA	26	Kruger Park, falls in two provinces

Source: Municipal Demarcation Board (2000c).

The result was that the board was able to analyze where people lived and where they worked.

The analysis revealed that the board's boundaries captured the vast majority of people's activity spaces. Ninety-five percent of Cape Town's population lives and works in the metropolitan area, while the Durban equivalent is 86 percent. In Gauteng, where there are greater leakages due to migrancy and the economic interdependence of the province as a whole, the figures for the East Rand, Johannesburg, and Pretoria metros are 87 percent, 64 percent, and 84 percent, respectively. In North Cape, more than 90 percent of the people within the four District Council areas live and work within that area, the Northern Province equivalent is 80 percent, and the North-West figures are over 90 percent (Municipal Demarcation Board 1999b, 15-19).

Due to the time constraints, the board did not have discussions about appropriate theoretical models of demarcation that could guide the process. They were nevertheless influenced implicitly by some of these models, notably the settlement pattern (or sociogeographic approach).

Figure 11.2

Provincial and municipal government boundaries, South Africa

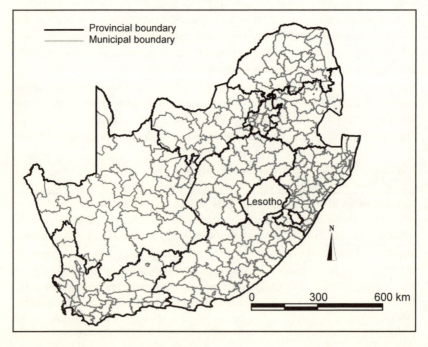

Source: Municipal Demarcation Board (2003).

John Meligrana introduces in Chapter 1 the notion of over- and underbounded municipal territories. Here there is a direct correlation between activity spaces and administrative structures. More commonly, administrative structures are "underbounded," whereby the activity space crosses over many local government boundaries, with resultant spillover problems. "Overbounding" occurs where the activity space is only a small part of an administrative division (Bennett 1989, 34-35). There are problems in achieving "truly bounded" administrative spaces. For example, there is no consensus about the level of aggregation of preferences and activity spaces that is required. Another problem is the frequency of journeys and activities. There are also different types of activity, such as commuting, recreation, and shopping (Cameron 1999a). Nevertheless, it is still a useful approach.

Historically, South Africa's local government boundaries were underbounded because of apartheid fragmentation. As discussed, the results of provincial demarcation during the interim phase were quite uneven. Some boundaries were truly bounded, others became less underbounded, and some were as fragmented as they were under apartheid.

The board primarily used commuting patterns as a means of dealing with the illogical spatial apartheid distortions that theoretically should have led to truly bounded boundaries. Arguably, the metro boundaries conform to the truly bounded approach. However, for Category B, the board also used minimum area sizes of 3,500 km^2. Underpinning this assumption was the contestable economies of scale argument, which posits that efficiency will be enhanced by enlarging local government areas (Smith 1985; Keating 1995). This has arguably led in some cases to overbounded boundaries in that communities with little in common were amalgamated. This not only signalled a retreat from the more logical settlement pattern approach but also has led some new municipalities post-2000 to complain that their areas of jurisdiction are too big to service properly.

Evaluation of the Demarcation Process

In this final section, an evaluation will be taken of this demarcation process. This section will be divided into factors that facilitated good demarcation and those that impeded the process.

One major factor that helped to facilitate the board's demarcation was a highly sophisticated Geographic Information System (GIS) that captured spatial data from a variety of sources, including census data from Statistics South Africa, Project Viability, and municipalities. The board in fact won a Special Achievement in GIS Award at the Environment Systems Research Initiative (ESRI) annual conference in San Diego, California, in July 2002. The board was selected to receive this award from over 100,000 Web sites worldwide (see www.demarcation.org.za).

The board's information technology consultants, Data World, did a commendable job in assimilating data and coming out with a variety of spatial options on a nation-wide basis. This work expedited the board's task, and it is doubtful whether the board could have completed its work within the extremely tight time frames without the logistical support of Data World.

The board also generated a great deal of local government data. They included information on urban conurbations, institutional capacities, powers, and functions in district municipality areas, and local government finances. In some cases, the board generated more data than the line departments responsible for the function. This information was not only a useful data source for the board but also a reference point for government departments and urban researchers for years to come.

The board was also extremely cost effective in its operation despite having a limited budget (R33.5 million) in its first full year of operation. This cost effectiveness was achieved by having a small administrative corps located in the board's head office in Pretoria and by using consultants at a relatively cheap rate. There was certainly none of the profligate payment of consultants that has characterized some other state institutions in South Africa.

What factors worked against the board? There was the constant complaint from stakeholders throughout the country about the ridiculously tight time frames that had to be adhered to, with the limited time given to make submissions a particularly contentious issue. One could not help feeling sympathy for these people. To meet the deadline, the board worked under tremendous pressure. For example, this author had as much time to demarcate the whole of the Western Cape province for the 2000 elections as he did to demarcate one district in the province as part of the 1994-95 provincial demarcation. However, the board ended up bearing the brunt of criticism for something beyond its control. It was a constitutional requirement that boundaries had to be demarcated before the next local government elections.

A related issue was the question of consultation, with many local actors complaining that the board had not consulted them during the demarcation process. What is correct was that the board did not consult individually with the existing 843 municipalities in the country. That was not the intention of the act and, in any event, was physically impossible given the tight time frames. Consultation occurred through various stakeholders: the provincial ministers of local government, SALGA and its provincial affiliates, and the provincial houses of traditional leaders.

The board held numerous workshops with these stakeholders in which process, policy, draft boundaries, final boundaries, and ward delimitation were discussed. One problem was that many of these stakeholders did not convey information gleaned at these workshops to their constituencies. The lack of knowledge on the ground about the demarcation process can partially be attributed to communication problems within some of the above-mentioned organizations.

The GIS approach was in fact a double-edged sword. It enabled the board to use nationally generated statistical data as the basis of its demarcation. However, this quantitative approach was sometimes dismissed by communities that argued that the board was using a "top-down" approach and did not know the circumstances on the ground.

Resistance to boundary reorganization by both councillors and officials is a common phenomenon internationally (Keating 1995). This was certainly the case in South Africa, where the rationalization from 843 to 284 municipalities meant that there were fewer political and managerial jobs available. It was not surprising that there was resistance to change.

Many (although not all) traditional leaders were critical of the board's demarcation process. The KwaZulu-Natal Provincial House for Traditional Leaders, the National House of Traditional Leaders, and the Congress of Traditional Leaders (Contralesa) were particularly vocal in this regard. The Inkatha Freedom Party leader, Mangosuthu Buthelezi, also chair of the House of Traditional Leaders, as early as April 1999 stated that "the chairman of the Demarcation Board has always made no secret of being a communist, and he utterly despises the institution of traditional leadership." He then called on traditional leaders to oppose the demarcation of their areas of jurisdiction into municipalities (1999, 4).

During the demarcation process, traditional leaders argued vociferously that the inclusion of their areas into municipalities would undermine their status. As pointed out, "areas of traditional rural communities" comprised one of the factors that the board had to take into account when demarcating the municipalities. The board decided that it would not split traditional areas. This meant that, even when only parts of traditional areas had functional linkages with neighbouring cities and towns, the whole area was included in the urban cities and towns. However, this approach did not satisfy traditional leaders. The interesting thing was that, although there was constant criticism of the board, few alternative proposals came from this group. The reason soon became apparent. The concern was less about demarcation than about the Constitution, which made provision for wall-to-wall local government. The bottom line was that traditional leaders did not want elected local governments in their areas, fearing that they would lose powers and functions to such bodies.

The board informed them that this was a constitutional issue that should best be raised with the president. A meeting was held with the president, and it was agreed that further discussions on the role of traditional leadership should continue, particularly in light of a (then) recently released government discussion document on traditional leadership. However, the demarcation process had to continue. A further concession was that up to 20 percent of councils could consist of nonvoting traditional leaders (Department of Provincial and Local Government 2000; Mbeki 2000).

Another serious challenge that the board faced was opposition from the Department of Finance to the board's demarcation proposals. A memorandum by the director general of finance to the board argued that the board's proposed boundaries would structurally weaken the fiscal positions of nonmetropolitan cities and towns and, as a consequence, constrain rather than enhance their ability to raise capital and develop infrastructure (water, power, etc.), their key responsibilities.

An analysis was made of three existing towns. It was shown that nonmetropolitan towns generally would face a marked structural decline in their fiscal positions as a result of the inclusion of extra territories into their areas. The board was asked to fundamentally look at its demarcation of nonmetropolitan towns and cities. The department implied that the board did not look at financial viability properly (Department of Finance 2000).

The board's response to this memorandum was to dispute the methodology used by the department. No indication was given of which powers and functions were being analyzed against available income; the report ignored the fact that the smaller the boundaries the greater the spatial inequalities and the greater the correlation to the old apartheid order, and it incorrectly presumed that boundary demarcation is a primary determination of financial viability and creditworthiness. The board did not change its boundary recommendations (Municipal Demarcation Board 2000c).

This attack on the board was in effect a challenge from the department's macroeconomic framework, GEAR (Growth, Employment, and Redistribution), which had a strong emphasis on financial and fiscal austerity. It involved inter alia cutting government expenditure and creating an investor-friendly environment. The board's proposals were seen to be inimical to this framework.

The board also had its own internal problems, such as its organization. The board was formally inaugurated only in February 1999. For its first few months of existence, its secretariat was handled by the Department of Constitutional Development officials. It was only in the second part of the year that it appointed its own staff and moved into its own accommodation. In fact, it was already October 1999 before the board's manager assumed duty. Because of the extremely tight time frames, there was virtually no time to develop the systems and procedures of the office to deal with demarcation. The board had already commenced with its demarcation, in fact, before any permanent staff was appointed. The result was that the office was in many ways undercapacitated to deal with the huge workload that it immediately found itself with. For example, the failure to organize meetings properly, process submissions, and deal with correspondence in a timely manner led to much criticism. In addition, the board fired its manager for misconduct after less than a year in the position.

A similar problem was the calibre of consultants. While some consultants were of an extremely high calibre, others were decidedly poor. Because of the tight time frames and the lack of capacity of its own staff, the board had to use consultants to undertake demarcation investigations.

Finally, there was the problem of what can be termed "reorganization fatigue." The Constitution makers had decided in 1993 that local government transformation should be divided into three phases: pre-interim, interim, and final. Some municipalities, such as Johannesburg, had already been reorganized twice (Mabin 1999). Many municipalities had only just completed the complicated functional, financial, and administrative restructuring required by the previous demarcation process. Frankly, there was little political support at the local level for large-scale local government reorganization. In retrospect, it would perhaps have been wiser to have gone in 1993 directly through to the final model of local government. The direct and opportunity costs of the interim local government reorganization were estimated in 1997 to be R5.4 billion (Western Cape Local Government Association 1997). After the December 2000 election, local governments are again busy reorganizing themselves. This is impacting negatively on service delivery given the scale of time and the resources required.

References
Bekker, S., and R. Humphries. 1985. *From Control to Confusion: The Changing Role of Administration Boards in South Africa*. Pitermaritzburg: Schuter and Shooter; Rhodes University Institute of Social and Economic Research.
Bennett, R., ed. 1989. *Territory and Administration in Europe*. London: Pinter.
Buthelezi, M. 1999. "Joint Meeting of the Executive Committees of the Houses of Traditional Leaders." Unpublished paper, 8 April.
Cameron, R.G. 1995. "The History of Devolution of Powers to Local Authorities in South Africa." *Local Government Studies* 21, 3: 396-417.
–. 1996. "The Demarcation of South African Local Government." *Local Government Studies* 22, 1: 19-39.
–. 1999a. *Democratisation of South African Local Government: A Tale of Three Cities*. Pretoria: J.L. Van Schaik.
–. 1999b. *An Overview of the Local Government Municipal Demarcation Act 27 of 1998*. Johannesburg: Electoral Institute of South Africa.
–. 2000. "Megacities in South Africa: A Solution for the New Millennium?" *Public Administration and Development* 20, 2: 155-65.
–. 2001. "The Upliftment of South African Local Government." *Local Government Studies* 27, 3: 97-118.
Cloete, F. 1995. *Local Government Transformation in South Africa*. Pretoria: J.L. Van Schaik.
Constitutional Court of South Africa. 1999. *In the Matter between the Executive Council of the Province of the Western Cape and the Minister for Provincial Affairs and Constitutional Development of the Republic of South Africa, the Municipal Demarcation Board*. Johannesburg: Constitutional Court of South Africa.

Department of Finance. 2000. *Municipal Demarcation Board Proposals.* Pretoria: Department of Finance.

Department of Provincial Affairs and Constitutional Development. 1998. *The White Paper on Local Government.* Pretoria: Government Printer.

Department of Provincial and Local Government. 2000. *A Draft Discussion Document towards a White Paper on Traditional Leadership and Institutions.* Pretoria: Government Printer.

Keating, M. 1995. "Size, Efficiency, and Democracy: Consolidation, Fragmentation, and Public Choice." In D. Judge, G. Stokes, and H. Wolman, eds., *Theories of Urban Politics,* 117-36. London: Sage.

Mabin, A. 1999. "From Hard Top to Soft Serve: Demarcation of Metropolitan Government in Johannesburg." In R.G. Cameron, *Democratisation of South African Local Government: A Tale of Three Cities.* Pretoria: J.L. Van Schaik.

Mbeki, T. 2000. "Municipal Government and Powers and Functions of Traditional Leaders." Unpublished memorandum, Pretoria.

Municipal Demarcation Board. 1999a. *Nodal Points for Metropolitan and District Council Areas in South Africa.* Pretoria: MDB.

–. 1999b. *The Determination of Metropolitan and District Council Boundaries.* Pretoria: MDB.

–. 1999c. *Policy on District Management Areas.* Pretoria: MDB.

–. 1999d. *The Board's Approach to the Determination of Category B Municipalities.* Pretoria: MDB.

–. 2000a. *Process of Determining Boundaries in KwaZulu-Natal with Specific Reference to Traditional Leaders.* Pretoria: MDB.

–. 2000b. *Budget Vote: March 2000.* Pretoria: MDB.

–. 2000c. *Memorandum: Municipal Demarcation Board Response to Department of Finance.* Pretoria: MDB.

Pycroft, C. 2002. "Addressing Rural Poverty: Restructuring Rural Government." In S. Parnell, E. Pieterse, M. Swilling, and D. Wooldridge, eds., *Democratising Local Government: The South African Experiment,* 105-22. Cape Town: UCT Press.

Smith, B.C. 1985. *Decentralisation: The Territorial Dimension of the State.* London: George Allen and Unwin.

Sutcliffe, M. 1999. "Opening Remarks at Inaugural Demarcation Board Meeting." Cape Town, February.

Western Cape Local Government Association. 1997. *Weclogo Workshop.* Bellville: WCLGA.

Wooldridge, D. 2002. "Introducing Metropolitan Government." In S. Parnell, E. Pieterse, M. Swilling, and D. Wooldridge, eds., *Democratising Local Government: The South African Experiment,* 127-40. Cape Town: UCT Press.

12
Conclusion:
Changing Local Government Boundaries in Different Political-Ideological Environments

John Meligrana and Eran Razin

Collectively, the case studies presented in this book reveal the complex factors involved in the restructuring of municipal boundaries. Municipal boundary change procedures are partly an administrative issue that involves considerations of efficiency, effectiveness, and equality in the provision of public services as well as aspects of planning and development. However, these procedures also have profound political significance on local democracy and local autonomy. Moreover, in multiethnic societies, the procedures can also be viewed in light of their impacts on interethnic relations, since they could serve to encourage integration, secure ethnic autonomy, or promote control of one group over the other. Viewing local democracy as a tool to promote and consolidate democracy at the national level would also influence policies of municipal boundary change and the choice of procedures.

Local government boundary change procedures are thus deeply embedded in the broader political-ideological environment and could also influence fundamental aspects of the state and society rather than solely aspects of local development and service provision. This chapter weaves together the information from each national case study in order to begin to come to a general understanding of the systemic and chronic issues regarding local government boundaries and their revision. The chapter is organized around the research questions posed in the introductory chapter. It answers each question based on the collective evidence presented by the case studies. It also revisits the ideas and theories regarding local government boundary reform introduced by Ronan Paddison in Chapter 2 and Andrejs Skaburskis in Chapter 3.

What Are the Goals and Objectives for Reforming Municipal Boundaries?

To answer this question, we examined the cases with respect to both explicit and implicit goals and objectives for redrawing local government territories. Explicit goals are revealed in the boundary reform procedures contained in official regulations, rules, or laws. Rules or laws may require the satisfaction of certain criteria as a condition for redrawing local government territories. Such criteria are explicitly stated within government annexation rules or laws. Implicit goals are reasons for local government boundary reform that are found "outside" the existing rules and laws. Such implicit goals could be overtly or covertly achieved via the reform of local government boundaries (see also the goals for local government restructuring plans found in Table 3.1).

Explicit Goals and Objectives
The cases presented in this volume reveal that the goals and objectives contained within boundary reform procedures run along a continuum from no criteria to very detailed ones. Criteria are used here to refer to specific reasons (e.g., geographic, economic, social, etc.) that warrant and justify the redrawing of local government boundaries. At one end of the continuum lie Canada and Israel, whose annexation/amalgamation procedures are not only rather simple but also silent with respect to any specific criteria that could trigger the redrawing of local government boundaries. At the other end of the continuum lies South Africa, whose Constitution and various pieces of legislation (e.g., Municipal Demarcation Act) contain complex and detailed criteria regarding the territorial revisions to local government boundaries (Chapter 11). Most of the other nations are located somewhere between these two extremes. For example, in the United States, some state governments require fiscal impact analyses of lands to be annexed (Chapter 4). However, in Spain, the only criterion is that municipal boundaries remain contiguous after additional land is annexed (Chapter 7).

At what level of detail goals and objectives should be articulated within actual boundary reform procedures is informed by Paddison's three propositions (Chapter 2). On the one hand, detailed criteria might detract from or mask local preferences and needs regarding the restructuring of local government boundaries (Proposition 1). On the other hand, the enumeration of detailed criteria within boundary reform procedures might help to focus the debate regarding redrawing local boundaries, thereby helping to ensure a process that is transparent and fair (Proposition 2). Furthermore, the third proposition, that boundary reform be wholly decided neither by central nor by local objectives, can be achieved with the proper development of and agreement on the criteria used to judge local government territorial reform.

Implicit Goals and Objectives
The case studies in this book reveal that redrawing local government boundaries remains a standard response to urbanization, particularly the

problems associated with urban-rural sprawl. This response involves two spatial strategies. One strategy is to capture urban developments within urban municipalities – that is, to maintain a system of "overbound" local governments as discussed in Chapter 1. This strategy implies the maintenance of rural and urban forms of local government. The alternative strategy is to create a hierarchy or nesting of different kinds of local government with various territorial dimensions. This usually results in the creation of metropolitan or regional governments. The creation of a hierarchy of spaces, in the form of a regional government, to provide cooperation among urban municipalities and between rural and urban areas represents a major territorial and functional redistribution within a city-region (Barlow 1991; Meligrana 2000). In some cases, a hybrid strategy of both enlarging local governments and creating a tiered system of local governments is undertaken.

The case studies can be grouped within each of the three strategies outlined above. Korea represents the hybrid strategy of using boundary reform to maintain "urban-rural separation" and later using reform to integrate urban and rural areas under one local government system. The Korean strategy contrasts with the American and Israeli strategies, whose annexation procedures were premised on maintaining a strict political division between rural and urban governments. The Canadian and Chinese experiences come between the Korean-American-Israeli model; these countries attempted to reform local boundaries to achieve objectives of both urban-rural separation and urban-rural integration. More complex spatial models of boundary reform are found in Robert Cameron's review of South Africa's annexation procedures.

An emerging trend is the use of local government boundary reform as an instrument to realize national economic and political goals. Thus, sweeping reforms to local government territories are sometimes associated with substantial changes to a nation's economic and political frameworks. For instance, the reunification of Germany, constitutional reforms recognizing local governments in Spain, radical economic transformations in China, and emerging (maturing) democracies in Korea and South Africa had important influences on the redrawing of local government boundaries. In related research, redrawing these boundaries in developing countries (Ghana in 1988 being a typical example) frequently materialized as part of broader political and economic reforms of democratization and structural adjustment (Razin and Obirih-Opareh 2000). At the least, national economic and political reforms accelerated the need to debate or institute new procedures to revise the local government map.

Thus, local government boundary reform is seen to service national economic and political goals. However, the theories and ideas put forward by consolidationist and public choice theorists (see Chapters 2 and 3) make certain assumptions about local and regional requirements regarding various local territorial configurations, but they are largely silent with respect to national requirements regarding local boundary reforms. The national necessity for cities that work well in the global economy needs to be injected into the theoretical debate regarding the reform of local government boundaries. These kinds of debates, for example, are found in the Canadian and Chinese national case studies, which have seen recent local government boundary reforms premised on the need to maintain or enhance the global competitive positions of each country's city-regions. Also, Israel has begun to show an interest in boundary reform as an economic development tool through the creation of local industrial councils. However, the redrawing of local government boundaries should not be solely in the service of national economic or political goals, as Paddison's first and third propositions indicate.

What Are the Procedures for Extending the Territory of a Local Government?

The case studies presented in this volume illustrate that the procedures used to redraw local government boundaries vary substantially from country to country, reflecting differences in prevailing ideologies and political-administrative traditions. Nevertheless, the issues at stake and the trade-offs inherent in choices about procedures are usually similar. The fundamental concern in debates over municipal boundary change procedures is twofold: first, achieving the appropriate balance between central control and local autonomy or democracy (Razin and Lindsey 2002); second, balancing competing local interests and claims over the appropriate territorial configurations of local governments.

In general, the procedures for redrawing local government boundaries can be divided between "top-down" and "bottom-up" origins, in which the senior level of government plays either a leading or a reactionary role (Meligrana 2000). Leading occurs in the sense that the senior government initiates various kinds of local government boundary reform, such as incorporating new municipal governments, altering their boundaries (i.e., annexations), amalgamating two or more municipal governments, or creating upper-tier regional governments. Reaction occurs in the sense that the senior government merely establishes the rules and regulations for possible types of reform, but the process is triggered by local stakeholders, such as local government officials.

The top-down/bottom-up distinction refers, however, not only to the identity of the initiator but also to the identity of the body that retains the authority to decide on boundary changes. In most decentralized options, the central state not only leaves initiatives of municipal boundary change to local stakeholders but also does not directly intervene in the decision, other than determining the framework and legal basis for municipal boundary changes. Popular determination, municipal determination, and judicial determination procedures, practised in most states in the United States, best represent such procedures. Intermediate situations are characterized by largely local initiatives to change boundaries, in which the central state, either the government or the legislature, retains the power to make the final decision, subject to specific procedures. Israel largely represents this situation, decentralized in initiatives for change and centralized in decision making. Ultimate top-down situations are those in which the central state both initiates and determines the redelineation of the local government map. Common in countries that lack deep democratic roots, this option is also practised in democratic systems, such as local government reforms in Britain since the 1970s. The recent reform in South Africa is an interesting top-down model in which establishment of a professional quasi-legislative board, with final decision-making powers, was intended to mitigate risks embedded in the extremely centralized model.

Collectively, the case studies reveal the tension between top-down and bottom-up procedures used to redraw local government boundaries. On the one hand, procedures are affording more opportunities for public participation, as is the case in the United States and Korea, and are proposed in Israel. Even in China, attempts are being made to foster bottom-up initiatives to redraw local territories. On the other hand, procedures are being streamlined, as in Canada, and are allowing for quick and dramatic reforms imposed by the senior level of government, as in Canada, Germany, and South Africa. All in all, most boundary reform procedures try to balance both top-down and bottom-up approaches to redrawing local government boundaries. This is a demanding balancing act and reveals how difficult it will be to achieve Paddison's propositions to make for a more just system of restructuring local government boundaries.

Local government boundary reform conflicts can also be divided into those waged on a horizontal basis (e.g., city versus countryside) and those waged on a vertical basis (e.g., boundary disputes between local and senior levels of government)(see Fan 1999; Shin 2000; and Terhorst and van de Ven 1990). The type of boundary conflict (i.e., horizontal or vertical) is largely conditioned by the arrangement of the various levels of government in each nation as well as the procedures established to redraw local government boundaries. However, the cases presented in this volume can be organized into three groups.

First are the countries where territorial disputes are largely horizontal or between various local governments. This horizontality heightens the zero-sum aspect of the redrawing of local government boundaries. The American and Israeli disputes are largely between urban and rural municipal governments. For example, Greg Lindsey notes in Chapter 4 that American cities are increasingly annexing land that is less populated, perhaps as a municipal strategy to annex lands in the path of least (political) resistance. In Israel, the battle over territory is usually between urban authorities and regional councils.

Second are the countries where the territorial disputes or debates are mainly between various levels of government. For example, in South Africa, the provinces have sought remedy from the courts to the actions of the Municipal Demarcation Board and the minister of local government. Similarly, the Chinese hierarchical administrative system provides the National People's Congress or the State Council with the ability to initiate top-down reforms to local government territories. Thus, in China, boundary disputes are among the various levels of government, but such disputes are rarely public.

And third are the countries where boundary disputes have both horizontal and vertical dimensions. For example, in both Korea and Canada, disputes during the 1960s were mainly horizontal ones between urban and rural forms of government. However, during the 1990s, the senior levels of government began to play a more aggressive role in dealing with their local governments to achieve boundary reforms. In particular, recent actions of the Ontario and Quebec provincial governments pitched them against their largest municipal governments, Toronto and Montreal, respectively. Dong-Ho Shin in Chapter 9 describes the rising antipathy in Korea between Kyungnam Province and Pusan City over the city's attempts to annex provincial land.

To summarize, local government boundary reform procedures contain two important aspects: first, top-down versus bottom-up origins of the procedures; two, vertical versus horizontal disputes. These two aspects are interrelated and become clearer when the roles and perspectives of key actors (stakeholders) are examined. The next section identifies four distinct actors common to most of the case studies: senior government, local governments (including lower- and upper-tier), independent boards, and regional groups with a strong attachment to place.

What Are the Various Roles and Perspectives of Different Stakeholders in Redrawing Local Government Boundaries?

Senior Governments as Proponents/Initiators of Boundary Reform

In general, senior levels of government are often strong proponents of the reduction or enlargement of the areal sizes of local governments. This suggests that public choice theory (see Skaburskis in Chapter 3) does not inform the senior government's perspective concerning the reorganization of local government boundaries. For example, Ontario and Quebec provincial governments, Korea's Ministry of Home Affairs, and some *Länder* governments in Germany strongly advocated using boundary reform to reduce the number of local governments. However, the methods and abilities to implement this objective varied among the national case studies.

Senior levels of government are not unified entities. Many of the cases reveal that agendas and perspectives regarding the objectives of boundary reform vary by the numerous ministries and government departments. Thus, the general trend toward reduction of the number and territorial enlargement of local governments is challenged by some state institutions, particularly political parties. The parties that have strong regional support often attempt to maintain the territorial status quo or assert a boundary configuration that maintains regional identities (as discussed below). For example, in Germany, the Christian Democrat Party advocated a more cautious approach to boundary reform as its traditional electoral support came from rural areas. Cameron also notes the influence of traditional (rural) communities in South Africa, which are the power sources for the Inkatha Freedom Party. Such traditional communities would likely resist whole-scale boundary changes insensitive to cultural-geographical boundaries. Thus, if the consolidationist approach finds favour with the senior level of government, the public choice approach to local boundary reform is often voiced by those at the regional or local level.

Senior levels of government attempt to achieve their consolidationist boundary reforms by either voluntary or imposed methods. Examples from Canada, Germany, and Korea show that the senior levels of government attempted to reform local government boundaries by establishing a series of recommendations to be voluntarily adopted by the affected local governments, usually within a specified time period. In some cases, certain financial incentives were offered to sweeten the deal (as in Canada). In these cases, the voluntary method did not achieve the comprehensive reforms wanted by the senior levels of government. This failure usually led to imposed reforms, mainly by legislative fiat or coercive measures, by the senior governments. The cases of voluntary reform in Canada, Germany, and Korea were, in reality, attempts by the senior levels of government to engineer a particular boundary reform: an enlargement of local government territories and a reduction in their numbers. The voluntary approach was simply a "yes" or "no" response to a reform option and not a debate regarding a variety of reform alternatives that may or may not have included redrawing local government territories. This strategy by senior governments to proffer the "voluntary" adoption of specific reform options under the threat of possible imposed reforms violates all three of Paddison's propositions, which attempt to promote a more just system of redrawing local government boundaries.

Other than political parties, government departments and ministries have varying views and perspectives regarding the redrawing of local government boundaries. For example, Eran Razin in Chapter 8 explains that Israel's minister of the interior has jurisdiction over municipal boundary changes, yet other ministries, particularly the Ministry of Finance, are asserting a stronger role in the redrawing of local government boundaries. This situation parallels Cameron's finding that South Africa's Department of Finance challenged boundary reforms put forward by the Municipal Demarcation Board on the ground that they would weaken the fiscal health of local governments. Perhaps the increasing role of ministries of finance in redrawing local government boundaries reflects a trend toward urban governance as a business, as suggested by some authors (Harding, Wilks-Heeg, and Hutchins 2000).

Independent Boards and Commissions

Many of the cases presented in this volume describe the use of commissions, boards, or task forces set up with the specific mandate to investigate and assist in the resolution of local government boundary problems. Such institutions are usually created by senior governments for a number of reasons: to remove the senior level of government from hotly contested local political battles; to institute a more rational approach to boundary reform; and to impose its reform agenda on the local government map. For example, the Korean Local Administration Research Institute attempted to develop principles and rationales that could guide the national debate regarding the reform of local government boundaries. However, its research and publications were funded and supported by the Ministry of Home Affairs, thus making it appear a tool for the central government's reform objectives.

The institutions also varied from advisory commissions, as in Germany, Israel, Spain, and Korea, to ones that have the power to make decisions, as in Ontario and South Africa. The Ontario Municipal Board and South Africa's Municipal Demarcation Board share similar attributes. Each was specifically empowered to investigate boundary problems and make binding decisions. Both approached the local government boundary problem in a rational manner by attempting to apply uniform principles and procedures. However, there are some notable differences. The Ontario Municipal Board reacts to annexation petitions from local governments, while the Municipal Demarcation Board undertook to investigate the redrawing of local government boundaries as part of a wider effort to overhaul and modernize South Africa's government.

Local and Regional/County/Provincial Governments: Hierarchy of Boundary Changes

In most of the case studies, there are two levels of local government, commonly referred to as municipal and regional (or county) levels. The cases suggest that boundary reform at both levels is often interrelated. There appear to be three models of boundary change.

First, concurrent and related changes are made to both municipal and regional government boundaries. It appears that the reform of regional government boundaries often coincides with changes to local government boundaries. It is almost impossible to redraw regional government territories without altering local government boundaries. Examples include China's creation of prefecture-level cities, South Africa's establishment of metropolitan (Category A) municipalities, Quebec's institution of regional municipal councils, and, in some cases, Germany's reform of county boundaries. The reform of regional boundaries challenges existing theories and ideas of local government boundaries and their revision, as noted by Skaburskis and Paddison. Most theories explain only changes to local (or lower-tier) governments. How such theories apply to the restructuring of regional government boundaries is not specifically addressed (Keating 1995).

Second, reforms occur at the local level, yet the regional boundaries remain static. Examples include the United States and Ontario, whose county boundaries have remained largely unaltered over an extended period of time. The county boundaries can be seen as fixed containers of local governments, and the alteration of their boundaries is usually spatially constrained by the county boundaries. However, in some cases, municipal boundary reform was complicated by provincial boundaries or international borders. Examples are South Africa's attempt to deal with local boundary configurations that straddle provincial boundaries and Spain's problem with municipal boundaries crossing international borders.

Third, limited reforms of either the local or the regional level of government occur. This type of reform is exemplified by the Spanish and Israeli experiences. Abel Albet i Mas discusses in Chapter 7 the numerous types of boundary change permitted by legislation but rarely implemented in Spain.

Groups with Strong Sociospatial Identification

The difficulty of redrawing local government boundaries is related to strong sociocultural attachment to place and local government. For example, Albet i Mas suggests that the Spanish people's strong civic pride and identification with local government make reforms difficult. In other cases, conflicts between ethnic groups complicate local government boundary reforms where such reforms may threaten or weaken the rights or identities of specific groups. This problem is seen in the resistance to reform from traditional communities in South Africa; English-French linguistic division in Montreal, Quebec; Arab-Jewish tensions in Israel; and the Basques in Spain. Thus, Paddison's first proposition, that local government restructuring meet local needs, suggests a sensitivity to local cultural geography.

Whereas aspirations to promote equality and to secure ethnic minority representation could be explicit objectives for reform, municipal boundary changes are frequently implicitly motivated by the aspirations of political parties or population groups to gain a political advantage from the new territorial configuration. Gerrymandering is the case of manipulating boundaries in order to reduce the electoral power of particular population groups, usually racial or ethnic minorities. Nevertheless, in multiethnic countries characterized by geographical segregation along ethnic lines, local government boundary changes can frequently be interpreted as influencing interethnic power relations. The desire to promote such change could be an engine for reform, but such sensitivities could also form high barriers for change, even when well justified by considerations of efficient service provision, economic development, or equality.

Have the Procedures Changed Radically over Time?

Waves of Reform

Local government boundary reform, for a number of countries, oscillated between major periods of reform and no reform. The period of such oscillation varied from five to thirty years. For example, Canada (Ontario and Quebec), Germany, and Korea dramatically altered their local government territories during the 1960s and 1970s only to revisit the issue to embark on more elaborate plans to restructure local boundaries during the 1990s and beyond. South Africa's reforms of the mid-1990s coincided with the transitional era in the nation's move toward democracy, while the reforms between 1998 and 2000 were more formal ("permanent"). However, a number of the other cases contained no period of extensive reform.

There are three main findings with respect to these waves of boundary reform. First, the first wave usually established the template and/or laid the framework for the next wave. For example, the model of boundary reform undertaken in West Germany during the 1960s was then (partially) applied to East Germany after reunification in 1995. Thus, one perspective is to view the second wave as completing the project of local territorial reform started during the first wave. Second, the first wave of reform is later viewed as flawed, necessitating a new round or wave of reform. For instance, in Ontario, the wave of boundary restructuring that occurred during the 1960s and 1970s to create two-tier local governments became the means by which unitary governments, via amalgamation, were carried out during the 1990s. Similarly, in Korea, the boundary reforms of the 1990s were seen as correcting for problems created by the reforms undertaken during the 1960s. And third, it appears that nations such as Israel, Spain, and the United States, which failed to achieve a first wave of reform, continue to have chronic boundary problems, with only piecemeal or ad hoc boundary changes taking place.

In all three cases, proponents of boundary change must articulate a position in support of or opposition to previous periods of reform or lack of reform. In other words, contemporary debates regarding the restructuring of local government boundaries are informed by varying interpretations of the historical record and achievement (or lack thereof) of previous changes to local territories. This temporal dimension of the redrawing of local government boundaries is often missed or neglected by theories (e.g., public choice, consolidationist) that tend to view boundary debates as static. Yet the case studies in this volume suggest the opposite.

The Role of the Political-Ideological Environment

Obviously, there is no single optimal solution to the dilemma of how to delineate municipal boundaries and to the preferred territorial configuration of local authorities. Outcomes are products not only of varying geographical, social, and economic circumstances but also of the prevailing political-ideological environment. The choice of procedures and the decision on solutions depend on normatively defined preferences, such as the weight given to instrumental considerations of efficiency and equality versus the weight given to local identities and the preservation of local democratic traditions, as a cornerstone of the national political system. The level of trust in the central state as an arbiter in local conflicts also varies from place to place. Changes in political circumstances and in prominent ideologies are no less important than spatial, demographic, and technological processes in explaining the waves of reform mentioned above.

A laissez-faire ideological environment, resembling prevailing ideologies in the United States, presents strong negative sentiments toward direct intervention of the state in municipal boundary delineation. Popular determination conforms best to laissez-faire ideologies, but the case of the United States demonstrates that this option is not accepted in a dogmatic and universal manner. Rather, a broad array of procedures is applied in the fifty states, and these procedures are modified from time to time.

A political-ideological environment that promotes competition and privatization could lead to very different results when the central state aims to bypass local governments in the provision of public services, mainly through their direct privatization or transfer of responsibilities to NGOs. Local governments, in this case, would be weaker and prone to centrally imposed territorial changes.

At the other extreme of democratic countries are liberal welfare states, where local authorities serve as a major arm for the provision of welfare services. Equitable provision of these services is a prime public concern, as is the ability of local authorities to provide these services efficiently. Thus, top-down alternatives would prevail, justified largely by equality and efficiency considerations as well as by rational patterns of land development, which justify changes in territorial structures of local authorities. Nevertheless, where prime emphasis is given to historical local identities and traditions of local democracy, the central state could refrain from reforms, thus either sacrificing some of the efficiency benefits of consolidations or attempting to provide solutions through regional levels of government or mechanisms of municipal cooperation.

Intermediate environments could follow two different paths. In the first, the state is less interventionist and less committed to extensive welfare state ideologies but still considered a fair broker, thus acting as a neutral mediator in local conflicts. The state in such an environment is less likely to initiate its own municipal territorial reform but acts as an arbiter in local boundary disputes, largely initiated by the local parties themselves. In the second, the state acts as a pluralist decision maker, performing as several stakeholders and undertaking a wide range of often conflicting actions. The state is rarely a monolithic organization, but in a multiparty coalition government structure a coherent national policy is particularly difficult to implement. Fragmented action of the central state is likely in particular when government ministers and members of the legislature represent diverse ethnic or religious groups. It is in this environment that tensions between the desire of the state to retain decision-making powers and the desire of local interest groups to decentralize the process toward popular determination are greatest.

Two different environments could characterize newly democratizing countries. Nondemocratic traditions imply extreme centralization in which the head of state usually has a major say in the determination of the local government map, even though formal responsibility could lie with the government or the legislature. Territorial reforms could be frequently associated with changes in the identities of power holders. Democratization and decentralization reforms could emerge from external pressures of donor organizations. Top-down alternatives of municipal boundary change would be maintained in this case, but pressures of donor organizations could have a major impact on the territorial structure of local government, particularly on the sizes of local authorities. However, in other circumstances, particularly where democratization emerges through internal pressures, local democracy could be viewed as an important practice to secure democracy at the national level. In this case, local autonomy considerations could have an overriding influence over efficiency and process (proper administration) considerations, and top-down alternatives would raise considerable resistance.

Normative principles, such as those defined by Paddison, could be regarded as universal, but their application would require sensitivity to the particular political-ideological circumstances, as demonstrated above.

References

Barlow, I.M. 1991. *Metropolitan Government.* London: Routledge.
Fan, C.C. 1999. "The Vertical and Horizontal Expansions of China's City System." *Urban Geography* 20, 6: 493-515.
Harding, A., S. Wilks-Heeg, and M. Hutchins. 2000. "Business, Government, and the Business of Urban Governance." *Urban Studies* 37, 5-6: 975-94.
Keating, M. 1995. "Size, Efficiency, and Democracy: Consolidation, Fragmentation, and Public Choice." In D. Judge, G. Stoker, and H. Wolman, eds., *Theories of Urban Politics,* 135-59. London: SAGE Publications.
Meligrana, J. 2000. "Toward a Process Model of Local Government Restructuring: Evidence from Canada." *Canadian Journal of Regional Science* 23: 509-30.
Razin, E., and G. Lindsey. 2004. "Municipal Boundary Change Procedures: Local Democracy versus Central Control." In D. Wastl-Walter and M. Barlow, eds., *New Challenges in Local and Regional Administration.* Aldershot: Ashgate.
Razin, E., and N. Obirih-Opareh. 2000. "Spatial Variations in Fiscal Capacity of Local Government in Ghana before and after Decentralization." *Third World Planning Review* 22: 411-32.
Shin, Dong-Ho. 2000. "Governing Inter-Regional Conflict: The Planning Approach to Managing Spill-Overs of Extended Metropolitan Pusan, Korea." *Environment and Planning A* 32, 3: 507-18.
Terhorst, P., and J. van de Ven. 1990. "The Territorial Strategies of Amsterdam." *Tijdschrift voor Economische en Sociale Geografie* 81, 4: 267-79.

Contributors

Abel Albet i Mas, PhD in geography, UAB 1993, is an associate professor at the Universitat Autònoma de Barcelona. His teaching and research interests are focused on geographical thought (history of geography and geographers, new trends and methodologies, new regional geography), on urban and regional planning (urban planning, regional analysis, problems and evolution of cities and metropolitan areas, the case of Barcelona), and on local government (municipal boundaries, metropolitan administration). He has published in national and international books and journals. He is co-director of the academic journal *Documents d'Anàlisi Geogràfica*.

Robert Cameron is an associate professor in the Department of Political Studies, University of Cape Town. He has published extensively on local government and boundary demarcation. He has published in *Local Government Studies, Public Administration,* and *Public Administration and Development*. He has written a book on local government reorganization in South Africa. His latest publications include *An Overview of the Local Government Municipal Demarcation Act 27 of 1998* (Johannesburg: Electoral Institute of South Africa, 2000); with Chriss Tapscott, "The Challenges of State Transformation," *Public Administration* 20, 2 (2000); and "Megacities in South Africa: A Solution for the New Millennium," *Public Administration* 20, 2 (2000). He is a member of South Africa's Municipal Demarcation Board, which redemarcated the country into new local government boundaries for the 2000 local government elections.

Raphaël Fischler is an associate professor in the School of Urban Planning at McGill University in Montreal. His academic work concerns the history and theory of planning as well as planning and governance in the Montreal region. His professional work pertains to design review, community planning, and public planning at the city and regional levels. Among his recent works are a co-edited volume on urban design and planning in Israel and a research monograph on metropolitan development and transportation in the greater Montreal region.

Greg Lindsey is the associate director of the Center for Urban Policy and the Environment and the Duey-Murphy Professor of Rural Land Policy at the

School of Public and Environmental Affairs, Indiana University–Purdue University, Indianapolis. He has twenty years of experience in environmental and land use planning and has published in the *Journal of the American Planning Association* and *State and Local Government Review*. Among other activities, he recently completed an assessment of annexation policy for the Indiana Advisory Commission on Intergovernmental Relations.

John Meligrana is an assistant professor of urban and regional planning at Queen's University in Kingston. He has been an advisor to several municipal and provincial governments with respect to contemporary annexation disputes. He has published extensively on issues of annexation and municipal government in Canada. His publications can be found in the *Canadian Journal of Urban Research* (1998 and 2000), *Applied Geographic Studies* (1998), *Transportation* (1999), and *Urban History Review* (2000). He received his PhD from Simon Fraser University in 1998 and a master's degree in urban and regional planning from Queen's University.

Ronan Paddison is currently head of the Geography Department at Glasgow University. He has held appointments at Trinity College, University of Dublin, and at the Planning School, Glasgow School of Art. His primary research interests are in urban and regional government. He is working on an ESRC Cities Project, looking at issues of urban governance in central Scotland. He is currently managing editor of *Urban Studies* and also edits *Space and Polity*. He has published extensively on the topic of local and regional government.

Eran Razin is an associate professor and head of the Department of Geography, The Hebrew University, Jerusalem. His recent publications focus on the impact of local government organization on development and disparities *(Environment and Planning C, Urban Studies, Urban Affairs Review, Political Geography, Third World Planning Review)* and on immigrant entrepreneurs in different urban milieus *(International Migration Review, Urban Affairs Review, Urban Geography, TESG, Journal of Ethnic and Migration Studies)*.

Jianfa Shen is an assistant professor in the Department of Geography, Chinese University of Hong Kong. He got his PhD from the London School of Economics in 1994. His research interests are on urbanization and migration, urban and regional governance, and urban and regional development, with a special focus on China. He has published in *Geoforum, Progress in Planning, Environment and Planning A, Environment and Planning C, Regional Studies,* and *Geographical Journal*. His recent co-edited book is *China Review 2000* (Hong Kong: Chinese University Press, 2000).

Dong-Ho Shin is an associate professor of regional analysis in the Department of Urban and Regional Planning, Hannam University, Taejon, Korea. He was trained as a regional planner at the University of British Columbia, Vancouver. His past research focused mainly on two streams: interregional planning practices and science policies. His recent publications include "Governing Inter-Regional Conflict," *Environment and Planning A* 32, 3 (2000): 507-18, and "An Alternative Approach to Developing a Science Park," *Papers in Regional Science*

80, 1 (2001): 103-11. Currently, he is conducting research on regional innovation systems of various countries, such as the Silicon Valley in the United States, Ulm in Germany, Tsukuba in Japan, and Taejon in Korea.

Andrejs Skaburskis is the acting director of the School of Urban and Regional Planning at Queen's University. He has published numerous articles, book chapters, monographs, and reports on the economic factors bringing about demographic changes and affecting rental markets as well as on the determinants of sprawl. He has recently published (with Dennis Keating and Michael Teitz) *Rent Control: Regulation and the Rental Housing Market*.

Jeanne M. Wolfe is a professor emeritus of the School of Urban Planning at McGill University in Montreal. She is the author of numerous articles and reports on urban and regional planning, housing policy, and planning theory and history, both in Canada and in the developing world. A former planner with the City of Montreal and with the Province of Quebec, she was also a member of the *Commission d'étude sur les municipalités* (the Parizeau Commission of 1985 on municipal government) and has served as a board member of several community organizations in Montreal.

Hellmut Wollmann is the director of the Teaching and Research Unit on Public Policy and Public Administration at the Institute of Social Sciences of Humboldt University in Berlin. He is a co-editor of the social science journal *Leviathan* and a member of the editorial board of *Policy Sciences, Theoretical Politics, Knowledge,* and *Policy*. He has published extensively on the topic of local governments, particularly in Central and Eastern Europe.

Index

African National Congress, 209
Ahnyang (South Korea), 12, 172, 177-79, 182, 185
amalgamation, 5, 6, 8, 9, 12-14, 27, 29, 38, 39, 40, 41, 43, 47, 48, 50-52, 76, 78, 81-83, 85, 91, 92, 95, 96, 99, 100, 102-4, 110, 113, 114, 118, 121, 124, 126-28, 133, 141, 143, 144, 160, 165, 167, 170, 179, 181-87, 207, 215, 216, 228, 236. *See also* annexation
annexation, 2, 4-7, 9, 12-17, 20, 29, 31, 34, 38, 39, 50-76, 78-80, 83-87, 88, 91, 99, 101, 102, 132-34, 141-43, 148, 151, 156, 159, 167, 172, 180, 189, 193-95, 204, 228, 229, 230, 234. *See also* amalgamation
Arab, 156, 163, 164, 170, 235
Arab-Jewish, 235
Arab-Palestinian, 164
Australia, 26, 27, 30

Barcelona (Spain), 133, 149
Basic Regulatory Local Government Act (Spain), 139-41
Basque Country (Spain), 135-38, 140, 145, 147
Beijing (China), 192
Berlin (Germany), 110
boundary commission: Canada, 91; Israel, 58, 85, 160, 161, 165-69; Scotland, 32-33
Boundary-line Regulation Act (Spain), 143
British High Commissioner (Israel), 159, 163
Bund (Germany), 107

Canada, 1, 5, 17, 26, 31, 75, 85, 101, 170, 228, 231-33, 236
Cape Town (South Africa), 209, 213, 219

Catalan Municipal Act (Spain), 9, 132, 142, 143
Catalonia (Spain), 134-40, 142, 143, 145-48, 151
central city, 40
China, 1, 12-14, 17, 18, 20, 34, 189-201, 203-5, 229, 231, 232
Christian Democrat (Germany), 116, 233
citizens, 5, 21, 22, 25, 27, 28, 36n5, 53, 71, 91, 97, 118, 128, 130, 151, 164
city-region, 15, 30, 88, 97. *See also* metropolitan
Commission for Territorial Boundaries (Spain), 143
community, 9, 23, 40, 42, 43, 45, 47, 68, 69, 73, 81, 82, 97, 100, 107, 109, 134-38, 142, 145-47, 151, 178, 183, 189
consolidation, 29, 30, 41, 48, 49, 81, 82, 91, 96, 99. *See also* amalgamation
constitution, 9, 56, 75, 107, 108, 113, 131, 132, 139, 144, 190, 191, 200, 203, 206-10, 212-14, 216, 217, 223, 225, 228

decentralization, 12, 26, 29, 34, 89, 92, 140, 154, 162, 164, 169, 170, 172, 181, 185, 186, 202-4, 238
demarcation, 14, 34, 79, 206-16, 218-26, 228, 232, 234
democracy, 14, 21, 22-23, 28, 34, 41, 42, 44, 89, 91, 124, 151, 167, 186, 206, 227, 230, 236, 238
density, 20, 38, 47, 61-64, 66, 67, 72, 73, 114, 115, 117, 122, 123, 125, 195, 197, 212, 214, 215, 218
development, 3, 8, 10, 13, 15, 18, 20, 24, 27, 29, 35, 38, 39, 48, 60, 61, 67-69, 73, 76, 77, 79-81, 83, 84, 89, 90, 94, 97, 100, 116, 124, 130, 132, 141, 150, 156, 160, 168, 180, 189, 191, 195, 196, 199,

244   Index

201, 202, 204, 208-12, 214, 215, 217, 218, 224-28, 230, 236, 238
dynasty (China), 11, 175, 177, 190

economy, 12, 24, 35, 38-39, 41-43, 97, 119, 150, 179, 180, 197, 204, 212, 230
elections, 22, 36n4, 101, 124, 126, 128, 139, 181, 186, 206-9, 217, 222
employment, 29, 184, 211, 219, 224
enclaves, 9, 142, 143, 146-48
England, 21, 22
environment, 16, 38, 47, 50, 52, 59, 64, 68, 86, 97, 112, 154, 155, 161, 164, 210, 221, 224, 227, 237-39
equity, 4, 30, 44, 67, 99
ethnic, 25, 45, 192, 227, 235, 236, 238
Europe, 20, 21, 29, 30, 118

farmland, 89. *See also* rural
Federal Constitution (Germany), 107, 108, 113
Federal Republic (Germany), 7, 106, 110, 111, 115, 117, 118, 120, 122, 124, 126, 127
federalism, 41, 42, 50, 56
finance, 162, 165, 169, 224, 234
Foshan City (China), 201
fragmentation, 9, 11, 12, 27, 28, 30, 41, 44, 45, 46, 47-49, 81, 96, 97, 101, 134, 146, 151, 154, 164, 165, 168-70, 176-78, 181, 184, 185, 186, 187, 188, 212, 218, 221, 238
France, 25, 77, 118, 130, 146, 148, 150
Fujian (China), 199

GDP. *See* gross domestic product (GDP)
Geographic Information System (GIS), 221, 223
Germany, 1, 7, 8, 36n3, 106, 107, 109-11, 113, 118-21, 123-25, 127, 229, 231, 233, 234, 236
gerrymandering, 14, 209, 236
GIS. *See* Geographic Information System (GIS)
globalization, 18, 38, 46, 51
governance, 11, 12, 14, 15, 18, 20, 22, 26, 28, 30, 31, 34-36, 41, 43, 46, 47, 64, 65, 73, 80, 88, 97, 106, 120, 172, 174-77, 181-84, 186, 189, 195, 203, 208, 210, 212, 234
government, 1-36, 38-57, 60-62, 64-66, 73, 75-85, 87-99, 101-7, 109-14, 116, 118-22, 124, 126-33, 139-43, 145, 147, 148, 150, 152, 154-59, 161-92, 195-97, 199, 200, 202-4, 206-15, 217-39
Greenbelts Area (Seoul), 178

gross domestic product (GDP), 177, 196
growth management, 2, 15, 39
Guangdong (China), 199, 201

High Court (Israel), 10, 166-68, 170
housing, 29, 30, 39, 92-96, 100, 110, 164, 168, 180, 191

ideology, 41, 114, 131
Illinois (USA), 62, 63, 65
Indiana (USA), 5, 59, 61, 62, 67, 68, 71-74
infrastructure, 65, 78, 81, 112, 134, 150, 201, 204, 211, 212, 224
Inkatha Freedom Party (South Africa), 209, 223, 233
Israel, 1, 10, 16, 17, 34, 154-57, 159-61, 163-67, 169-71, 228, 230-32, 234-36

Japan, 179
Jerusalem, 156
Jewish, 154, 156, 163, 164, 170, 235
Jiangsu province (Korea), 195, 204
Johannesburg (South Africa), 209, 213, 219, 220, 225
joint authorities, 8, 114, 116, 118, 120-22, 124, 126

Knesset (Israel), 161, 162, 171
Korea (South), 1, 11, 12, 16, 17, 172, 174, 176, 178, 180-82, 185, 187, 188, 229, 231-34, 236
Korea Local Administration Research Institute (KRILA), 182, 186
Kyungki Province (Korea), 11, 177, 178
Kyungnam (Korea), 11, 12, 172, 179-81, 183, 232

*L*änder (Germany), 7, 8, 107-10, 112-18, 120-28, 232
local democracy, 21, 44, 91, 167, 227, 238
local government, 1-32, 34-36, 38-49, 51-55, 64, 75-81, 83-85, 87, 89-93, 95-99, 101-7, 109-14, 116, 118, 119, 121, 124, 126-33, 139-41, 143, 147, 154-59, 161, 163, 165-74, 176, 181, 184-88, 200, 203, 206-15, 217-19, 221-39
local government boundaries, 1-3, 14, 17, 18, 24, 29, 30, 36n5, 36n14, 49, 75, 84, 127, 155, 157-59, 161, 163, 165, 167, 169, 206, 208, 209, 221, 227-35, 237
local government territories, 3, 17, 76, 106, 107, 111, 229, 232, 233
London (UK), 26, 29, 32-34, 213, 216

Madrid (Spain), 132, 133, 135-38, 149
metropolitan, 11, 20, 24, 25, 27-29, 35,
  39, 44, 80-82, 95, 97-101, 138, 139,
  144, 145, 149-51, 156, 158, 172,
  174-77, 179-81, 183, 207-9, 211-16,
  218-20, 229, 235
Minister of Interior (Israel), 159-69
Ministry of Civil Affairs (South Africa),
  192, 196, 199
Ministry of Finance (Israel), 162, 165,
  169, 234
Ministry of Home Affairs (Korea), 12,
  176, 181, 183, 186, 232
Ministry of Municipal Affairs (Ontario),
  5, 6, 76
Ministry of Municipal Affairs (Quebec),
  5, 78, 81-83, 101
Montreal (Canada), 77, 78, 81-83, 91,
  97-101, 232, 235
Municipal Demarcation Board (South
  Africa), 207-10, 213-16, 218-20, 224-26,
  232, 234
Municipal Ordinance, 159, 160
municipal segregation, 142

Nanhai City (China), 201
National People's Congress (China) 190,
  191, 203, 209
nation-state, 23
negotiations, 69, 71, 84-89, 93, 202, 206,
  217

OMB. *See* Ontario Municipal Board
  (OMB) (Canada)
Ontario (Canada), 5-7, 41, 75-77, 79, 80,
  84-86, 93-96, 101-4, 127, 232, 234-36
Ontario Municipal Board (OMB)
  (Canada), 6, 7, 76, 79, 80, 84-87, 101,
  234
Ottawa (Canada), 95, 96
Outaouais (Canada), 81, 83, 91, 100

Parti Québécois (Canada), 89, 97
People's Republic of China, 190
planning, 3, 7, 16, 27, 29, 30, 38-40, 45,
  47, 49, 52-55, 67-69, 75, 79, 80, 83, 85,
  89, 90, 97, 99, 100, 111, 114, 116, 119,
  133, 134, 139, 144, 145, 166, 176,
  179-81, 202, 211, 212, 227
political boundaries, 2, 24, 25, 31, 35, 43,
  68
politics, 10, 17, 23, 25, 34, 41, 91, 128,
  170, 175
power, 3, 5, 10, 13, 17, 22-27, 31-33, 35,
  40-42, 47, 50, 51, 56, 62, 65, 66, 72, 75,
  79, 84, 86-88, 90, 92, 94, 102, 112, 131,

134, 139, 144, 145, 154, 159, 162-67,
  169, 170, 176, 190, 191, 195, 199, 200,
  202-4, 207, 224, 231, 233, 234, 236, 238
prefectures, 196, 202, 204
Pretoria, 213, 219, 220, 222
privatization, 28, 46, 91, 237
procedures, 1-6, 8, 10, 12, 14-19, 23,
  31-33, 51, 56, 57, 61, 64, 72, 75, 76,
  85-88, 90, 91, 93, 101, 102, 128, 132,
  133, 141, 154, 155, 159-63, 166-71,
  186, 189, 190, 192, 203, 224, 227-32,
  234, 236, 237
property taxes, 71, 156, 162
public choice theory, 22, 28, 29, 47, 52,
  91, 96, 229, 232, 233, 237
Pusan (Korea), 12, 172, 174, 178-81, 185,
  232
Pyrenees (Spain), 134, 147

quasi-legislative, 58, 60, 163, 231
Quebec (Canada), 5-7, 75-78, 81-83,
  89-92, 97, 99-104, 127, 232, 235, 236

RCM. *See* regional county municipalities
  (RCM)
reforms, 2, 5-8, 11-13, 29, 34, 76, 83, 91,
  101, 102, 106, 108-10, 112, 113, 116,
  118-22, 124, 126-29, 154, 155, 170-72,
  174, 177, 181, 182, 186-88, 190, 196,
  203, 229-36, 238
regional county municipalities (RCM),
  89, 90, 98, 102
regional planning, 7, 40, 111
restructuring, 3, 5, 8, 9, 15, 16, 21-28, 34,
  38, 39, 41, 43, 45, 47-51, 75, 86, 88,
  91-96, 101-4, 111, 112, 124, 131, 172,
  182, 187, 227-28, 231, 235-37
rural, 11, 13, 15, 16, 19, 20, 29, 39, 68,
  76-78, 81, 83, 84, 90-92, 99, 111, 114,
  116, 118, 124, 131, 150-52, 156, 159, 164,
  166, 168, 172, 177-79, 182-84, 186, 187,
  189, 190, 192, 193, 196, 197, 201, 203-
  8, 211, 213-17, 223, 229, 231-33

Scotland, 32
Sengstock, Frank, typology, 61, 64
Seoul (Korea), 11, 174, 175, 177, 178, 180
Shanghai (China), 192
Social Democrats (Germany), 114, 116
socialist, 119, 122, 131, 154
socialist state, 119, 122
South Africa, 1, 14, 17, 34, 206-13,
  215-23, 228, 229, 231-35
Spain, 1, 8, 9, 17, 34, 130, 131, 133-38,
  145-50, 228, 229, 234-36
Spanish Constitution (1978), 9, 139

sprawl, 39, 149, 229
stakeholders, 3, 86, 164, 200, 209, 218, 222, 230, 232, 238
state, 2, 5, 7, 12-14, 19, 21-24, 26, 30, 33, 34, 36n6, 40, 45, 46, 51, 56-58, 61-69, 72-75, 109-12, 116, 119, 120, 122, 126-29, 131-33, 139, 140, 154, 155, 159-61, 163, 164, 170, 190-92, 195-98, 200, 202-5, 217, 218, 222, 227-28, 230-33, 237, 238
State Council (China), 13, 190-92, 195-97, 200, 202, 203, 232

Tel Aviv, 156, 158
territorial reforms, 8, 106, 108, 110, 112, 113, 116, 118-22, 124, 126-28, 170, 238
territorial restructuring, 112
territoriality, 23
territories, 1-3, 6, 8, 17, 25, 48, 57, 75, 76, 78, 84, 93, 96, 106, 107, 110, 111, 122, 139, 140, 151, 174, 221, 224, 228, 229, 231-33, 235-37
Tianjin (China), 192
Tiebout, C.M., 28, 46. *See also* public choice theory
Toronto (Canada), 41, 80, 95, 232
transportation, 93, 97, 100, 164, 174, 178, 216

tribunals, 17, 31, 60, 72

Uiwang (Korea), 178, 179, 182
Union of Municipalities of Quebec, 91
United States, 4, 16, 17, 33, 56-59, 61-63, 65-67, 69, 71-73, 107, 163, 228, 231, 235-37
urban, 2, 3, 5, 6, 11-16, 18-21, 23, 27, 30, 31, 35, 38, 39, 42, 59, 64-66,68,69, 75-84, 86, 89, 91, 96, 97, 99, 100, 102-4, 111, 124, 131, 133, 141, 143, 149-51, 155, 156, 159, 160, 166-68, 172, 174, 176-80, 182-84, 186, 187, 189-206, 208, 214-16, 222, 223, 229, 231, 232, 234
urban governance, 31, 234
urban settlements, 155, 191, 204
urbanization, 11-14, 20, 38, 89, 110, 114, 121, 156, 172, 189, 196, 201, 203-5, 228
urban-rural, 16, 156, 172, 177, 182-84, 187, 201, 204, 229

villages, 62, 77, 83, 96, 97, 130, 131, 134, 145, 147, 155, 156, 161, 214, 216

welfare, 7, 39, 42, 44-46, 49, 52, 77, 111, 151, 237, 238